EXPOSED

Also by Jane Velez-Mitchell

IWANT: MY JOURNEY FROM ADDICTION AND
OVERCONSUMPTION TO A SIMPLER, HONEST LIFE

SECRETS CAN BE MURDER: THE KILLER NEXT DOOR

ADDICT NATION: AN INTERVENTION FOR AMERICA

(with Sandra Mohr)

EXPOSED | THE SECRET LIFE OF JODI ARIAS

JANE VELEZ-MITCHELL

HARPER

An Imprint of HarperCollins*Publishers*

HARPER

An Imprint of HarperCollins*Publishers*
195 Broadway
New York, New York 10007

First Harper mass market printing: September 2014
First William Morrow hardcover printing: September 2013

Visit Harper paperbacks on the World Wide Web at
www.harpercollins.com

10 9 8 7 6 5 4 3 2 1

To Travis Alexander and his siblings

CONTENTS

AUTHOR'S NOTE

The writing of this book posed an extraordinary challenge because the person at the very center of the horrific events is a habitual liar. Adding to the dilemma, Jodi Arias made her upbringing, her interactions with previous boyfriends, and her relationship with murder victim Travis Alexander a huge part of her defense strategy. Tragically, Travis is not alive to give his side of the story. Additionally, many of the individuals Jodi maligned in her testimony and/or her journals, including ex-boyfriends and members of her own family, never took the stand to offer their version of events. Given these remarkable circumstances, the reader is strongly advised to regard everything that Jodi Arias claims, as recounted in the following pages, with skepticism and suspicion. She has earned her reputation as a pathological liar. While many of her claims have been exposed as outright lies, like all accomplished fabulists, Jodi Arias seamlessly wove actual events into her fabrications, often making it impossible to determine where truth ends and fiction begins. Hopefully these mysteries will add to the adventure of the reader's journey through these pages. Because of the passions and social media frenzy surrounding this case, and the unreliability of her testimony and writings, the friends and ex-boyfriends Jodi Arias references are identified only by their first names unless they testified in court or spoke out publicly.

FOREWORD

by Nancy Grace

There are some messes in life you can clean up. Murder is not one of them. The decision to kill is irrevocable. There is no turning back the clock. Not ever. Not even if you lie about it.

This universal truth seemed to escape the enigmatic Jodi Arias, but then again, Arias always has a difficult relationship with the truth. Her decision to commit the premeditated murder of Travis Alexander was not just one bad decision—it was the culmination of a series of bad decisions. Those choices reflect a lifetime of warped logic and twisted beliefs. In the following pages of this book, you will learn the secrets of Arias's long journey to murder. Her life story features self-delusion, self-pity, grandiosity, and above all, a sense that nothing in this world could take her down.

The Jodi Arias story does not begin with the murder of Travis Alexander. She was never your typical "woman scorned," victim-turned-killer, victim of circumstance, or whatever lie she may tell next; instead, she was something far more insidious. She was the manipulator, the deceiver, and the deviant hidden behind the guise of placid beauty, who spent years building up her own reality until it all came crashing down.

Jodi Arias is a liar and a murderer, but what is perhaps

most terrifying about her is that she still believes she will get away with it. This is a woman who thought she could lie her way to freedom. From the first time that she spoke to police until her final day on the witness stand, she treated the truth with disdain. In the process, she shamelessly and repeatedly denied the proof that was so apparent to everyone else, while dragging her innocent victim through the mud. Through all the photographs, the DNA, and the testimonies, Arias never once thought she could be convicted. She matched each mounting piece of evidence with another outlandish lie, holding on stubbornly to her fabrication. Arias then turned to her next lie with a faint smile and a dry tissue for her "tears."

Arias's claims will be repeated in the following pages in all of their lurid detail, just as they came out in her police interrogations and at trial. But the question the reader must always ask is: How much of it is true? When it comes to what Travis and Jodi did behind closed doors, the full story may never be known. Everything that she has said—both about her own life and about her relationship with Travis Alexander—must be questioned. We can never forget that, with Travis dead, Jodi has become the sole author of their affair. When the only source of information is a proven liar, it is our duty to find the truth for ourselves.

Pathological liars like Arias are inherently dangerous because they perfect a psychological strategy that allows them to lie convincingly on a moment's notice. Arias's lies were so brazen, so patently ridiculous, that her ability to deliver them with a straight face and a convincing look—under oath, no less—became a subject of fascination for HLN viewers across the country. Arias seems to have mastered a mental technique that allows her to believe her own lies. Put another way, in her mind, factual truth is irrelevant. Truth is redefined as survival. Arias would say anything in her desperation to survive.

While Arias's endless, rambling tales never added up to the truth, one certainty was clear: there was something unquestionably wrong with her. Something about this woman made the world's skin crawl, from her own family and friends to trial watchers in their living rooms. This book dissects Arias's behavior to discover the connection between her past and her mysterious relationship with Travis Alexander. She did not come out of the womb evil. So what happened during her life to make her the person she became? Paranoia, obsession, and manipulation are what catapulted her from man to man and eventually into the arms of Travis. When the time came, as it inevitably did, Arias was always prepared with a new variation on the same story: suspicion, betrayal, and abuse. She starred as the victim in each scenario.

Arias's calculated manipulation was never more obvious than during her affair with Travis Alexander. Alexander was successful, loved, and happy, everything Arias wanted for herself. Their relationship was undeniably fueled by intense sexuality and endless deception. Arias's sexual prowess was overwhelming, and Travis fell for each devious move she made. Taking advantage of Travis's Mormon beliefs, which prevented him from exposing their sex affair, Arias built a wall between him and the truth.

But Arias's manipulation could bring her only so close to Travis, and, when faced with rejection, she got angry. Instead of facing reality, Arias created a convenient new truth: Travis was no longer her lover but rather her tormentor and source of humiliation. A jealous rage overcame Arias, and, suddenly, she wanted revenge, taking days, maybe even weeks, to plot out Travis's murder. She thought through and planned all of the logistics of how she would kill the supposed love of her life.

Perhaps the most disturbing aspect of the crime, beyond its grisly nature, was that, in the weeks following Travis's death, Arias carried on with her life, living as though his blood was never on her hands. There was no sign of remorse, no sign of grief or self-loathing for the heinous crime she committed. Not even when police confronted her with the overwhelming evidence of her culpability was she willing to accept the burden of the truth and own up to her role in his death.

With this book, Jane Velez-Mitchell goes behind the scenes of what has become one of the nation's premiere case studies on killers who lie and liars who kill. She sets out to uncover the real Jodi Arias, decoding the mind of a killer. In the coming pages, she unpacks this case in full, from Arias's childhood to the stunning guilty verdict.

By diving deeper into the facts of this case, we can all learn a life lesson. While most of us are honest, straight-forward, and trusting, predators exist who are the exact opposite—deceitful, cunning, and dangerous; three words that perfectly describe Jodi Arias.

PROLOGUE

As she sat on the witness stand, only one thing about Jodi Arias was clear: the woman was a chameleon.

Once upon a time, before the trial had begun, before she'd been taken into custody, before she'd killed her ex-boyfriend Travis Alexander, Jodi Arias had been a bombshell. During her relationship with Travis, her hair had been dyed blond; her makeup had been tasteful, with just the right amounts of lipstick, blush, and mascara; and her alluring face had been radiant.

The woman on the witness stand bore little resemblance to that Jodi. She wore no makeup, though her skin had grown pale from lack of sunlight. Her mousy brown hair had returned to its natural state, with thin, wispy bangs cut right at the eyebrows. When she dated Travis, she hadn't worn glasses, but during her trial a large, unavoidable pair of glasses was often fixed on the bridge of her nose. It was unclear whether she actually needed the glasses, but their presence had the unmistakable and deliberate effect of making her look like a librarian—a librarian who happened to be on trial for murder.

There was nothing subtle in this transformation or in the public's fascination with it. From the first words of the defense's opening statements, people had been clamoring for more, and most days the gallery was packed to the gills with spectators eager to witness this chameleon firsthand and hear the inner workings of a case that was more sexually charged than any in memory—possibly ever. Indeed, though this was a murder trial, the sexual exploits of Jodi and Travis were the bedrock of the case, with both the prosecution and defense alike putting the most intimate details of the pair's sex life on full display for the jury. The fact that cameras were permitted in the courtroom to broadcast the stories of their steamy sex to the world made things even more lurid. Voyeurs everywhere came out of the woodwork, and outside the court, gallery tickets were briefly scalped for hundreds of dollars until court officials cracked down.

But this wasn't just about sex. A brutal crime had been committed—the cruel, bloody slaughter of Travis Alexander, who at thirty years old had been an active member of the Mormon church. Not only did he possess athletic all-American good looks, he was adored by his community—and people were hungry for justice. According to the prosecutor, Jodi had killed him three times over on June 4, 2008, leaving him with twenty-nine knife wounds and shooting him in the right temple. Even though the gunshot was probably a gratuitous postmortem act, two of the twenty-nine knife wounds were definitely lethal: the fatal stab to the heart, and the six-inch slice across Travis's throat, a gash that went three and a half inches deep from ear to ear and severed his airway and carotid artery. Five knife injuries on Travis's hands were defensive wounds, sustained in his desperate effort to fight off his attacker.

Fueling the graphic details of the murder was the fact that Jodi had already admitted responsibility for it. Jodi's two court-appointed lawyers promised jurors there was a reasonable explanation for all of this. Her testimony had been littered with implications of self-defense or perhaps battered woman's syndrome; however, Jodi's credibility was extremely suspect. In the early days of the investigation, she had denied being anywhere near Travis's house on the night of the killing. Then she changed her tale, admitting she was there but insisting that two strangers, a man and a woman dressed in ski masks had done it. Finally, she'd come around to admit she was solely responsible, only this time she concocted a new story alleging that abusive behavior by Travis had pushed her to kill him.

For his part, the prosecutor, Juan Martinez, was confident that the evidence would prove Jodi Arias was guilty of premeditated first-degree murder, even though the defense wanted to paint her as a woman left dazed and disoriented by acute stress disorder, dissociative amnesia, and post-traumatic stress disorder after an angry, violent encounter. The stakes were enormously high for both sides. Jodi's life and the lawyers' careers rode on the outcome. Though the death penalty was on the table, it could be considered only with a conviction of murder in the first degree.

The fascination with both Jodi and the case had started at the murder, crescendoing steadily for four and a half years. By the time the trial started on January 2, 2013, it was at a fever pitch. After Jodi's attorneys had rolled the dice, calling Jodi herself to the witness stand on February 4, it had become insane. From that moment forward, the crowd of devoted true crime followers and regular folks at the courthouse mushroomed, with more and more people trying to witness up close the testimony of this femme fatale.

In the fifteen days during which Jodi had been testifying, she had been addressing questions from both sides, fending off attacks from Prosecutor Juan Martinez and spinning her version of events with the help of her own lawyers, Kirk Nurmi and Jennifer Willmott, who fed her carefully phrased questions. What emerged was a graphic, often uncomfortable level of detail about the sex life that Jodi and Travis had shared. She had described in full color every kinky sexual behavior she and Travis had ever engaged in. They had anal sex; they tried bondage; their fantasy sex play made porn writers blush. In a phone sex recording played in open court they talked about zip-tying Jodi to a tree with her dressed as Little Red Riding Hood while they performed wild sex acts outdoors. Jodi had recorded the late night conversation between the two that went on for more than half an hour. On the tape, Travis's voice, sleepy, baritone and raspy, is in sharp contrast to Jodi's soft, young, giddy tone. They delightedly recall the time they had experimented sexually with Pop Rocks and Tootsie Pops; the pleasures of oral sex; their sex in a bubble bath; the lubricants and bikini waxes; and the mutual masturbation on both sides. The moans of orgasms could be heard at various points of climax. The entire courtroom, jurors and gallery alike, had sat in awkward self-conscious silence as this extremely private pillow talk was broadcast as evidence. Some in the audience had been visibly embarrassed.

The explicit testimony seemed especially hard on those who knew and loved Travis. His sister, Tanisha Sorenson, a fixture in the gallery pretty much every day since the trial had started on January 2, took in the information as stoically as she could. She was not one to keep her feelings about Jodi to herself. "I know this might sound creepy, but I hope to get to watch her die someday after she's on death row," she had told a reporter early on. Tanisha was joined in the gallery every day by her sister Samantha and her brother Steven. The other four siblings were there less often, but all of them had to travel great distances to hear the secrets of their brother's sex life spilled into open court.

The graphic nature of the sexual content was amplified by the fact that both Travis and Jodi were Mormon, though Jodi had not been a Mormon when she and Travis first met in September 2006. By most accounts the connection between them was immediate and electric, and within two months, Jodi had converted to the Mormon faith, with Travis performing her baptism. But her conversion didn't change the fact that out-of-wedlock sex acts are absolutely forbidden in the Mormon religion. The church's Law of Chastity couldn't be clearer: "Before marriage, do not do anything to arouse the powerful emotions that must be expressed only in marriage. Do not participate in passionate kissing, lie on top of another person, or touch the private, sacred parts of another person's body, with or without clothing. Do not allow anyone to do that with you. Do not arouse those emotions in your own body." All this can be found in chapter 39 in *The Book of Mormon*.

According to Jodi's testimony, Travis had told her all about the Law of Chastity and its taboos. His explanation was that "vaginal sex was the ultimate place to not go until marriage," but any other sex acts, while not being condoned, were in a gray area that might make them okay. The very night of her baptism, Jodi claims, the two went to the gray area, with abandon.

After fifteen extraordinary days of Jodi on the stand, it seemed to many in and out of the courtroom that there could be nothing left to ask of this strangely mesmerizing defendant. Both her attorneys and the fiery prosecutor had finally run out of questions. But, now, on Day 16 of Jodi's testimony, it was time for a different set of questions—from the members of the jury.

In Arizona, criminal trial court proceedings allow time for interaction between a witness and the jury, giving the jury an opportunity to ask a witness direct questions through the judge. Arizona is only one of a handful of states that routinely allow juries to do this, the thinking being that such exchanges encourage jurors to be engaged and attentive during the trial. Each juror writes his or her questions on a piece of paper while the witness is testifying. They are then placed anonymously in a wire basket in front of the jurors to be vetted and read by the judge at the end of each witness's testimony. Both the prosecution and the defense attorney are allowed to argue against questions they deem inappropriate or irrelevant, but ultimately the judge makes the final decision on what gets asked. Then the attorneys are allowed another round of follow-up questions of the witness based solely on the scope of the jurors' questions.

Maricopa County Superior Court judge Sherry Stephens was on the bench, and she would be the reader of the jury's questions. Over the course of the trial, Judge Stephens had turned neutrality into an art form, her monotone voice and bland expression studiously avoiding any hint of what she might be thinking. Given the barrage of questions that the defense and the prosecution had already asked of Jodi Arias, the number of new questions the jury had for her was astounding. More than two hundred additional inquiries had been picked from the hundreds in the basket of jury questions. The eleven men and seven women on the panel, with no one identified as "alternates" until after closing arguments, had been busy. Without much emotion, the judge turned to Jodi, seated in the witness box, and read the first question.

"Did Travis pay for a majority of your trips?" she asked.

The juror's question was referring to the many small trips the two had taken together over the almost two years they had known each other. Jodi listened carefully, seeming to want to process the question before making a snap response, which she might later regret. She swiveled her chair to look at the jury face-on. There were no signs of fatigue or stress in her face, despite her often-emotional testimony during the previous three and a half weeks. Many days on the stand, she doubled down with her head in between her hands. Today she was much more composed. Her puffy, short-sleeved blouse was starch white, like the top half of a schoolgirl's uniform. Only the top of her hair was pulled back in a scrunchie, the rest of it falling down straight to her shoulders.

"Fifty-fifty," she replied, indicating that, at least for travel, she and Travis were on equal financial footing.

After two more follow-up questions about the trips they took, the line of inquiry from a juror went right to the murder. A juror wanted to know why Jodi had put Travis's camera in his washing machine right after she killed him. Again, Jodi paused to consider the question carefully. She relied on the answer she had repeated so often during her time in the witness box, namely that she couldn't remember. She claimed she had no memory of anything that happened after Travis lunged at her and she shot him. Throughout the long period of jurors' questions, she answered over and over that she couldn't remember. Finally on the seventy-fourth question, the issue of her memory loss was dealt with head-on.

"Why is it that you have no memory of stabbing Travis?" the judge asked, reading from a juror's question.

Jodi took a long pause. She looked at the jury, prepared to answer, then hesitated again before any sound came out. She raised her hands from her lap, lifted them into the air, spread her fingers, and began using her hands to help her with her emphatic points.

"I can't really explain why my mind did what it did," she said in a tone no more emotional than if she had been asked where she had last seen her car keys. A pause of at least three seconds ensued. "Maybe because it's too horrible. I don't know."

PART I

CHAPTER 1

DEAD AT HOME

On June 9, 2008, at just before 10:30 p.m., officers for the Mesa Police Department in Mesa, Arizona, responded to a 911 call at 11428 East Queensborough Avenue. It came from a five-bedroom, well-maintained Spanish-style house in a quiet residential area of town where the homes were variations of each other, based on a handful of tasteful models. The owner of this particular home had been found dead in the shower of the master bathroom. The caller stated she had no idea how long he had been there.

"A friend of ours is dead at his home," the young female voice told the dispatcher, her words shaking in her throat. "We hadn't heard from him in a while and came to check on him. We think he is dead. His roommate went to check on him and said, 'There is blood everywhere.'"

Responding officers found the man, later identified as thirty-year-old Travis Alexander, crumpled naked and lifeless on the floor of his shower stall. His body was well into the decomposition process, and although it was unclear how long he had been there, there was no doubt it had been at least a couple of days. Officers observed large amounts of blood beyond the shower as well, splattered around the floor, walls, and sink. Police observed a large laceration to the man's throat, which appeared to cross from one ear to the other.

A fairly hard-edged town with a violent crime rate above the national average in pretty much every category, the city of Mesa had seen its share of disturbing deaths. Twenty-five years earlier, in one of Maricopa County's most heinous crimes ever, a transient by the name of Robert "Gypsy" Comer had murdered a man he had never met before at a campground near Apache Lake, then kidnapped a woman one campsite over and sexually assaulted her for twenty-four hours. He had been sentenced to death, and he was executed by lethal injection in May 2007.

Unlike the Apache Lake crime, this new Mesa murder did not have the markings of a random crime, though at this early stage, nothing could be ruled out. Travis owned and occupied the house, but being single, he liked to rent out bedrooms to friends and roommates for the income. He currently had two boarders, Enrique Cortez and Zachary Billings, who told police it had been four or five days since they had last seen and spoken to him. However, they hadn't suspected anything was wrong, because he had a trip planned to Cancún; they'd just assumed he had already left.

It was the planned trip to Cancún that had prompted the search for Travis in the first place. Unable to reach him, Marie "Mimi" Hall, the friend Travis was supposed to be traveling with, had become increasingly concerned, especially since they were scheduled to leave in the morning. That evening, she'd gone to his house, knocked, and waited in vain. When no one came to the door, she went home and called her friend Michelle Lowery and Michelle's boyfriend, Dallin Forrest. All three entered the house by using the keypad code at the garage. Mimi immediately detected a foul odor, something she initially blamed on Travis's dog, Napoleon. Inside, they were surprised to find Zach and his girlfriend, Amanda McBrien, in Zach's bedroom. They had not heard the doorbell. Now that they knew Travis was missing, Zach tried to turn the doorknob to his room, discovered it was locked, and went to retrieve the spare key to the master bedroom suite. As the door opened, a huge bloodstain could be seen on the carpet at the entryway to the hall leading to Travis's en suite bathroom. The smell of death was undeniable. That was when all of them knew the search was not going to end well.

It was ten minutes to midnight when homicide detective and lead investigator for the case Esteban Flores arrived at the address. By then the residence had already been secured with yellow police tape, and a police guard was in place to monitor the comings and goings in the house.

The scene in the bathroom was gruesome. By the blood spatter and smears on the walls, there definitely appeared to have been a struggle between the victim and the assailant. It was difficult to assess a cause of death because of the high number of wounds visible across the victim's upper torso and head. The victim was hunched in a sitting position on the shower floor. The body looked like it had been rinsed off in the shower some time after death. A .25-mm bullet casing was carefully removed from atop caked blood on the floor near the sink, but the handgun it came from was nowhere to be found. Blood swabs, fingerprints, and hair samples were collected from the bathroom baseboards and floor.

Nothing in Travis's bedroom looked particularly out of place. His well-organized closets and drawers had not been disturbed, and there was no indication that the room had been entered in any forced manner. Of note, however, sheets and blankets had been stripped from the bed and removed from the room, although it couldn't be determined by whom or why. The hallway between the bedroom and master bathroom had blood smears and one latent bloody palm print, which would be cut from the wall and analyzed later at the crime lab.

With the preliminary assessment of the crime scene complete, Detective Flores turned his attention to the friends or housemates who had been present when the body was discovered—Mimi Hall, Michelle Lowery, Dallin Forrest, Zachary Billings, Amanda McBrien, Enrique Cortez, and Karl Hiatt. After being ruled out as suspects, they might be able to provide information about other people who knew Travis and maybe had a grudge or a score to settle. The fact that the other two boarders were not only unharmed, but had actually been living several days in the same house as their dead landlord, allegedly without knowing it, seemed to suggest that Travis had been a very specific target. Among Travis's friends, there was a lot of buzz about Jodi Arias, a vindictive ex-girlfriend who lived in California. She would need to be located, but at the moment, the six at hand all agreed to go to the Mesa police station to be interviewed.

Flores chose to speak with Mimi Hall first, as she had been the first on the scene and was Travis's intended guest for the trip to Cancún. She told the investigator that she had met Travis a year earlier in a singles ward of the Church of Jesus Christ of Latter-day Saints, although the two had only been getting to know each other better in the past few months. She thought Travis may have had a romantic interest in her, but she had told him that she wanted the relationship to be platonic and would understand if he wanted to replace her with someone else on the business trip to Mexico. Travis had declined, promising he would respect her boundaries. She reported she hadn't seen him in church on Sunday and had been trying to call him for days before she finally went to his residence.

When asked about Travis's roommates, Mimi didn't know much. Zach had been there a few months but frequently stayed with his girlfriend, while Enrique had moved in only a couple of weeks earlier. Both were from the church, but she didn't know them well enough to provide an assessment of their personalities. When asked about Jodi Arias, she had to rely on hearsay, but there had certainly been a lot of chatter about Jodi: she was a "stalker ex-girlfriend"; Jodi would crawl through Napoleon's doggie door to get inside when she wasn't invited; after the two broke up, Jodi had stolen some pages from a journal Travis kept, something he had been hoping to turn into a memoir. Mimi was aware that Travis had talked to Jodi as recently as the previous week to confront her about hacking into his Facebook account. In Mimi's opinion, even though she had never met her, Jodi's obsession with Travis was concerning.

"I was worried because he had told me about an ex-girlfriend who had done some psychotic obsessive things to him and his friends," she said. She told Flores she even had her sister on the line when she went to the house in case something was seriously wrong. "I was actually afraid that the girl might be there," she told the detective.

The next person interviewed was Zachary Billings, one of Travis's two tenants. Zach had met Travis a couple of years earlier when Zach had been on a Mormon mission in Arizona in 2006 and had come to Travis's home to talk to one of his roommates. More than a year later Zach was back in Arizona and looking for a place to live. In January 2008, Zach had moved into Travis's house as a boarder.

Though the likelihood of Zach's being the killer was slim—who would live in the same house as his victim for that many days without trying to get rid of the body?—he could have easily seen or heard something that might prove critical. It was almost four in the morning when the interview with him began. Despite the hour, Zach was quite forthcoming and relaxed, respectfully answering all questions. He paid Travis $450 a month for his room, and with that rent, he had free range of the house. Though Zach did not know the new roommate, Enrique, very well, he did know that Enrique was also from the church. The house was strictly a living arrangement, not a social one, and each man kept pretty much to himself—in fact during the four and a half months Zach had been there, he and Travis had not had dinner together once. Because Travis traveled on business frequently, it was common for Zach to go days without seeing his landlord.

The last time he thought he had seen Travis was the Thursday before the body was discovered, but he didn't think anything of Travis's absence. Zach knew Travis was going on a trip, and not knowing the specifics, Zach assumed he had already left. At this point, Zach accounted for his whereabouts from the time he had last seen Travis alive, which had been in the house, till the time the body was found. For the most part, he had been with his girlfriend, Amanda McBrien, at her house. Other than that, he said he had been going to church, running errands, or working at McGrath's Fish House, at the intersection of Stapley Drive and U.S. Route 60, about fifteen miles from the house. At one point, he had texted Travis about a mailbox key, but was not concerned when there had been no reply.

Detective Flores asked Zach if he had noticed anything out of place or unusual. Zach said maybe some furniture had been shifted ever so slightly in the living room. This had a reasonable explanation. Travis had purchased a floor cleaning machine somewhat recently, and because the machine was also in the living room, he assumed Travis had a maintenance project in mind.

Turning to more general questions about his landlord, Flores asked questions about Travis's physical well-being. According to Zach, Travis was in overall good health and exercised regularly, either riding his bike, running, or kick-boxing.

When it came to Jodi Arias, Zach had a lot to say. He said she had once been Travis's girlfriend, but they had broken up before Zach began living with Travis. It was after the two split up that Jodi moved from California to Mesa to be close to him, which seemed rather weird since most people would move farther away following a breakup. Zach wasn't sure where Jodi lived now—whether she was still in Arizona or back in California with her family. Travis had sometimes paid Jodi to clean the house, maybe because she didn't know many people and he felt sorry for her. Other times, she came over uninvited or called at inappropriate times to ask for advice, which led to heated arguments between them. Travis had had two girlfriends since Jodi, but one had broken up with him in February, in part because she said Jodi was always hanging around and Travis needed to deal with it. Zach was more than willing to give a buccal swab for a DNA sample and be available in the future for questioning.

Travis's second roommate, Enrique Cortez, was confused about the exact day he had last seen Travis. He described for Detective Flores unusual observations from the week before. One evening when he had gotten home from work at 6:00 P.M., he had noticed the front door was locked. It was unusual that he had to enter the house through the garage. Like Zach, Enrique had noticed that the living room furniture was pushed aside, and the floor cleaner stood in the middle of the floor. The dog fence was also out of place, set up across the stairs. Though he had been living there only a few weeks, Enrique had never seen Travis restrict his pug Napoleon's movements around the house. The dog was free to roam everywhere. Enrique also noticed that Travis's bedroom and office doors remained closed for days. He didn't detect an odor in the house until about an hour before Travis's body was found.

As night turned into morning, the interviews with the other people who had been at the house revealed similar themes. As far as Travis's having any enemies in his social circle, profession, or church, nobody could think of anybody beyond the obsessed jilted girlfriend with a penchant for showing up unannounced. The boarders had not seen any strange, suspicious characters lurking around the bushes or casing the neighborhood in the days before the murder. Of course, Jodi was no stranger.

CHAPTER 2

YOUNG JODI

Despite the intense media coverage, there is surprisingly little known about Jodi Arias's upbringing. Many of the supposed "facts" about her early life come from Jodi herself, making them unreliable and subject to an understandable amount of scrutiny. However, if we sift through the concrete and established aspects of Jodi's past, it becomes clear that much of her youth was marked by her family's relocations and her parents' strict, controlling behavior toward her.

Jodi Ann Arias was born on July 9, 1980, in Salinas, California, to parents William "Bill" and Sandra Denise (nee Allen) Arias. A tall, muscular man, with a well-trimmed mustache and beard, Bill Arias was a restaurateur, and took pride in his buff physique. He had dreams of opening a chain of restaurants, while Jodi's mother worked as a waitress at the family's restaurants. Her heritage on her father's side is Mexican, while her mother's background is German and English.

For Jodi, growing up in Salinas was close to ideal. Known for its flowers, vineyards, and temperate climate, the city is located in Monterey County in the middle of the California coast, about eight miles inland from the Pacific Ocean. Jodi attended Los Padres Elementary School on John Street, and to hear others tell it, she was a happy kid, well liked by a large circle of playmates and friends. She loved art, especially drawing and coloring, and was happiest when she was near a pile of Crayola crayons and some pieces of blank paper. She was also an avid reader, who took flute and karate lessons. Around age ten, she took on photography as a hobby.

The oldest of her parents' four children, Jodi had two younger brothers, Carl and Joey, and a younger sister, Angela; she also had an older half sister from her father's first marriage.

Beth Hawkins was a weekend babysitter for the household for almost a year, around the time Jodi was five or six. She claimed she had sometimes observed Jodi behaving aggressively toward her younger brother, Carl. She recounted one incident in particular, when Carl began screaming from another room. She asked him what was wrong, and at first, the child could not explain. Eventually he admitted that his sister had struck him in the back of the head with a baseball bat. When Beth asked Jodi if she had hit her brother, she was struck by Jodi's response of "I don't know why he is crying."

Recalling it more than two decades later, Beth said she was surprised by Jodi's lack of empathy for her brother, who had clearly been hurt. It could have been an early indicator that Jodi suffered from some sort of detachment disorder.

Years later Jodi would say she was subjected to disciplinary beatings from both her mother and her father, claiming her mother hit her with a wooden spoon that she carried with her in her purse, and that her father used a belt to dole out punishments. But others disputed this, insisting Sandy and Bill never reacted with violence. To that end, these claims of abuse have never been substantiated by any school or health authorities, nor have any of her friends come forward to say they saw evidence of abuse. Aside from Jodi's own statements, there has never been any evidence to suggest domestic violence in the Arias household. What people have said is that Sandy and Bill were particularly strict with their daughter from a young age, a trend that would continue well into her teenage years, until Jodi moved out.

When Jodi was about eleven, the Ariases moved for the first time in Jodi's life, going 157 miles south to Santa Maria, California, where Bill had a restaurant called the Branding Iron. Jodi seemed to adjust well to her new surroundings, developing a tight circle of six or seven girlfriends and taking to middle school easily. She attended the eighth grade at Orcutt Junior High School, on Pinal Street not far from Mary Grisham Park. One thing that friends at the time noticed was that Jodi always seemed to be babysitting the youngest two siblings, Angela and Joey. She carried around a diaper bag and was often seen pulling them around in a red cart. It was a lot of responsibility for a girl in junior high, and friends say she was often a no-show at the school dances and sporting events.

Still, Jodi loved school. Once again displaying an affinity and natural talent for art, she drew inspiration from her art teacher, Mr. B, whom she credits with giving her "the creative freedom to veer from the linear syllabus and follow my own inclinations." Though she was still in middle school, her year in Mr. B's class solidified her love of the creative process. In part because of him, but also because of her friends, Jodi had really settled into her community, hanging out a lot with a best friend named Patti, with whom she was very close.

It was not to last. About four years after the family moved to Santa Maria, Jodi's mother found something that put an irreversible trend of suspicion into the mother-daughter relationship. Sandy discovered that a piece of her Tupperware was missing from the kitchen. In no time, she discovered that Jodi had taken the container to the roof of the house, where she was using it to grow a marijuana plant. Upset by the discovery, Sandy and Bill Arias decided to call the sheriff's office to turn their daughter in. They felt they had to do something and hoped involving the police would scare her straight.

Retelling the story recently, Jodi's friend Patti, who was also in on the rooftop scheme, said the incident was blown completely out of proportion. "We took a pot seed and we planted it in a little Tupperware and it bloomed like one little leaf on it. And another little tiny leaf almost grew . . . and we put it on top of the roof so the sun would hit it. And then the neighbor told on us."

Patti said the cops came over and sternly lectured both girls, warning them they could end up in juvenile hall. Patti was also grounded by her father after Sandy called him. Beyond being embarrassed and ashamed, Jodi felt betrayed by her parents and, using the emotion many teenagers throw around with abandon, told friends she now hated them. Up until this point, friends said Jodi was not a rebellious teen and had not been acting out in a way that would have made her parents afraid that their child was getting involved in drugs and other kinds of teenage risk-taking behavior. But Bill and Sandy Arias were not taking any chances. In many ways this overkill response was indicative of the kind of strict parenting they would continue to display as Jodi got older.

Indeed, Sandy Arias seems to acknowledge that this event marked the beginning of the deterioration of Jodi's relationship with her parents. Afterward, Jodi grew distant and even paranoid. She began claiming that her parents would constantly search her room, making it so that she would never trust them again. For their part, her parents have insisted they did not continue to snoop in her room, even though Jodi was convinced they were always looking for something on her. Jodi started becoming dishonest, at least with them. Sometimes, Jodi was physically violent toward her mother. There was even an incident where she got so mad at her mother she kicked her for no reason during a family dinner.

Around the same time, Jodi's parents decided to move the family again, further complicating their family dynamic. This time, they moved 556 miles north, to Yreka, California, near Mount Shasta and the Oregon border. According to Patti, the news devastated Jodi. First, she was betrayed by her parents when they called the cops, and now they were ripping her away from her tight circle of friends, especially her very best friend, Patti.

Recalling that difficult time, Patti said, "The last night Jodi was in town . . . she was crying and she said, 'The reason I'm moving is because me and you get into too much trouble together,' and I was just absolutely heartbroken because we were good kids. We didn't do anything to get in trouble."

This was the third home in several years, a difficult situation for any teenager who wanted to be part of her school crowd. Jodi had to redefine herself with each move to fit in to the new culture and community she had been transported to.

Yreka was a big change from both Santa Maria and Salinas. Santa Maria and Salinas were ethnically mixed agricultural towns, while Yreka, predominantly white and Anglo, was a more upscale tourist town for visitors interested in the historical period of the California gold rush. If her parents thought they were improving their lifestyle, it was an intimidating environment for the new teenager in town. The problems in the family would at least be *inside* the house and not be apparent or visible from outside the family's white two-story home on Oregon Street, with the nice yard and gravel driveway in a well-kept neighborhood near the village.

Jodi began the ninth grade at Yreka Union High School. People who knew her during that time had only nice things to say about her. They saw her as a good girl, kind and caring. According to her friend Tina, Jodi had a good sense of humor and wasn't the least bit violent; in fact she actually had a kind and gentle spirit. Some who were students at the time said Jodi was not only accepted but even became popular at the school.

Apparently that's not how Jodi saw it. In Jodi's telling of events, she never fully adjusted to life in Yreka. A while after arriving in town, Jodi wrote a letter to Patti, spilling out on paper how miserable she was and how she couldn't make new friends in a small town where everybody else seemed to have known each other since birth. Jodi had just turned fifteen when she wrote the letter, dated September 16, 1995. It reads: "My dearest Patricia, I miss you so much. Nobody up here could ever take your place. No one up here listens like you do . . . Everyone here is pretty much the same as down there, except for one thing: I don't feel like I belong . . . I can't even join in the conversation because I don't know what they're talking about. They'll say something to me like 'can you believe so and so's going with so and so, and they look so funny together' and I'll be like 'no.' I don't even know who the hell they are. So it doesn't matter to me. And that brings up another complaint. The only thing people do around here—I figured out—2 different groups or types of people: getting stoned—the stoners—and the gossips . . . preppy snobs."

"The move broke her," Patti said years later, pausing as she recalled the letter.

Jodi ended the letter by telling a story about the family van overheating. She painted a portrait of an average family juggling everyday challenges, but as a team, taking on obstacles in optimistically good spirits. There was no hint of an abusive family; rather, a loving family in it together for the long haul. In the midst of these moves and adjustments, another stress may have been weighing on Jodi: her father had been struggling with serious medical issues. He would later get a kidney transplant, but his persistent illnesses could have been very hard on Jodi and the rest of the family, as the man of the house was preoccupied with saving his own life.

One friend said Jodi's father was warmer than her mother. The friend said Bill liked to laugh, while Sandy was quieter and more reserved. Of course, with Bill in poor health the enormous burden of raising the sizable family was Sandy's.

No wonder Sandy might have seemed pensive, and no surprise that Jodi would have to take on more than her fair share of rearing her younger siblings.

Through all this, art seemed to be Jodi's one reliable outlet. In the letter to Patti, Jodi explained how she had just bought an oil painting set that strained her teenage budget, saying she took the leap because she was determined to paint more. "I'm going to start oil painting. I went and got a few supplies and in total it was $50.28. This stuff is outrageous. I got paints, I got paint thinners and canvasses to paint on."

Jodi's interest and talent in art was well known in the school. Many years later, her high school art teacher remembered her with praise, recalling how conscientious, mature, hardworking, and smart she was. He also thought she was extremely talented, with a mastery of all media. Not only was Jodi the first to complete his assignments, but she presented herself with perfection, not a hair, piece of clothing, or application of makeup out of place. He told a local paper, "She was the perfect kid; the kind of kid you would want your son to date because she just seemed so clean cut."

Despite appearances, things were far from perfect for Jodi. Sandy Arias said she found herself on the receiving end of hostile tirades from her fifteen-year-old daughter. The outbursts were baffling to both her parents, but Jodi felt her parents imposed too many restrictions, given that she was now in high school. Jodi's friends agreed that her parents were on the strict side. While other freshmen and sophomores were allowed to stay out until nine or ten o'clock in the evening, Jodi had a dinner hour curfew of 6 P.M., and she couldn't go out again after dinner. The rule was not bent to allow for even the evening after-school activities.

Perhaps her parents were uncomfortable with Jodi's emerging sexuality. She was changing fast, both physically and emotionally. She was a beautiful young woman who was beginning to realize that boys were attracted to her. She must have experienced the rush of power that many attractive young women feel when they first understand their effect on the opposite sex. Nevertheless, Jodi still felt insecure and like an outsider in Yreka. That could have been why she chose another outsider for her first romantic experience.

In the ninth grade, she formed a friendship with a young man named Bobby, three years older than she, whom she'd met at a state fair. It had been the middle of summer, and the temperature was in the triple digits. Dressed in an eighteenth-century long black suit and wobbling along on crutches, Bobby was a standout in the crowd. A self-identified Goth, he was clad in all black, and everything about him from his hair to his eyes was dark and exotic. That night, he invited her to ride with him on the Zipper, an adrenaline-provoking ride that rotated while spinning the individual cars for two. Bobby lived six miles away, huge to a young teenager. After the ride at the fair, they didn't see each other until a few months later, when Jodi saw him at a homecoming football game. She sauntered over to him and asked if he remembered her, he said yes, she gave him her number, and he soon called.

In the beginning, Jodi and Bobby were just friends. He already had a girlfriend, so nothing could happen until those two broke up. When that eventually happened, Jodi and Bobby grew closer and unofficially started dating. Jodi's dating rule was that young men who wanted to go out with her had to agree she was their one and only. Bobby, already graduated from high school but currently unemployed, had lots of free time. He would meet Jodi near the high school, and they would hold hands. Bobby had big dreams. He wanted to be an actor, but Jodi said he also had wild ideas about vampires, and he wanted to move to San Francisco to find them. According to Jodi, he wanted to stay with her forever.

But others said Jodi was the one who really latched on to Bobby, beginning a pattern that would continue throughout her dating life in which she would abandon her interests and concentrate on the guy she was dating. *His* friends would become her friends, and *his* interests would become her interests. In Bobby's case, he was into martial arts and friends say Jodi soon got into them, too. Small behaviors like this already showed that Jodi was exhibiting a tendency to obsess about the man in her life. This made her romance with Bobby tumultuous. There were dramatic breakups and ecstatic reconciliations; each dramatic breakup was supposed to be the last one.

In the final quarter of tenth grade, perhaps to get her away from what they saw as bad influences, Jodi's parents arranged for her to take part in a cultural exchange program in Costa Rica, ostensibly to learn Spanish. In no time at all, Jodi was dating the son of her host family, Victor, who was also sixteen. While Jodi's friends believe she had passionate feelings for Bobby, Jodi described Victor as her first experience with the "warm fuzzies." She said she wasn't in love with Victor, but it was her first taste of feeling warm about somebody.

Jodi celebrated her seventeenth birthday in Costa Rica with Victor. When she returned home and the two corresponded by mail, Jodi was on the receiving end of long, romantic letters, written in Spanish. Before long, Victor came to the States for a monthlong visit, two weeks of which he stayed with Jodi and her family. It was then that he gave her a promise ring to express his devotion. She was so in love she gave him a promise back—she would move to Costa Rica when she could and they would live there and start a family together. The thought was romantic, but completely unrealistic.

As it turned out, Victor was rather jealous and old-fashioned, according to Jodi. He would make Jodi walk on the inside of the sidewalk to make her less visible to other men who might be driving by. One time, she spotted a male classmate at a drive-through restaurant and said Victor got upset. Not being able to handle his jealousy, she broke up with him over the phone during October of her junior year. She'd already complained that she had a controlling father; she definitely did not want a controlling boyfriend on top of it.

As she neared the end of eleventh grade Jodi was clearly floundering. The small town, the insular high school, and the rigidly controlled home environment were just too much to bear. She wanted out. Though she was of well above average intelligence, Jodi's grades were deteriorating. She told a friend, "I got my report card recently and my grades were bad. I've got to get with the program and raise them." But Jodi also revealed to her friend that she was thinking of joining the army and even took the military's popular test, the

Armed Services Vocational Aptitude Battery, designed to help young adults assess what occupations they might be suited for. Jodi added, "Then, a few days ago, some guy from the army called me and asked what I planned on doing after graduation and I told him I wanted to study medicine and he said judging from the results on my test I could probably go into any medical field I wanted to. Cool, huh?" But, she added, her mother and father immediately poured cold water on her explorations. "When I told my parents they got all mad and said that those people will say anything just to recruit a person."

Jodi desperately needed an escape route and, just in time, along came Bobby back into the picture, and they reconnected. They took a drive out to a little white chapel with a tall white steeple, where they decided to give their relationship another try. When Jodi's parents got wind of it, they were totally disapproving. They had heard rumors that Bobby was into the occult. Jodi disagreed. She told her parents he was beautiful inside and out. He was just a sensitive soul who was searching. He was still eccentric and friends say he loved to play the Dungeons and Dragons board game. But at least he wasn't chasing vampires anymore.

Though Jodi's parents didn't like him, Jodi seemed long past caring what they thought. She was tired of their control. At every turn, she felt that they were on her case. She claimed that she once skipped class in order to study for an exam she thought was more important, and her father found out. After an administrator told him about the unexcused absence, he tracked his daughter down and grounded her until her eighteenth birthday, still three months away.

Jodi made up her mind that she was going to drop out of school when the academic year was over in May. She was already getting a lot of D's and F's, and the fun of school was long gone. She may have just gotten tired of trying to fit in, being neither a stoner nor a preppy. She claimed her parents didn't support her interest in art, the subject she loved the most, and she was sick of fighting with them. She interpreted their strictness as a rejection of her artistic abilities and this became a reason to blame them for her academic failures.

While most teens act out, Jodi's behavior already seemed to have diverged into something more serious. Friends say she wasn't into drugs or alcohol, but rather appeared to have some escalating personality dysfunction. It had started about a year earlier, when she had gone around warning her friends about the Apocalypse and the Second Coming of Jesus Christ. Jodi had been raised as a nondenominational Christian and wasn't particularly religious, but an older man who frequented her father's restaurant, where she sometimes waitressed, had done the math and determined that the catastrophic event would occur in September 1997. The idea that Jodi would get invested in this story and take it seriously enough to warn others raised doubts about how grounded in reality she was. To Jodi, the man in the restaurant seemed to be a reliable, valid source of prophecy, as he always carried a dog-eared pocket version of the New Testament and quoted Bible stories with authority. To others he might seem like a nut.

Perhaps the story gave Jodi the opportunity to drum up some fear and excitement, creating unnecessary drama. At this point, signs were beginning to emerge that Jodi thrived on drama and knew how to create it. Was her willingness to believe fantastical stories a hint of why she would soon develop an uncanny ability to lie with abandon? Whatever Jodi's relationship with the truth was at that point, the tension with her parents built to a head around age seventeen, just before she decided to move out of the house altogether. One of the unsubstantiated claims of physical abuse that precipitated the move was her father pushing her, causing her to hit her face on a doorpost and lose consciousness, only to wake up to her mother telling her father to be more careful. Jodi would maintain that this final abuse was what pushed her to move out of the house at seventeen and in with Bobby.

In the aftermath of Jodi's decision, Sandy and Bill Arias were beside themselves. Even when Jodi had been struggling, they had always had high hopes for their eldest daughter. Jodi was smart, pretty, and poised, and they believed she was going to accomplish something of importance in her life. They did not understand her rebellion. Simple statements or requests would become twisted, resulting in frivolous battles. Jodi seemed to misconstrue everything they said. They were at a loss as to how to turn things around and recover the daughter they loved. Possibly the intensity of her emotions frightened them, and rather than intervene by finding her professional help, they continued to employ futile, simplistic fixes. Her father had even resorted to disconnecting the car battery to keep her home, which was successful short term, as Jodi did not understand the workings of a car engine. But as it turned out, the Ariases were unable to stop their daughter from taking the drastic step of leaving home for good that summer.

Jodi recalled the night of her escape from her parents' home. She had packed up what little she had. She knew she had to check her car to see if her father had unhooked the battery again. She was as far as the living room when she heard one of her parents upstairs, so she jumped onto the couch and pretended she was asleep. She ended up dozing off and woke up to find her mother in the kitchen making breakfast. Not to be foiled, she then said that she was going to school, so luckily her mother didn't see her grabbing her cat as she headed out the door. In a flash, Sandy and Bill's beautiful but willful child was gone.

CHAPTER 3

FIRST WORDS

This is Jodi."

The voice on the other end of the phone was girlish, almost pleasant. It had been a late night of questioning for Travis's roommates and friends, but by the following morning Detective Flores had begun to expand his interviews. It was clear that investigators would have to speak with Jodi Arias soon; what was unexpected was that Jodi would be trying to get a hold of them. Word of Travis's death had spread quickly among his friends and colleagues, and Jodi had received a late-night call, informing her of what had happened. A friend of Travis and Jodi's, Dan Freeman, called her at 11:00 P.M., just thirty minutes after Travis's body was found. Jodi became silent, then broke down sobbing when he told her Travis was dead. After a few moments, Dan cut the call off because Jodi wanted to "be with herself."

Less than two months earlier Jodi had abandoned Arizona after living in Mesa for ten months and had moved back to California. Being hundreds of miles away from this tragic news, she spent the rest of the night calling long-distance to Arizona, reaching out to Travis's friends there to find out what was going on. At one point as Travis's friends gathered outside his house, Jodi called one of them, who happened to be standing next to Detective Flores at the time. He asked the detective if he should answer the call. It seemed almost all of Travis's friends already had their fingers pointed squarely at Jodi. The question was whether the police would come to the same conclusion.

In addition to calling Travis's friends, Jodi had been busy calling police headquarters twice, leaving a number where she could be reached. With Jodi probably aware that it would only be a matter of time before the police came knocking on her door in Yreka, California, perhaps she thought she could deflect attention away from herself by offering to assist them. At a minimum, she needed to know what the police knew.

Finally at 10 A.M. on June 10, less than twelve hours after Travis's body had been discovered, Detective Flores called her back.

The detective introduced himself. "I have a message from one of my patrol officers that you needed to talk to me about something?"

"Well, I just wanted to offer assistance . . . I don't know a lot of anything, but . . ."

"What have you heard so far?" the detective asked.

"I heard that he was, that he passed away, and it was, I don't know . . . I heard all kinds of rumors," Jodi said. She stuttered over the few things she claimed she had heard. "There was a lot of blood, his roommate found him, his friend found him, people were . . . I'm sorry, I'm upset, but um . . . I heard that nobody's been able to get a hold of him for almost a week, and that was about the last I spoke to him, too, and that's why I thought . . ."

Flores listened attentively, trying to glean from her conversation either inconsistencies or things only the killer could know. This early in the investigation, she was no more a suspect than anyone else. Nobody had seen her near Travis's home in a while, and as far as Flores knew, she might have an airtight alibi.

Jodi continued her assistance. "I . . . my friend said I should call you anyway and let you know of the last time I talked to him."

"Yeah, absolutely," Flores replied with encouragement. "I mean, any help we can get from anybody who contacted him . . ."

Jodi didn't wait for him to finish his thought. "I used to talk to him quite regularly," she offered. "I used to live there [in Mesa], but I live in Northern California now. I moved a few months ago. After I moved, we kept in touch regularly . . . a couple of times a week. I hadn't heard from him. I talked to him on Tuesday night. I looked at my phone records on the Internet to check, and I definitely talked to him Tuesday night."

Flores was increasingly interested. "That Tuesday night, do you remember the time?" he asked.

"I wanna say like a quarter after nine, but probably between eight thirty and nine thirty."

"What did you guys talk about?"

"Um, it was brief. He was, I was driving out to Utah, and you know, he was like 'are you gonna come out and see me?' And I was like 'no.' He was supposed to make a trip up here at the end of the month. We're doing this thing called 'one thousand places to see before you die,' and it's been featured on the Travel Channel. We sort of got into it last year, where we're starting to see all these different places on the list 'one thousand places.' It is a lot to see, but we each had that goal, and one of those was the Oregon coast. And so he was gonna come up here for that, and we were gonna go see that . . . crater lakes [*sic*]."

"Was that trip already scheduled or was it just something you guys talked about?"

"It wasn't officially, like dated, but I was planning to make the trip down there. But it was supposed to happen in May, and then it was supposed to happen last week, but that didn't work out. And he was going to Cancún today and um, and then he said as soon as he gets back from Cancún, he was going to drive up the coast and when he reaches me, we'll do some things, and then he'll continue up the coast to Washington and see some friends up there. And then I guess that was to happen in July, that he was supposed to go to Washington, D.C."

Flores could sense that Jodi was projecting a portrait of a relationship where all was rosy between Travis and her—very different from what he'd been hearing from Mimi Hall and Zach Billings. In Jodi's version, it appeared she and Travis talked regularly, they were going to see a thousand places together before they died, presumably of old age, and they couldn't have been more compatible. Undeterred by this discrepancy, Flores turned his attention to any potential suspects she might know of.

"Okay," Flores said, "did he have any issues with anybody here in town? Any enemies?"

"You know, he got his tires slashed," she declared. "It was last year, he said he was worried about that. And I was worried, too. He never locked his doors, and I would tell him 'lock your doors,' and he said 'you're not my mom.' And he comes from a bad city, Riverside, California, violent. And I come from a similar neighborhood, and my parents always said to lock doors. He doesn't have that habit, because he lives in a great neighborhood, and it's never been an issue. Nothing's ever been stolen."

The truth of the matter was that the murder did not look like it was motivated by burglary. Valuables had not been reported missing, and things that could have been taken weren't. Not only did the intruder have enough time to drag Travis's body from the bedroom into the shower and rinse it off, but there had been time to run a load or two of laundry. This was not a botched or panicked burglary. Because Travis's body had sustained so many brutal knife wounds, many in the back, it seemed very passionate and personal.

Flores was curious about Jodi's view of her rapport with Travis. "How would you describe your relationship with him?" he asked.

Jodi seemed to be forthcoming. "We dated for like five months. And we broke up, and we continued to see each other for quite a bit. You know? Right up until I moved," Jodi said, referring to her recent return to California.

"When did you guys break up?"

"We officially broke up June 29 of last year. But we . . . even though we broke up and decided to remain friends . . . I feel embarrassed talking about this but it was . . . but it wasn't boyfriend and girlfriend . . . it was more like kind of buddies . . . you know what I mean?"

"You guys were not like romantically together at any time?"

"We were intimate, but I wouldn't say romantic as far as relationship goes. We were in no way headed toward marriage." Jodi answered the questions with a frankness that bordered on detachment.

"When you say intimate, does that include like a sexual relationship with him?"

"Yeah, it does."

"Kind of embarrassing to talk about . . . ?"

"Yeah. And if you could keep it kind of confidential? It's really looked down upon in that church, I mean, I'm telling you this to help you in any way I can."

Raised in both the Catholic and Mormon churches, Flores

had knowledge about how the Mormon church would have viewed this relationship. In many ways, Detective Flores was the exact opposite of the hard-drinking, smoking, raunchy detective that Hollywood scriptwriters love to create. He'd been married to the same woman for more than two decades and had five children with her. A homebody who loved to cook for his kids, Flores chose to identify with the Mormon church when he married his wife, who was also Mormon. He knew plenty about the religion, including the rules that Jodi and Travis were breaking by being intimate.

Now that Flores had Jodi admitting she and Travis had been lovers, he was in a better position to get her to reveal other crucial details. "I appreciate it," he said, using the classic technique of seeming to befriend the person being investigated. The detective moved the conversation along, looking to map out a timeline. "So you moved back to California a couple of months ago."

Jodi guessed that she had moved back on April 10.

"Did you stop by his house to say goodbye to him?"

"Oh, yes," Jodi replied. "I was completely moved out of my house, and I stayed at his house for about a week. I practically lived there. I spent the night there several times a week when I lived there. I came over and I cleaned his house a lot. He paid me a little bit to keep his house nice and clean. Sort of like a housekeeper."

The detective asked if Jodi had ever met any of Travis's roommates, to which she replied that he'd had several. One guy who had been there moved to Utah, she thought, and one had moved to Phoenix. She said that she and his current roommate Zach, a returned Mormon missionary, had "sort of connected" because they communicated by instant messaging. She claimed not to know if he still lived at the house, and Flores confirmed that he did.

Flores used the opening to expand on the profile of the

renter. "What do you think about Zach . . . what was his relationship with your ex-boyfriend?"

"He seemed like a nice guy when I first met him," Jodi stated. She explained that she had met both Zach and his girlfriend at the house.

With the Mormon religion on the table, Jodi talked about Travis's position on substances. Mormons don't drink alcohol and don't use tobacco, drugs, coffee, or tea, she stated. "He was just super strict on that," she told Flores, referring to Travis. "He wouldn't even take Excedrin for headaches because it had caffeine. I'm a little less strict on that . . ."

"There are a lot of Diet Cokes in the fridge," Flores commented.

"Yeah, they're not Travis's," Jodi responded. "I can guarantee you that. He wouldn't even touch Coke."

The conversation returned to contact between Jodi and the victim. "And that was around April that you last saw him, right? You haven't been back in town since?"

"No, I haven't at all," answered Jodi.

"Somebody had mentioned your name, that you had been back in town for like a week, a couple of days."

Jodi said that she had been planning on going, but hadn't acted on it, but Flores was on to something. "You haven't been physically down here since you left?"

"Since I moved, no, I haven't. I was gonna go this week actually and stay at his house while he was in Cancún, but it's just not in the budget."

"Is that something you guys had scheduled?" Flores questioned.

Jodi went on to explain that Travis frequently let his friends stay at his house, and that according to Jodi's calendar, she was going to stay at Travis's place the following week. She had emailed him about it, being so last minute. Now that Jodi's timeline was getting closer to the murder,

Flores's interest increased. "And when was that email sent out?"

"Just a few days ago," Jodi replied. "I'm in front of the computer, so I can check right now. Let me log in to my account." In a few moments, she had her answer. "I sent one on June 7. He got a little upset when I told him I wasn't driving out. He gets upset really easily . . . I don't know, we kind of . . . guilt each other."

"So you guys have a decent relationship as friends?"

"We did. We had . . ."

For the first time, Flores let Jodi know her name had come up in the investigation. "Because the people we talked to, they said your relationship was kind of rocky, got a little crazy at times . . ."

"It did. What happened was when I broke up with Travis last year, it was kind of dumb. It was a bunch of drama . . . I had the suspicion that he was cheating on me, so I looked in his phone . . . it all blew up and we realized we couldn't trust each other. We broke up at that point, but we were still attracted to each other . . . still loved each other. So, it wasn't the best thing, but we still hung out all the time together. And it didn't really help either of us to move on.

"I haven't really dated anyone since. And he told me he hadn't dated anyone since, but then after that, he had. So, it's all been kind of weird because we kept our dating life sort of from each other. Like a 'don't ask, don't tell' policy. And I figured, 'Okay, if he didn't have a girlfriend, then it was okay me coming over.' And if he didn't think that I was with anybody, then that's fine, too. So the less we knew about each other, the better off we were."

Flores moved the interview from the relationship to the crime scene. "You stayed in the house, knew the surroundings," he continued. "Can you describe his bedroom bedding and stuff for me?"

"Um, I spent a lot of time in there," Jodi answered confidently. "I don't know if it's Egyptian cotton or what, but it's really nice." She went on to describe what should have been a five-thousand-dollar bed, a California-king-sized Intelli-Gel sleigh bed, but Travis had picked it up for really cheap. She was quite familiar with the bedding as well, knowing that his down comforter was encased in a brown-striped duvet cover with a button closure and that the sheets were more of a cotton/linen material in a brown-checked pattern. She described the many times the two had to reposition the comforter inside the duvet cover, grabbing corners and shaking it out to distribute it.

Once those details were established, Flores moved the conversation to people and contacts other than Zach Billings, asking Jodi how she'd heard of Travis's death and what people around Travis were saying about the death. When Jodi said that she'd heard it was being treated as a "suspicious death," Flores cut in.

"I can tell you that we're investigating it as a homicide," Flores stated. "It's not a suspicious death anymore. And it's important to find out why someone would want to do harm to him. What kind of stuff he was involved in . . . or maybe it was as simple as a burglary or an intruder."

Jodi picked up on how hard it would be to overpower him. "One thing," she added, ". . . when they said suspicious death, I thought, well he's trying to shed pounds so he looks good for Cancún, so he looks good in boxers and in a bathing suit, swim trunks or whatever, so I know he takes supplements and he works out really, really hard. It's a very intense routine . . . he had these heavy dumbbells that he uses . . . he's so strong, there are a couple of kinds that he uses, we tried to wrestle for fun and he showed me some moves . . . unless there were two people, I don't see how anyone could have overpowered him." It wouldn't be the last time Jodi spoke about it requiring two people to take him down.

"Yeah, he was a pretty good-sized guy," Flores said, having only seen him dead and crumpled over with little blood left in his veins.

"Close to two hundred pounds," Jodi stated.

"Why would somebody want to hurt him?" Flores continued. "Money worries? Concerns?"

"He did owe people money, but they were good friends," she said, before proceeding to launch into a prolonged discussion of Travis's finances and the fact that Jodi had recently written him a small check toward the BMW he had sold her. Flores let her talk, but sooner or later the conversation would have to shift back to their relationship. Finally he saw an opening.

"We've been talking to people . . . don't want to make you feel bad, but they didn't have the best things to say about you," Flores said, putting the rumors about their relationship on the table for the first time.

"Okay."

"They said that you were either taking advantage of him, or hanging around when you weren't wanted. They mentioned that sometimes you would end up going into his house. You were in his house when he didn't want you there, and you were asked to leave, but you would continue to return. There was also some talk about you spying on his email, Facebook accounts, those types of things."

Jodi had a reasonable defense. "He gave me his Facebook password and his Myspace password. And I gave him my Facebook password and Gmail account password. And we did that a few months ago to reestablish trust between us . . . It just didn't work, and he got upset and we changed our passwords after that . . ."

"How long ago?"

"Not long ago . . . two weeks ago, maybe? I don't know about his because I wasn't going to try to get back into his accounts anymore . . . And as far as ever getting into his emails, that never happened. He would just have his computer on, and he'd leave his Gmail window up, and there were times where I went on his computer to look up other things, and if his Gmail window was open, I would just close it."

"We are getting a search warrant for his email, but we can tell where those things were accessed from. I just wanna make it clear that if you did access it from somewhere else at a certain time, we're gonna know."

Jodi was not intimidated. "I'll tell you right now that I did," she said assuredly. "He gave me his passwords . . . but I only accessed Gmail and Myspace because those were the only passwords."

Jodi had just contradicted herself, because seconds earlier, she had mentioned she also had his Facebook password. Flores pretended to ignore her slipup.

"How long ago?" Flores wanted to know. "When was the last time?"

"Weeks ago. We had a conversation where like, he made it clear he wasn't comfortable with that anymore. And I changed my Gmail password again, and he saw another guy's email there and gave me a hard time about it . . . We're both trying to move on . . ."

"There seems to be a lot of jealousy issues."

Jodi seemed to know where this was leading, so she went on the offensive. "I think it was jealousy on both parts," she responded. "For me, it wasn't so much jealousy as it was, I just wanted him to be honest. And one of the reasons I moved was because we were spending too much time together, we weren't moving on. I guess I could have dated other people, but our social circles were so small that any time he heard about something . . ."

"Okay. Did you move down here . . . because of him?"

"Yeah, because of him primarily . . . because of Travis."

"People were saying to call you because you probably know what happened and possibly had something to do with it." The question came out of the blue.

"Oh gosh, no, I . . . ," Jodi stammered.

"Yeah, that's how bad it was getting at the scene. I needed to talk to you to see why they would say something like that, why they would start pointing fingers in your direction."

"I don't know, maybe because I'm the ex-girlfriend?" The conversation had clearly taken a turn for the worse, but Jodi tried to face it head-on. "We had a lot of fights."

"Were there a lot of issues? Obviously, it wasn't a great relationship."

"It was a great relationship until we started fighting . . . I had a suspicion . . . that he wasn't being faithful, and I found a bunch of text messages that were no good. And rather than being an adult about it and confronting him, I kept it in and let it fester, and I was miserable . . . I realized this is no kind of relationship, so it finally all just came out. He was really apologetic, but we both just realized that neither of us could be in an adult relationship. And that was the end of a black year. So at that point we continued to see each other, a long time after that."

"I'm glad I did get a hold of you," Flores commented. "It clears up a lot of the concerns that I had. I don't think it's what these people thought was going on."

"I should probably tell you that when Travis got upset, he would send me text messages and things. You'll probably find Gmail, Facebook, you're welcome to access all of my accounts."

"We're probably going to subpoena all of his Facebook

and Gmail and everything to see who he was communicating with. I'm not sure how far back we go, usually six months to a year . . . I hate telling people over the phone, but it is a homicide, it was an angry situation. When we see something like this, we think, these people hated each other. Somebody went in there to hurt him, and they did, and they hurt him really bad."

CHAPTER 4

JODI'S MEN

Jodi never returned to high school after her junior year. Instead, she took a series of waitressing jobs, and Bobby eventually got a job busing tables. Between them they made enough to make ends meet.

Bobby did not have his own place; he lived with an elderly couple whom he considered his grandparents. The property was in bad shape—cigarette smoke hazing the interior light, linoleum buckling in the kitchen, and an unkempt lawn begging to be mowed. Inside, the house was a complete mess, with stuff hoarded in every corner. Amid that chaos, Bobby had carved out a bedroom of his own, and when Jodi moved in, she shared that space with him.

At first things seemed to go well, until Jodi claimed she discovered that Bobby was being unfaithful. According to Jodi, Bobby was exchanging affectionate emails with another girl, which Jodi admitted she discovered with a little sleuthing on Hotmail. Jodi said the two would go to the library so they could each check their respective personal email accounts. While there, Jodi happened to see an email from another woman in Bobby's inbox. In an early sign of

Jodi's penchant for espionage, or perhaps fabrication, she said she left the library with Bobby under the guise that she was heading to work, but secretly returned to the library, where she was able to access his account. She then printed the letters at the library and formulated a plan to confront him.

Impulsively, and seething with jealousy, Jodi called in sick to her job, found Bobby, and handed her evidence to him. While Bobby was understandably shocked that Jodi went to such lengths to trap him, Jodi said she felt righteously angry, calling it her first experience with being jilted and deceived by a man.

Despite her discovery, Jodi didn't leave Bobby, possibly because of her fear of abandonment. Jodi said the two broke up so many times that she found herself constantly packing and unpacking all of her things. But she hadn't reached the point where she wanted to end it for good. Something in her wouldn't let her detach. What ailed Jodi would become a source of great debate. The entire nation of amateur armchair psychologists and professionals would weigh in on it. Was Jodi bipolar? Did she have borderline personality disorder or detachment/attachment disorder? Did she suffer from narcissistic personality disorder, or was she a sociopath or even a psychopath? These psychological issues would be fodder for speculation both inside and outside the courtroom, with opinions on it at every turn.

Jodi seemed to make a lot of self-destructive choices, and several claimed that she changed completely after moving in with Bobby. One visitor to their place expressed shock at their living conditions. Others insisted Bobby wasn't the problem, that some other emotional or psychological issue was rising up in Jodi as she matured into her teenage years. A friend recalled the night Jodi called very upset after an argument. Jodi later claimed that Bobby had tried to choke her during an argument, using his martial arts training to put her in a stranglehold that almost made her pass out. She claimed she had even called 911 for assistance, but said Bobby had taken over the call and had given the operator an excuse. Jodi said she brushed off the assault as an isolated incident and continued to live with him. You have to wonder, given her propensity toward violence, if perhaps Jodi was the one who was violent. She seemed to have a penchant for relationship turmoil.

Eventually, circumstances pulled Jodi and Bobby apart. Bobby, possibly wanting to get some space between himself and Jodi, relocated across state lines up to Medford, Oregon, fifty miles north. He lived with a roommate named Matt, while Jodi headed south to live for several months with a good friend back in Santa Maria, the town she still loved best and had always missed ever since she had been stripped away from it at the end of eighth grade.

Living space at her friend's house was tight, as the family already had five members sharing cramped quarters. Still, they embraced Jodi and lovingly welcomed her into their home. She arrived in the summer of 1999 and stayed through Christmas. She found a job waitressing at a local Applebee's, but soon became quite lonely. Her best friend had started college that fall and was busy with her studies and playing on the college softball team. With her friend otherwise occupied, Jodi probably began to realize the consequences of her decision to drop out of school and leave her parents' house. She had tried to re-create the good feelings she remembered from her childhood in Santa Maria, but this was now a different time. Jodi was lost, and she needed to find something or someone to hang on to, to make her feel grounded in the world.

Perhaps that's why Jodi just couldn't seem to get her mind off Bobby. Acting on the possibly faulty notion that

Bobby had no car, no food, no money, nothing, that didn't deter her from reinitiating contact with him. Santa Maria was ten hours from Medford, Oregon, but she made her way to his doorstep with a bagful of groceries left anonymously for him to find. Jodi claimed Bobby instantly knew the care package was from her and called to thank her, but others saw Jodi's mysterious delivery as a creepy move. Creepy or generous, she would complain that Bobby wasn't nice to her, but she was soon making the long drive up to Medford on the weekends to hang out with him anyway.

Jodi was getting a little disheartened with Bobby, however. When she observed how chivalrous and kind Bobby's roommate Matt was with his girlfriend, she realized she was not being treated well. In her journal entries, she wrote of her growing friendship with Matt and his ability to "spiritually help others."

In January 2000, Jodi confided her dissatisfaction with Bobby to friends who suggested she make a list of pros and cons to see if the relationship was worth saving. She came up with three pros right off the bat: "made me feel beautiful," "could make me laugh," "would scrape the ice off my car in the winter while I stayed inside and warmed up." Next, she moved to the cons column. The list stretched for more than three pages: "unsympathetic when I need a shoulder to cry on," "tells me to 'fuck off' on a weekly basis," "trashes my name to anybody who will listen," "tells me he loves me but takes it back minutes later," "trashes my family and my friends." The list went on and on. She accused Bobby of flirting with other girls on "the party line, the Internet, and at parties and bars," and claimed he had called her "the worst, filthiest, most unimaginable names in the dictionary.

"The list doesn't even begin to mention the fact that he likely cheated on me . . . including all aspects of an alternate love affair," she wrote. "But if he wanted me to go away so badly, why didn't he just tell me?" Given Jodi's intense neediness, maybe Bobby had already told her to leave him alone, but she hadn't listened. After all, he was the one who had moved to another state and she was the one who pursued him again.

Jodi's next move would be her strangest to that point, and it would also foreshadow odd behavior in her future. Even though things weren't going well with Bobby, Jodi moved to Medford, Oregon. She said she liked it and wanted to relocate there. Her unhealthy pattern had begun: she would complain about an ex-boyfriend, but then would move very close to him in spite of the turmoil that he'd supposedly brought into her life. Perhaps it was her fear of abandonment. Or maybe she wanted to be near Bobby to whip up drama, such a staple of her relationships. She could distract herself from the self-loathing that often plagues those suffering from mood disorders. Or perhaps she already had her eye on Bobby's roommate Matt, whom she was lavishing with compliments in her journal. Regardless of her underlying reasons, her behavior had characteristics of stalking.

Jodi was still in touch with her parents, at least sporadically. She wrote in her journal that her parents were exasperated at her life choices and begging her to focus on achieving something. Jodi wrote about a day spent in Yreka with her father. "Patterns of thought. I hope I don't fall into any and I hope I can uproot those which I've embraced since childhood," she began. "Went to Yreka today. I was sitting with my dad in the little Jodan Karate Dojo and we were watching the kids warm up for class when somehow he and I got on the subject of my life for the past two years. He just kept shaking his head disbelievingly, stating that he couldn't believe I had just wasted my life and thrown away two years. I responded by telling him that it wasn't a waste, and that I've taken a lot from that experience . . . But he couldn't believe it and kept repeating and objecting, stating that two years is such a long time, such a waste, and that I was just being rebellious by not listening to anyone."

The Ariases later confided that they sometimes debated whether their beautiful, promising, but clearly troubled daughter was suffering from bipolar disorder, which is characterized by wild mood swings. Based on their later interviews with law enforcement, it seemed they were wondering if they would ever be able to reclaim their daughter, a hope that was quickly dashed when they learned she had moved in with Matt.

Jodi had started dating Matt not long after she got to Medford, perhaps remembering how chivalrous he had been with his former girlfriend. But, given Matt's connection to Bobby, it was beyond awkward. Jodi had to have known it would cause her former boyfriend emotional pain for her to hop in bed with his roommate, but she did so nevertheless. She found yet another job at Applebee's and when she had enough money, she and Matt rented a one-bedroom apartment together. On occasion, she would run into Bobby. Such encounters with him were inevitable given she had chosen to move to his town. But Jodi went further at times, calling Bobby repeatedly, both at home and at his job, and even leaving mysterious things on his doorstep. Sources have said that Bobby even became quite fearful of her and they regarded him as a stalking victim. Bobby has chosen not to go on the record with the author, so the only account of his and Jodi's relationship is Jodi's alone, which should always be met with skepticism. Nonetheless, Jodi had begun her pattern of relationship obsession and of vine swinging from one boyfriend to another, bitterly disenchanted with one man as she grabbed on to the next. In Jodi's world, it seemed a lover was either wonderful or horrible, with no in-between.

Matt and Jodi were together for a couple of years. Matt

described her as gentle and caring, someone who would go into the bathtub to rescue a bug so it wouldn't get washed down the drain. With Matt, Jodi continued her odyssey through the spiritual world she had begun at age eighteen. Despite being raised as a nondenominational Christian, Jodi, through one boyfriend or another had taken a curious interest in alternative religions—fundamentalist Christianity, Wicca, Buddhism, and Hinduism, to name four. Matt had a few books on witchcraft for the purpose of seeking spiritual alternatives. He had once even dabbled in it, but he had already moved into studying the mystical Eastern religions by the time Jodi started dating him. They explored the spiritual world together, taking "New Age"–type meditation seminars with roots in Hinduism or Buddhism, best described as a modern version of transcendentalism. Sometimes the seminars were quite a distance, as far away as Portland, four hours north of Medford, or San Francisco, six hours south.

Jodi believed she was in love with Matt, and for a time things between them seemed good. She wrote of feeling "blessed" to be with a man so kind and caring. "It is simply incredible, the fact that we are here building our dreams together," Jodi wrote in her journal, dated February 6, 2000. "I can't even imagine trying to pull something like this off with [Bobby]. In fact, I can't even imagine having wanted to do such a thing. Living with him was a disastrous nightmare. Yet, putting up Christmas lights in February with [Matt] is so close to heaven-sent, that even now I still question what I ever did that was considered worthy enough for God to make this union between us a reality.

". . . I guess I'm still not quite used to this feeling of loving a person, a beautiful soul, so completely and actually have that love returned, no, not just returned, but reciprocated at a level which actually matches mine, if not exceeds it. That is something I had always sought in [Bobby], but never found."

But just three months later, in May 2000, Jodi sounded like a different person. Her emotional instability was apparent in her journals as she wrote about missing her times with Bobby. "He was my dream, he was my all, my everything," she said in her entry dated May 11. She added, in a somewhat ominous reflection, "Why do I feel like we still have unfinished business?"

By July she had seesawed back to loving Matt. "How grateful, how lucky, and how privileged I am to walk by his side in this lifetime," she noted on July 12. But by October, Jodi had become disillusioned. "I feel utterly fucking worthless, useless and destructive," she began her entry of October 8, 2000. "Like maybe I am failing at life, failing at my karmic lessons and failing at my relationship with my beloved."

January 2001 saw Jodi's relationship with Matt beginning to crumble. "So often, it seems like Matt really doesn't give a shit. Sometimes, I feel like I'm just some stereotypical 'woman' who sits at home and isn't important," was her entry on January 3.

Later that month, Jodi consulted her mother about her feelings of disillusionment. Sandy Arias told her daughter that she liked Matt, but Jodi needed to realize that "he's never going to change." In her journal entry dated January 18, 2001, Jodi complained about his housekeeping. It infuriated her that he left the house such a pigsty, and expected her to pick up after him. She also expressed annoyance at his constant lack of money. She wrote of feeling put upon by his continued inability to pay his share of the bills, and that they had to cancel evenings out with friends due to Matt's lack of financial resources. To remedy the situation, the two decided to get their own places. But Jodi feared it was not a permanent solution, "just running from the problem." The man Jodi had envisioned as her Prince Charming had turned into a disappointment. This would happen over and over again, with man after man.

Jodi claimed their relationship ended when Matt started secretly dating a colleague of his named Bianca. Matt had gotten a job at a resort in Crater Lake, Oregon, and had been living there in employee housing. Though Jodi had suspected that Matt might be straying, she had no proof until, she claimed, a friend broke it to her. Hysterical, she drove an hour and a half north to confront the other woman. When relationship drama was at the finish line, Jodi's urge to confront became single-minded, overpowering her common sense. Bianca confirmed the rumor, prompting Jodi to break up with Matt for good. That didn't mean there wasn't the final attempt to persuade him to come back to her, as she suggested in her goodbye email to him, hoping it might encourage him to stay with her. But the relationship was over. Indeed, some say Matt had already ended it with Jodi before she confronted Bianca, which would put a totally different spin on Jodi's behavior, making her seem angry over the rejection.

Not long after things with Matt went south, Jodi moved from Oregon to Big Sur, California, five hundred miles away, and it was there, in the fall of 2001, that she took a job as a waitress at the chic Ventana Inn & Spa in Carmel. Darryl Brewer, the resort's food and beverage director, was in charge of hiring and training the restaurant's employees. Darryl was handsome, thin, fit, and well groomed, and though he was her boss, Jodi harbored a secret crush for a year, calling him a "George Clooney type." He always presented himself in a sophisticated, professional manner, his brown hair neatly combed and his blue-gray eyes appearing gentle behind rimless glasses.

Jodi didn't want a workplace relationship, but it appeared that there were feelings on both sides, and some romantic type of relationship was slowly blooming. Finally it became unavoidable. Jodi says she began filling in as a wedding co-ordinator at the Ventana Inn, while Darryl resigned from management. Finally free to date, the two became a couple in 2002.

Jodi had never been in a relationship with anyone like Darryl. For one thing, Darryl was much older than Jodi—almost twenty years older. With Jodi twenty-two and Darryl forty-two, it was a real May-December romance. Besides the age difference, Darryl was also divorced with a four-year-old son. Jodi would go on to develop a good relationship with Darryl's son, saying he felt like a little brother to her. The end result of both these things was a relationship that, at least on the outside, looked far different from those she'd had with Bobby and Matt.

Although Jodi seemed to be experiencing a normal, well-balanced relationship with a gentle, soft-spoken, caring man, in retrospect some now see disturbing patterns in her behavior from that time. Those who knew Jodi back then said she seemed very intent on mimicking Darryl's ex-wife, an attractive blonde and successful career woman who had put herself through college by working at the chic Carmel restaurant where Jodi would eventually work. And then there was Jodi's physical appearance. Darryl's ex had blond hair. Jodi soon dyed her hair bleach blond. After Darryl's ex got breast implants, so did Jodi. It went so far as Jodi even getting the same kind of car that Darryl's ex had. It was as if Jodi were trying to become the woman who was standing with Darryl in his old wedding photo. Jodi seemed obsessed with the idea of getting married and getting financial stability, talking to those in the know about IRAs and other savings vehicles.

Jodi and Darryl had been dating for a while when Jodi learned that her childhood best friend Patti was getting married and wanted her to be a bridesmaid. Jodi was waitressing to pay the bills so couldn't afford to splurge on a bridesmaid's gown or store-bought gift. Patti's dad paid for Jodi's bridesmaid outfit, and Jodi's gift turned out to be a photo album that she created by snapping the photos herself. Those who've seen the wedding album say it was professionally done and quite artistic.

A couple of years into the relationship, Darryl and Jodi decided it was time to put down roots and buy a house together. Jodi, the woman who a year earlier couldn't afford to buy a dress for a wedding, suddenly was eager to become indebted to the tune of hundreds of thousands of dollars. Maybe co-homeownership was a way to lock in what she hoped would be her future, with a home and husband. Jodi was also suckered in by the way home prices were going in only one direction, up, and everybody's dream was to invest and watch his or her investment multiply during the now-infamous real estate bubble gone bust of the mid-2000s. Like millions of other starry-eyed Americans, Jodi wanted to get in low and flip high. Friends said she couldn't stop talking about real estate prices and mortgage rates. But there was no way Jodi and Darryl could afford to buy near the exclusive Ventana Inn, an area with some of the most expensive real estate in America.

Darryl's ex-wife was friendly and supportive of their relationship. She actually gave them some financial advice and factored in Jodi and Darryl's goals when she and her new husband bought a second home in the Palm Springs area. Everybody's decisions revolved around making sure both Darryl and his ex were close to their son. Darryl and Jodi found what seemed like a reasonably priced house in nearby Palm Desert. It cost $350,000, and they intended to treat it as an investment. When they closed in June 2005, their hope was to live in the house for two years, and then flip it for profit when the time was right. It would turn out that they had jumped into real estate near the peak of the market and were soon saddled with a house worth less than the outstanding mortgage, which ballooned from a monthly obligation of $2,400 to $2,800 at its first adjustment.

Despite the challenges and Jodi's behavior mimicking Darryl's ex-wife, Darryl and Jodi created a life together in Palm Desert, hiking, camping, and enjoying the outdoors. Darryl considered Jodi a responsible caretaker for his son, and he would often leave her alone with the boy, who came to view her as an aunt figure. During this time, Darryl said he observed Jodi grow as a person and considered her to be mature beyond her years and a responsible financial partner, working two jobs to contribute to the household expenses. He also appreciated her developing artistic talents.

Jodi felt they were making a nice, stable life together, but when she envisioned marriage and children, their relationship hit a wall. Darryl said the two discussed marriage and starting a family, and although he considered it for a fleeting moment, he ultimately decided he could not make the commitment. He already had a child and a job that demanded a lot of his time, and he did not believe he had room in his schedule for another child. Jodi said she understood, and according to Darryl, she was okay with their arrangement as it was. But others said it was obvious from talking to Jodi that she was focused like a laser beam on three goals: marriage, family, and financial security. When Darryl made it clear he was not going to tie the knot with Jodi, joint mortgage or not, their relationship started slowly unraveling.

As Darryl started pondering a return to Northern California, Jodi started looking around for options, which was when she discovered an opportunity called Pre-Paid Legal. Pre-Paid Legal Services, Inc. (PPL) encouraged individuals who represented them to sell legal insurance to others. The more people you signed up to sell legal insurance, the bigger your take, and the higher you rose in the company's ranks. To some the corporate structure seemed to look a little like a pyramid. To others it seemed like a fun way to make money while meeting lots of new people. There was a social aspect to PPL that was very attractive to those who got involved. It felt a lot like being part of a club.

From Darryl's perspective, it all looked like magical thinking. Jodi was thinking positive thoughts but stopped paying her share of the bills. Jodi started putting her half of the mortgage on her credit cards. Instead of getting better, her financial situation was becoming even more precarious. But Jodi appeared to be counting on Pre-Paid Legal to solve it all, and in September 2006 she decided to attend PPL's Las Vegas convention, where a chance meeting with Travis Alexander would change the rest of her life.

CHAPTER 5

THE CRIME SCENE

Temperatures had already climbed into the nineties by 9:30 a.m. on June 10, 2008, and the forecast was calling for a high of 105 degrees. Under mostly cloudy skies, Detective Flores and his team prepared to execute a search warrant on the Mesa home of Travis Victor Alexander. The two-story southwestern-style residence had been secured with yellow tape and was under steady police guard. No one was allowed to enter or leave the premises without signing a log. It was a little before 10 a.m. when homicide investigators, donning plastic booties and latex gloves, climbed the carpeted stairs of the home and entered the master bedroom suite through double entry doors.

Investigators had been instructed to focus primarily on the victim and the surrounding area where his body had been discovered, basically the master bedroom and master bath. The team had been briefed that the homeowner had been found dead in the master bathroom shower, and it was unknown how long he had been there.

The master suite was quite large and tastefully decorated in a soft palette of browns and yellows. A beige cut pile carpet covered the floor. A dark wood sleigh bed, matching end tables, and identical black table lamps with tiny white shades gave the room a homey feel. A comfy upholstered love seat was nestled in front of a big window, its matching ottoman draped by a cozy blanket. Hanging in a dark wood frame over the bed was a piece of traditional art. The master bedroom had a large walk-in closet, and a long tiled hallway led to the master bath, which had a cherrywood vanity topped by a double sink, a big Jacuzzi-style tub, a stand-alone shower, and a separate toilet area.

A huge bloodstain on the carpet at the entrance to the bathroom hallway immediately caught the detective's attention. He noted that the blood was dry and appeared as if it had been there for several days. There was also a large amount of dried blood on the floor tiles leading to the bathroom, and along the entire length of both walls. Upon closer examination, the detective observed a slight strip of blood down the center of one tile, which he could not immediately explain.

Since the hallway was awash with blood, the officers entered through the large walk-in closet, which had a second door that also led into the bathroom. While the closet itself was pristine, with Travis's shirts, pants, and shoes meticulously arranged on built-in cabinets, the bathroom on the other side of the closet door was a scene of carnage. There was blood everywhere—on the light brown tiles of the floor, on the walls, even on the window blinds. The gruesome sight of a man's bloody and bloated body crammed into the shower was compounded by the horrific smell of decomposing flesh that permeated the room. The position of Travis's body was particularly odd; he was crumbled faceup on the shower floor, his legs bent in a froglike position, and his neck and head bent forward and to the side, exposing a gaping wound to his neck. It looked as if he had been stuffed into the shower and left there to rot.

Detective Flores first noted the large amount of spatter on the northernmost sink and on the mirror above it. Sections of the blood appeared to have been diluted, as if water had been dropped there, while other areas looked like heavy spurting from an artery. There was also a mix of diluted blood and heavier spatter inside and around the sink. Flores determined the faucet must have been running and then was switched off at some point while the victim continued to bleed. Smears of blood on the counter in front of the sink looked as though bloody hands had gripped the area. The investigators searching the bathroom took special care as they maneuvered around the large, thick pools of dried blood all over the floor. They observed that the blood on the floor had a similar pattern to the blood in the sink, a combination of light, diluted areas beneath heavy areas of spatter.

To explain this unusual pattern occurring all over the bathroom, Detective Flores scoured the room, looking for a clue. What he discovered was a cardboard box in the linen closet next to the sink that was stained with a reddish watermark a few inches up from the floor. The location of the stain told him that the bathroom floor had been drenched in water at some time after the killing.

A spent shell casing in one of the dried blood puddles near the sink had not been immediately visible. Flores carefully collected it from the floor and studied it, trying to determine its caliber. He knew it had come from a small-caliber weapon, likely a .22 or .32. Only later was it determined to be a Winchester .25-caliber. An exhaustive search of the home turned up no firearms, no ammunition, and no other evidence that Travis had owned a gun.

DNA swabs, fingerprints, and hair samples were collected from the dried blood on the baseboards and floor of the master bathroom. Of particular note was one latent print found in a bloody area at the entrance to the bathroom hall. The print was waist-level, and police believed it might belong to Travis's killer. It was found near several blood swipe marks that had been identified in the same general vicinity. The section of the wall where the prints had been found was cut out and inventoried as evidence.

Multiple hair fibers were also collected from the floor and baseboards. Detective Flores noted that one of the hairs was particularly long and did not appear to belong to Travis. It, too, was cataloged as evidence. The homicide team photographed and collected a number of items from the shower area, knowing that any evidence that might be present would be contaminated once the medical examiner's team entered the room and removed the body. As the items were being collected, Detective Flores made a curious observation. The plastic cup on the floor of the shower had very little blood on it. In fact, it was fairly clean, further confirming his suspicion that Travis was murdered in a different location and dragged to the shower after his death.

An examination of the southern end of the bathroom revealed more blood droplets on the window blinds; some were found just below waist level and others were collected from the very top slat, which was over six feet high. Blood was also discovered on the lower half of the wall beneath the towel rack, as well as all over the door leading into the toilet area. There was even blood around the base of the toilet.

This massive amount of blood throughout the bathroom, hallway, and entrance to the bedroom told a tale that would soon be understood. There was clearly a lot of movement between Travis and his killer. The blood spatter, smears, castoff, and drips indicated that knife wounds were inflicted while Travis was in various parts of the bathroom. Low spatter meant he was on the floor or on his knees near the toilet area. There was spatter under the bathroom scale, several feet from the shower. Most telling was the northern sink, where it appeared that Travis had valiantly stood, his bloodied hands smearing the counter. It was obvious he had already grabbed the blade of the knife at least once, maybe twice, earlier on in the attack as he had staggered around. Blood spatter was on the mirror shelf and mirror over the sink, indicating he had been stabbed repeatedly from behind in his back and also in the back of his head, as he stood over that sink, where he was more than likely spitting blood as well. As his head hung down over the sink, he dripped blood into the drain. From the scene, it looked like Travis hadn't really fought back; he was just trying to get away from his killer.

But the stabbing assault continued; it was vicious and furious. Travis wasn't dying fast enough for his killer. He stumbled away from the sink and down the twelve-foot-long hallway that led to his bedroom. He knew the door that led out of the master suite was just to the left at the end of the hall. It was just a few feet away. If he could just get out of the bedroom, maybe a roommate would be home to save him. Maybe he could get downstairs and out the front door—to safety. But his killer knew not to let him leave the bedroom for these same reasons. Travis had already lost a lot of blood. He was dying as he neared the end of that bathroom hall. He left an arc of smeared blood on the wall of that hallway as he fell, maybe to his knees, unable to make the last few feet out of his bedroom. Was he conscious when his killer drew the knife across his throat for the final, brutal coup de grâce?

It was precisely 11 a.m. when Detective Flores gave the two investigators from the Maricopa County Medical Examiner's Office the go-ahead to enter the bathroom and help with the removal of Travis's body. Photographs were taken to document Travis's exact position, and then he was carefully prepared for transport. It was at this time that the extent of Travis's injuries became glaringly apparent to everyone in the room as the cluster of stab wounds to his back and head were now visible.

As the investigators from the ME's office began the process of removing the corpse from the shower, Detective Flores and his team continued their evidence collection in the master bedroom. They noticed that there were no sheets or blankets on Travis's king-sized bed. A search of the entire bedroom, including the walk-in closet and dresser, yielded not a single sheet, blanket, or pillowcase, which the detectives found extremely odd.

The answer to the puzzle was downstairs in the laundry room, where investigators discovered a set of brown-striped sheets in the dryer. Apparently, someone had washed them after the murder and then run them through the dryer. A reddish stain on the inside rim of the washing machine tested positive for blood. Inside the drum, detectives found a Sony DSC-H9 digital camera mixed in with several articles of Travis's clothing, undergarments, sweatpants, shorts, towels, and T-shirts. They determined the camera had been run through a wash cycle and had severe water damage. Remarkably, the digital card was still intact. Little did anyone know how critical to the case the photos on the digital card would become.

Detective Flores was able to determine that the camera had belonged to Travis. In an interview with Travis's roommate, Zachary Billings, he learned that several months before the murder, Travis had consulted Zach on the purchase of the camera, and its box was found in the downstairs office. Investigators found the camera bag and unused strap in the upstairs loft near the master bedroom door.

During an inspection of the home office, detectives recovered Travis's laptop computer. Members of the Mesa police Computer Forensic Unit were able to determine that it had last been used to access email at 4:19 P.M. on June 4. Travis's cell phone was also located in the room. A cursory review of the call log showed his last communication was made at 12:13 P.M. on June 4. It was a text to his close friend Chris Hughes. There had been other incoming calls and texts to the phone after that, but they had all gone unanswered. Detective Flores spoke to Chris and confirmed that he had received the text message. Chris said it had been a confirmation of the important conference call that Travis was supposed to be hosting in the evening of June 4. The call was scheduled for 7 P.M., but nobody had heard from Travis and no one could get a hold of him.

Chris mentioned that he and his wife, Sky, were supposed to meet Travis in Cancún on June 10 for the Pre-Paid Legal seminar and business vacation. Before departing, he had tried to reach Travis, but his cell phone mailbox was full and he had not been answering. Chris assumed that his friend was probably busy, and that they would catch up once they were together in Mexico. It wasn't until he and his wife were in bed in their Cancún hotel room that they got the call that Travis was dead. Sadly, Travis's last known communication had been his noontime text message.

It was close to 4:30 P.M. when the crime scene investigators concluded their search of 11428 East Queensborough Avenue. Detective Flores's final chore was to secure the premises and turn them over to Travis's next of kin. Police had been able to locate one of Travis's sisters, Samantha Alexander, a police officer with the Carlsbad Police Department in Carlsbad, California. But it wasn't until the following day that Detective Flores was able to meet with a member of the Alexander family. Travis's two older half brothers, Greg and Gary, had traveled from Riverside, California, after learning of their brother's death. While Travis was always in their hearts, both men confided that they hadn't been keeping up with their kid brother's day-to-day life since his move to Mesa. More important, neither man had any inkling of who could have perpetrated this horrific crime.

The morning of June 12, 2008, Detective Flores arrived at the office of the Maricopa County medical examiner to attend the autopsy of Travis Victor Alexander. The office was located in the Forensic Science Center, a state-of-the-art facility on West Jefferson Street in downtown Phoenix. Dr. Kevin Horn, a medical examiner for the county, would be conducting the postmortem exam. Blessed with movie-star looks, the slim, dark-haired doctor was nevertheless pensive and somber. He had been with the ME's office since 2001, joining the staff six years after his graduation from the University of Maryland School of Medicine, in Baltimore. His role as ME was to examine deceased individuals and certify a cause and manner of death.

As is protocol, Dr. Horn was present when the seal of the zippered body pouch containing Travis's body was broken and the body was laid onto the steel table. Dr. Horn's general examination found a "slightly heavy-set" Caucasian male, "69 inches in length and weighing 189 pounds." There was evidence of "moderate decomposition" as indicated by "bloating, green discoloration, and multifocal skin slippage with purge exuding from the nose and mouth." A visual examination of the body did not yield any scars, tattoos, or other identifying body features. A modified sexual assault kit was collected. However, no trauma or other abnormalities of the mouth, anus, or genitalia were observed.

The savagery of the victim's injuries was not lost on Dr. Horn, or Detective Flores, who was standing off to the side and anxious to learn if the doctor's findings would reveal any helpful pieces of evidence or other information that would aid in his homicide investigation. Dr. Horn found that Travis had multiple lacerations and punctures, as well as a single gunshot wound to the head. He also observed numerous sharp-force injuries of the head, neck, torso, and extremities.

An examination of the head revealed two "oblique linear full thickness incised wounds of the right and left posterior scalp." Each measured two inches in length. There was also a 1¼-inch stab wound on the lower scalp, just below the right earlobe, and a 1¼-inch shallow incised wound on the upper left forehead, within the hairline.

The wounds on Travis's neck were the most severe, with a number of shallow stabs around his upper neck along with a gaping incision that stretched across the upper neck. The slit of Travis's throat measured six inches across. It was determined that this incision both transected and perforated the entire upper airway, the strap neck muscles, the right jugular vein, and the right carotid artery. Basically he had been cut ear to ear, and all the way down to his spine. Dr. Horn determined that Travis was still alive when his throat was cut, because of the large amount of hemorrhage, which requires a beating heart.

A number of sharp-force injuries were also discovered on the torso. Of particular interest was a cluster of nine stab wounds on the upper right and left side of Travis's back that ranged in size from three-quarters of an inch to 1½ inches. The wounds were all concentrated within a 6-x-5½-inch area, with blunt and sharply incised ends that penetrated the soft tissue of the back and impacted the ribs and lateral aspects of the vertebral bone, but stopped short of penetrating the chest cavity. They were clustered together between his shoulder blades; were similar in size, depth, and direction;

and appeared to have been done in rapid succession, likely when Travis had his back to his attacker.

Stab wounds also littered Travis's upper and lower chest, the most severe of which was a 1½-inch gash to the right chest that both penetrated and perforated the area near the sternum at the third and fourth right ribs. This wound was about 3½ inches deep and penetrated a major vein near the base of the heart.

An examination of Travis's hands, which had been enclosed in paper bags to preserve any evidence, tested negative for gunpowder residue. His fingernails were short, and none appeared to be broken, except for the right thumbnail, where an incised wound approximately of one-quarter inch had clipped off a portion of the nail. A 1¼-inch-deep incision had penetrated the group of muscles at the base of the thumb, near the wrist, partially severing the muscles and tendons at the base. Horn determined a "sharp-edged object" had made the injuries, all likely defensive wounds. The presence of hemorrhage associated with some of the wounds led him to determine that the injuries had occurred while the victim was still alive.

Moving on to the gunshot wound, X-rays of the head were performed to determine the location of a bullet that had entered the body just above Travis's right eyebrow. Dr. Horn noted a one-eighth-inch circular gunshot entrance wound. There was no apparent exit wound. Dr. Horn determined the wound trajectory was right to left and downward, with the track of the bullet indicating that it had perforated the front skull, then reentered the facial skeleton near the midline, terminating at the left cheek. He was able to recover the small-caliber projectile where it had lodged behind Travis's face. The medical examiner photographed it and retained it as evidence to be turned over to police.

In his initial report, Dr. Horn concluded that the lacerations and puncture wounds found on Travis's body were consistent with a single-edged weapon at least five inches in length. The lack of stippling, gunshot residue, or soot around the gunshot wound indicated the gun was fired from no closer than two to three feet away. The knife wounds to his back had not entered the chest cavity, so they also were not fatal. Obvious defensive wounds to his hands showed that he had attempted to protect himself during the attack. According to Dr. Horn's report, the fatal wounds inflicted on Travis were the single stab wound to the center of his chest, which punctured his superior vena cava, a major vein, and the final throat slicing. The official cause of death was determined to be "sharp force trauma of the neck and torso." The manner of death was homicide.

CHAPTER 6

T-DOGG

Travis Victor Alexander was unlike any man Jodi had ever encountered. All of her previous relationships had been with men who were either unconventional, uninterested in marriage and children, or unable to offer financial stability. Travis appeared the antidote to all that; he had looks, charisma, confidence, solid religious beliefs, an interest in finding a wife and starting a family, and he was financially successful. Being someone who wanted to help others, he seemed willing to share himself with Jodi. He managed to be conventional, almost princelike, yet he was exciting and energetic.

Part of Travis's need to help those in trouble came from his own difficult and abusive upbringing. He was born on July 28, 1977, the first child of Gary David Alexander and Pamela Elizabeth Morgan Alexander. Pamela was Gary's third wife. She was twenty-four and Gary was twenty-nine, with two children from a previous marriage, when their beautiful green-eyed boy arrived, joining half brothers Gary and Greg. Pam and Gary Alexander would go on to have two daughters, Samantha and Tanisha. The family lived in Riverside, California, a large inland city in Southern California, about sixty miles east of Los Angeles, with the reputation of being one of the nation's most polluted "smog belt" communities.

By all accounts, this was not one big happy family. Travis's parents were both drug addicts, hooked on methamphetamine, one of the hardest addictions to treat. Pam and Gary were both self-absorbed and controlled by their addictions, and their children suffered tremendously in their care. In the self-help memoir Travis was in the process of writing at the time of his death, titled *Raising You,* he spoke of a father who was rarely around, and who eventually abandoned the family. He described his mother as a woman who, despite good intentions, had started a family too young. Once she became addicted to drugs, she was incapable of providing reliable, loving care for her children, not even able to meet their most basic needs. The children had no one to cook a hot meal, do the laundry, clean the house, shop for food, help with hygiene, or care for them when they were sick. Pam would go on weeklong drug benders, then crash in bed for days. Meth turned her into a monster.

Travis, being protective of his kid sisters, took on a lot of responsibility, beginning a pattern of caring for people that would continue throughout his life. Travis described terrible beatings at the hands of his mother, who would go after any child who dared to wake her as she slept off her latest high. To endure the wrath, Travis mastered a way of twisting in such a way as to deflect the blows to less sensitive areas of his body, such as his back and arms, where not only did it hurt less, but the bruises could be hidden from the school's teachers and other concerned adults.

With his mother sleeping off the drugs, he and his siblings were left to fend for themselves in a filthy house on Allwood Drive. There was very little food and no prepared meals, and the children would hunt through the kitchen for anything that was edible. They often had to eat things that were spoiled. Travis recalled once scarfing down a piece of moldy bread he had scavenged from the refrigerator. He spoke of feeling teased by the canned foods in the cupboard, which he longed to eat, if only he had known how to use a can opener.

The filthy conditions in the house encouraged cock-roaches. "My sisters and I found some amusement in the fact that an entire colony of albino roaches had broken out so that the house looked like a bunch of moving salt and pepper crawling on everything," he wrote. "To this day I only have one phobia, roaches. There was nothing more disgusting to me than to wake up to feel roaches crawling on my body."

With neither parent working, the family eventually lost the house. They moved to an old, beat-up camper shell in an aunt's backyard. The shell was four feet tall by five feet wide by six feet long, and was situated next to the garage, where the washer and dryer were kept. The washing machine was not hooked up to the plumbing, so every time somebody did wash, dirty wash water pooled in the backyard, creat-ing a swampy, germ-infested mess that the children had to muddle through whenever they left their "shell."

Travis recalled that his sisters, his mother, and he had lived in that camper shell for more than a year. There was no shower, so they would have to go for days without washing. Travis said he didn't mind being dirty. He said he was actu-ally afraid of bathing because one time he had spilled some water in a bathroom and his mother accused him of urinat-ing on the floor. Furious, she had shoved him into a wall.

The unpredictable family violence, fueled by drug abuse, left the children perpetually frightened and apprehensive. Travis recalled countless fights between his mother and father that required police intervention. He remembered a time when his mother emptied a revolver into his father's car, and according to Travis, he was standing on the other side of the front door when his father kicked it down and stormed into the house. His father then retaliated by chopping up his mother's belongings with an axe. Gary and Pam Alexander separated when Travis and his sisters were young, but as the years went by, Travis would welcome two more sisters, Hillary and Allie, and another brother, Steven.

School did not provide a respite for Travis. He was a shy kid, with few friends. "When your clothes are as dirty as the rest of you, and you stink and have lice, you don't make a ton of friends," he wrote of his school days. "Sadly, as you could imagine, I was mocked for my appearance. Nothing too harsh; nowhere close to what was said at home. I will not give much detail on that, as I feel it is inappropriate to state. I will say, though, I have never heard in any movie, on any street corner, or amongst the vilest of men any string of words so offensive and hateful, said with such disgust as was the words that my mother said to my sisters and me."

In spite of the hardship, Travis had fond memories of watching *Sesame Street* with his siblings, and of visiting his great-grandfather Vic, whom he credited with teaching him the alphabet. Vic was his mother's grandfather, and while she didn't have very much family, and fewer that she actually liked, she adored her grandfather. He lived only an hour south of them, but because Travis's mother did not want Vic to know about her addiction, they only visited twice a year. She'd get herself together enough to take the kids for a visit, which Travis always looked forward to. Vic would take everyone out for pizza or on walks with the dogs, then he'd challenge Travis to a game of checkers and pull out some of the other toys he kept at his house for the kids.

The goodbye hug was the moment Travis cherished the most. When it was time to go, Travis would run to hug

Vic goodbye. Vic's mood would suddenly turn serious. He would grab Travis by the shoulders, shake him, and utter the following words: "Travis, you need to know that you are special, that there is not anything that you can't do. There is something great inside you. You're special, Travis, don't you ever forget it." His words were always followed by a hug so tight and stiff, it would squeeze the breath from Travis's body.

Travis would channel these words from Vic whenever his mother's cruelty became too much. When she was coming down from drugs, she would be exceptionally nasty, telling her children how miserable and worthless they were and complaining how they had ruined her life. As hurtful as her words were, Travis found solace and inspiration in Vic's words of encouragement. "Every time I would feel her fist sink into my back, I could feel Grandfather's hands on my shoulders, and I knew she couldn't reach what was great inside of me," he wrote.

In Travis's account, he was six years old when he decided there was a God. He had spent the entire day screaming for his paternal grandmother to come and take him for the weekend. "I screamed so long and loud that I actually woke up my comatose mother long enough to beat me for waking her up," he recalled. "When she went back to bed I went back to screaming to God. Sure enough that evening [my grandmother] came and picked me up, while my mother slept." The problem was, he always had to return home when the weekend was over.

The filth, the beatings, the hunger, and the humiliation became almost too much for Travis. By the age of ten, no longer able to stand the conditions, he ran away. Even though he didn't go far, just a few blocks away to the residence of his father's parents, his grandparents Jim and Norma Jean Sarvey, he never planned on going back. He strode into the house, positioned himself in the middle of the living room, and announced, "I am going to live with you now!" to which his grandmother agreed. Though Travis's determination to escape his mother was clear, what was less clear was why there was no earlier intervention to take the children away from their abusive mother.

In many ways, Travis's decision to seek out his grandparents was not a surprise. He was particularly fond of his grandmother, whom everybody called Mum Mum. Born in the middle of the Great Depression near Oklahoma City, Norma Jean Sarvey was feisty and self-sufficient. She loved the outdoors and spent a good deal of her leisure time camping, fishing, hunting, and shooting. She liked to cook and attended church regularly. She was also a huge dog lover, with a particular affinity for pugs.

Norma was known for her broad smile and gave Travis the love, structure, and security he craved. She described him as an easy boy to raise. Travis had equal admiration for Mum Mum. According to friends, he liked to quote Abraham Lincoln when expressing his fondness for her. "All I am, or can be, I owe to my angel (grand) mother," he'd say, altering the quote just slightly to make it applicable to his grandmother.

Norma was also an active member of the Church of Jesus Christ of Latter-day Saints (LDS), and she introduced all of her grandchildren to its teachings. She belonged to the Jurupa Stake Center, the Mormon church on Serendipity Road in Riverside. At first the other kids in the ward viewed Travis as the kid who never came to church, but over time he became a welcome and regular member.

As he got older, Travis settled into a normal and wholesome life with his grandparents. He attended Rubidoux High School, one of four high schools in the district. The contemporary, one-story building on Opal Street had a brick façade and great views of Mount Rubidoux from its classrooms and playing fields. Travis kept mostly to himself there. He was introverted and shy and often chose to eat his lunch alone in the school library, away from the social scene in the cafeteria. Not the scrawny kid of his youth, he no longer smelled and was not dirty, but the memory of the pain of previous rejections still lingered.

At sixteen, Travis became more confident and self-assured, according to friends. They attributed the change to his involvement in the Mormon church, and as Travis became an active member of Jurupa Stake, he started to gain praise for his insightful ideas and his desire to help others.

Travis graduated from high school in 1995 and worked a string of jobs to save money for a church mission. The following year, he was called to serve in the Colorado Denver South Mission. Part of his two-year undertaking was volunteering to help the homeless in and around Denver. As someone who had spent a good deal of his life without essentials, Travis knew firsthand the plight of the people his mission was serving. He spent countless days handing out care packages to the less fortunate that contained food items and essential hygiene products. On each bag, Travis wrote a personalized note.

It was during his time in Colorado that Travis learned of the death of his father, who had perished in a motorcycle crash at the age of forty-nine on Travis's twentieth birthday. Travis's friends have said that Gary Alexander had been clean for more than a year when he died in 1997. By then Travis's mother had also stopped doing drugs and had been trying to get her life together. But her long history of drug abuse had taken its toll, physically and emotionally, leaving her morbidly obese with a number of health problems. Travis's friends complained that she was manipulative when it came to Travis, trying to make him feel guilty for not visiting more often or taking on the role of her caregiver. However, people around Travis were amazed that, despite everything his mother had done to him, he had found it in his heart to forgive her.

In 1998, around the age of twenty-one, Travis returned from his Denver mission and settled back in California, sharing a home with some other single Mormon guys. He joined the Riverside Singles Ward of the LDS, where everyone called him by his self-proclaimed nickname, T-Dogg. In the Mormon church, a ward is a local congregation presided over by a bishop, much like a pastor in other Christian denominations. Depending on the neighborhood, a ward can have anywhere between twenty-five to five hundred active members who live within a specified distance of a meetinghouse. Singles wards such as the one that Travis joined are found in areas where there is a high population of single adults. Also known as YSAs, or Young Single Adult Wards, they are created to serve unmarried members between the ages of eighteen and thirty. SAs, or Single Adult Wards, are for single members over the age of thirty. Family Wards are for married members *or* single members who are thirty plus. Either way, once a member is over thirty, the Young Singles Adult Ward is no longer an option. Members of the wards are taught the principles of the gospel, but a primary purpose of a singles ward is to give members the chance to mix with other Mormon singles with the goal of marriage. Travis was already keenly aware that in the Mormon religion, dating was for the sole purpose of finding a marriage partner.

At the Young Singles Ward, Travis made lots of friends, among them a young Mormon woman named Deanna Reid. They met in 1998 when Travis was on a date with her roommate. The girls in Deanna's house would hang out with the guys in Travis's house, and they all became friends. Travis and Deanna had already known each other for more than a year when they began dating in the spring of 2000. There was definitely a strong chemistry between them. In fact, friends said Travis wanted to marry her. Deanna wasn't ready, though, and at twenty-one she really wanted to pursue a religious mission in Costa Rica. After only a few months of dating, she left California for Central America. The two stayed in contact via mail, as phone calls and email were not permitted. The church had strict communication policies for members on a mission. They could only call family twice a year, on Christmas and Mother's Day, and they were forbidden to have telephone contact with boyfriends or girlfriends. There was no limit, however, to how many letters Deanna could write, but she was very busy and didn't have a lot of free time.

Deanna had been away for more than one year when she received a letter from Travis in the summer of 2001, telling her that he was seeing someone else. "I was sad at first, really sad," she recalled. "But I kind of expected it. I actually thought it would come a lot sooner. I kind of expected him to say that all along that he wanted to date other people. I even told him before I left that I didn't expect him to wait around for a year and a half. I've seen that happen. All of my friends went on missions. I know what it's like when the person you were dating starts dating someone else. It just happens all the time."

In June 2001, Travis had fallen in love with a young woman he had met at the Young Singles Ward in Riverside. Linda Ballard was nineteen and a student at Brigham Young University in Provo, Utah. Travis and Linda had met once before while Linda was still in high school. He had even flirted with her, but her sister scolded him that she was still in high school and too young for him. When Linda came home for the summer after her freshman year, Travis reconnected with her, and the pair quickly became a couple. Their first date and first kiss were on June 4, 2001, exactly seven years to the day before he was murdered. Travis picked her up at her sister's house, where she was staying. On his car's dashboard was a picture of a young woman. "Who's that?" Linda asked.

"Oh, that's Deanna," Travis replied. "She's my missionary. She's in Costa Rica on her mission." Later, Linda learned that Travis had broken up with Deanna while she was in Costa Rica around the time they had begun dating.

From the start, Travis adored Linda. She was pretty, smart, and there was definitely an intense spark. She was quite beautiful, with full lips, and a radiant toothy smile. He was particularly attracted to her slender, petite frame. Linda, in turn, was taken in by Travis's charisma and his easy way with people. Travis was just a few years older than she. At that point, he was selling day planners at Franklin Covey, a retail store in Riverside that sells organizers and offers time management training for companies and individuals. According to Linda, he was very into organization. He didn't want to stay there long, as he had bigger plans for himself. Linda learned that he had been raised in poverty and she admired his determination to make something of himself. However, she was against his decision to forgo college in favor of finding a quick way to earn big money.

Before long, the relationship between Travis and Linda became serious. They started talking about marriage almost immediately. In August, Linda had to move back to Provo for her second year at Brigham Young. Travis wanted to go to Provo, too, saying he would find an apartment, so the two could continue dating. But Linda told him not to come yet, preferring to wait a semester before Travis made such a leap. She didn't want the pressure of having someone moving his whole life to another state for her. She wanted to date long-distance and visit each other as often as they could.

That fall, Travis was struggling financially. He wasn't making much at Franklin Covey, and his financial picture was growing increasingly bleak. He shared a house with several other young men, but he still had rent and bills to pay. He confided to friends that he was down on his luck. Though he had saved three thousand dollars to put away for a rainy day, he had spent most of it, and there appeared to be many rainy days still ahead. From his futon, he prayed to God for an answer to his troubles. He had dreams of financial independence, world travel, and even a career in politics at some point in the future.

One morning, Travis awoke with a strong urge to connect with a fellow church member named Chris Hughes, a tall, strapping man with a cheerful yet commanding presence. Travis had heard of Chris, but the two had never really spoken. That Saturday, Travis followed his premonition and sought Chris out. He learned that Chris was a salesman for a firm called Pre-Paid Legal, and as luck would have it, Chris was searching for someone as well. Chris was looking for a key person to help him build his business in Southern California. Although PPL was a great opportunity, Chris was new to town and needed to make connections. It was a perfect fit. Except for his mission, Travis had lived in Riverside his whole life and knew tons of people. Chris had an established team and a secure career. Both men liked to describe their initial meeting as "providence," with each searching for what the other had to offer. In the days that followed, Chris hired Travis onto his sales team at PPL.

As a sales associate, Travis had a gift for closing the deal. He used the story of his own childhood struggles to motivate potential clients. The strategy quickly won him financial rewards, and he was convinced he had found his ticket to success. But his success at PPL came with a price all its own: Linda wasn't comfortable with PPL's multilevel marketing approach, where every sales associate recruited people under him, and each of those people was expected to recruit more people, who would be under that person. The concept did not sit well with her. She found it awkward when Travis tried to sell the company's services to her friends. They'd be on a double date when Travis would turn the conversation to PPL and encourage the other couple to join. Linda began to feel uneasy when they were socializing with friends, but it wasn't enough to end the relationship.

Travis and Linda spent that Christmas with both of their families; first in Las Vegas with Linda's father and the rest of her family, then in Riverside for Christmas dinner with Travis's grandparents, Mum Mum and Grandpa Jim. Grandma Norma was sweet, laid-back, and easy to talk to. Everyone involved had a great time, chatting, joking, and enjoying each other's company.

Travis was enamored with Linda and enjoyed showing her off to all his friends—even introducing her to his barber. He also wanted her to meet his mother, Pamela. She was not in good health, and he was not sure how much longer she would be around. Linda knew about Travis's horrible childhood. He had told her about his mother's abuse and the powerful drug addiction she had ultimately conquered, explaining how he no longer harbored animosity or resentment toward his mother and earning Linda's admiration in the process. Still, Linda didn't know what to expect.

During the visit, Travis and his mother were polite and cordial to each other, although they were clearly not close. While she had kicked drugs, her small home was still quite messy. She seemed to be the polar opposite of her fastidious and motivated son. Linda and Travis didn't stay long, just long enough for Linda to smile, shake Pam's hand, and talk for a bit.

After Christmas break, the plan was for Travis to move

to Provo. That January 2002, the two caravanned to Utah, using walkie-talkies to stay in touch for the long drive. Linda had found Travis a house to share with other single Mormon men and helped him move in. His place was not far from the house she shared with several other young Mormon women.

The momentum of their relationship was powerful. The two would kiss and cuddle together, but they never went further. Both were intent on adhering to the tenets of their shared religion, but it was hard for them to control their desires. Travis was anxious to enjoy a sexual relationship, but because sex out of wedlock was considered a sin by the Mormon church, Travis wanted to wait to have marital intimacy. Still, he was sure he had found his soul mate. Months earlier he had even gone out and bought her an engagement ring, and had gone so far as to ask Linda's dad for his daughter's hand in marriage.

Although Linda knew that Travis wanted to get married, she was having doubts about making him her life partner. She was very young and not sure that she was ready to make the ultimate commitment. She loved him, but she just wasn't sure he was the one. She began praying over whether or not she should marry him, and the answer she got back was "no." On February 5, she went to Travis's apartment to end things. She told him she didn't feel right about getting married. She wasn't sure if it was because he wasn't the right one, or it was simply bad timing. She said she was still very young, and marriage was a big step. When she said they needed to break up and move on with their lives, Travis was devastated. He began crying uncontrollably. "I just can't picture my life without you," he said, tears running down his cheeks. She had never seen him cry so intensely, and it broke her heart.

Travis sent Linda an email later that night, telling her he didn't know if he would ever find anyone else like her and apologizing for not being worthy. "I wish that I could show my best self. I feel like I have so much to offer, and I feel like you haven't seen the best Travis that there is. I want to be better, and I want you to see my best self."

Linda felt terrible for him. For some reason, she was no longer sure how she felt about seeing him. "It's a timing thing," she told him in a reply email. "We'll keep dating." The two got back together within the hour.

"I want to marry you, and I will wait for you to make up your mind," Travis told her.

On February 10, Travis's grandfather had a heart attack, and Travis immediately flew back to California to be with him and Mum Mum. He even moved in with Chris Hughes temporarily to be near his grandmother in case she needed him. Later that month, Linda traveled to Riverside to visit. While there, Travis brought her to a PPL meeting. He was enthusiastic for her to find out more about it, hoping it would turn her less negative. It was there that she saw Deanna Reid, the girl in the photo on Travis's dashboard. Deanna had returned from Costa Rica, and apparently had been recruited into PPL as well. By now Linda knew about their past relationship, so she was curious about her.

After the meeting, Travis signed Linda up as a new recruit. She was uncomfortable with that, but he told her not to worry, he would do all the work. Although Linda accepted Travis's choices, she continued to feel that a college degree would serve him better and open more doors in the future. The day after the meeting, Linda came to see Travis at Chris's house, and the two had a long talk. They considered dating other people, but still while dating each other, too. Travis agreed, hoping that this meant there was still a chance that their relationship would work out.

On March 8, Travis flew back to Utah, and the two continued to date. Linda was still trying to decide how she felt about the relationship. For the next several months, Travis did all sorts of special things to woo her—cooking her dinners, baking her cookies, and taking her out on really nice dates. After all his effort, Linda felt torn. A part of her wanted to marry him, but some other part of her was still questioning a lifetime partnership.

That May, Linda and her friend Krista took a road trip from Provo to Riverside. While in Southern California, they went on a double date in Huntington Beach with Travis and his friend Mark. During the evening, Linda and Travis danced to Chris de Burgh's "Lady in Red," the same song the two had danced to on one of their first dates the previous June. Suddenly, as they slow-danced, Linda began to cry. All at once, reality hit her. This would probably be the last time the two would dance together.

Linda had decided to move on. Travis soon packed up his stuff in Provo and moved back to Riverside. After the breakup, Travis wrote Linda a poem, the gist of it being he only wanted the best for her, whether that meant staying with him or going their separate ways. He was heartbroken, but ready to move on with his life. Now Travis Alexander was going to put all of his considerable intelligence and drive into becoming a financial success.

The sweltering hundred-degree days of summer in Southern California did not slow Travis down. He was disappointed that his relationship with Linda had failed, but he found comfort in his work with PPL and in the arms of his old flame, Deanna Reid. In the spring of 2002, after Travis had returned from Provo to Riverside, the two began seeing each other at the Young Single Adult Ward functions, and they quickly found their romance back in full throttle. Deanna had even gone to visit him in Utah while he was still living there. She was Travis's rock, always there for him as a loyal friend and, when the moment was right, happy to become his romantic partner once again.

For the next three years, Travis and Deanna dated exclusively. While they lived separately—Deanna with her parents and Travis in a rented house with other single Mormon men—they were a regular couple around town. They were very social together, taking in movies, hiking, and hanging out with friends. Everyone, including Linda Ballard, was convinced they would eventually be married.

With Deanna back in his life, Travis felt a sense of security and stability. He could now focus on becoming his best possible self. He began each day with a motivational exercise. On a three-by-five-inch index card, he listed the six things he believed were essential to do every day: prayer; reading scripture; reading ten pages of a good book; listening to thirty minutes of personal development; working out; and making money. He wrote the same list on a new index card every morning, until the six items became a routine part of his day. As time went on, he added a seventh item to his list, and then an eighth, and so on. He also created other lists of things he wanted to do for fun or out of necessity. They could be anything from updating his calendar to thirty minutes of practicing Spanish. Once the lists were made, he studied them and asked himself, "If this was all to get done, would it be an amazing day?" Sometimes the answer was "yes," other times it was "no." Either way, he wouldn't start his day unless he could say that it was going to be "one for the ages." Travis claimed his morning index card ritual had increased his productivity fivefold. He was convinced it was because people tended to finish what they focused on. "Write down what you want life to bring you today, and chances are life will bring it to you on a silver platter," he posted online in his blog.

As with Linda, Deanna's involvement in PPL was mostly for him. She already had a full-time job, working in customer service for a security company in Irvine, California, where she was stuck in a cubicle all day. She wasn't crazy about the work, but the money was good. Still, she went to the PPL meetings, helped with the setup, and manned the sign-in tables. She even did some sales. While she wasn't as high in the ranks of the company as everyone else seemed to be, she did like the personal development aspect of it. More important, she liked what the company had done for Travis. He'd become more confident, and his public speaking skills had really improved. He'd always had a swagger, and running the meetings and speaking in front of large groups seemed to fit his personality. At last, he seemed to have found his niche.

Deanna and Travis were together for about a year when she told him she wanted to get married. She was twenty-four and ready to settle down and start a family. In the Mormon faith, she was already on the older side, with most couples marrying in their late teens or early twenties. Travis was not surprised by her request; they had discussed marriage before and had agreed it was a shared goal. Travis was one year older than Deanna, so he, too, was considered on the mature side for a single Mormon man. He knew that in the Mormon faith, dating was supposed to lead to marriage. But he told Deanna that although she would be a wonderful person to marry, he simply wasn't ready. She was disappointed, but remained hopeful that he would come around soon.

In 2004, Deanna learned that her company was relocating its operation to north Phoenix, Arizona. She could either move with them or be out of a job. At the time, Deanna was living with roommates in Huntington Beach, most of whom were either getting married or moving away, or both. On top of that, their lease for the share was up, making it a good time for Deanna to entertain a change. Moving to Arizona sounded kind of cool, and she liked the idea. When she told Travis about it, he also seemed open to the possibility. He told her he had been eager to buy a house somewhere, but real estate in Southern California was just too pricey, so Arizona had promise. The more they spoke, the better the idea sounded. Deanna decided to keep her job with the company, signing up with them for another year. If the job in Phoenix was horrible and she hated it, she could move back home in twelve months.

Travis's decision to relocate to Arizona was largely based on Deanna's choice. There was nothing making him stay in California, and he could do his PPL business from wherever he pleased. Once he had made up his mind, he traveled to the area several months ahead of Deanna to look for a property he could purchase. He looked first in Mesa, twenty miles east of Phoenix, because of its large Mormon population. It was home to the massive Mesa Arizona Temple, located on a twenty-acre piece of property on South LeSueur Street. Almost immediately, he found the five-bedroom house on Queensborough Avenue in Mesa. He liked the neighborhood and just about everything about the 4,500-square-foot Spanish-style house. Of course, he didn't need a house this big, but he thought it would be cost-effective; the more bedrooms, the more roommates he could have to help pay his mortgage. He would still have to contribute, but the amount was pretty much equal to what his roommates would be paying.

When Deanna arrived, she rented an apartment in Phoenix, not far from her new office. That Travis and Deanna were living in different geographical locations meant that they belonged to different wards of the Mormon church and saw different bishops. They still attended the same temple, as there were more wards in the Phoenix area than there were temples.

Typically, a Mormon temple is a big, beautiful sacred building for adults only, except for certain occasions when children can go. There are sacred ordinances performed in the temple, such as baptisms, endowments, and marriages. Worshippers must show a Temple Recommend, similar to an ID card, just to gain entry to an LDS temple. To obtain one, worshippers must first be interviewed by their bishop, who asks if the applicant is living up to the standards of the church and if he or she believes in its principles. Then, a decision is made. Recommends must be renewed every two years to assure church standards are being upheld. Both Deanna and Travis had their Temple Recommends.

In Mesa, Travis joined the local LDS church on Hawes Road, and quickly became a popular member of its YSA, Young Single Adult Ward. To help pay his mortgage, he rented out rooms to church members, friends, and singles looking for a monthly arrangement. It was not long before he had a full house, all young men whose commonality was Pre-Paid Legal and/or Mormonism. At times, when the house was brimming with lots of handsome young men, the UFC fight-watching parties on Wednesday nights were the nights to look forward to. One of Travis's first housemates was an ambitious young Mormon named Taylor Searle. Taylor had just returned home from a two-year church mission in Japan. He met Travis at a Pre-Paid Legal business briefing held at a local hotel. Travis was dressed in a gold pinstriped suit and was standing in the front of the room greeting people as they arrived.

Travis soon became Taylor's mentor at PPL, as well as his landlord on Queensborough Avenue. Seven other guys were living at the house when Taylor moved in. He recalled that it was basically like a hotel, with tenants coming and going, some leaving to get married or to move to more permanent housing. Travis had an open-door policy and friends said he never kept the house locked. Deanna had her own key and an open invitation to come by anytime.

Travis and Deanna enjoyed their thriving social scene. For Halloween that year, they attended a party with five other couples, all of whom were married. All the couples dressed up in complementary matching costumes. Travis and Deanna went as Johnny Lingo, a Polynesian trader, and Mahana, his Samoan wife, from the 1969 film *Johnny Lingo,* produced by the Church of Jesus Christ of Latter-day Saints. Travis wore a sarong and let Deanna smother him in self-tanning lotion. At the party, everyone played the Newlywed Game. Deanna and Travis couldn't believe they had come within two points of winning, even though they were the only ones who were not married. They often laughed about how they had outscored couples who had been together for years. Yet, despite their obvious compatibility, Travis could not fully commit himself to Deanna. Several of his room-mates said that he adored her, but he just had reservations. Ironically, the ambivalence Linda had felt regarding Travis a couple of years earlier, Travis now seemed to be experiencing regarding Deanna.

What no one knew was that Travis and Deanna had begun having sexual relations, in spite of the church's strict Law of Chastity, which forbids sexual activity out of wedlock.

"Because we were sleeping together and we weren't married, that was a violation in the church," Deanna recalled in a telephone interview. "You're not supposed to do that." Travis and Deanna kept their intimate relationship secret for more than a year. Eventually, they agreed to go to their respective bishops to confess. There wasn't a big fear in the church of going to the bishop, as letting him know what was going on was better than harboring the secret.

In the Mormon church, confessions take place face-to-face in the bishop's office. First, the repentant person reveals his or her sin, at which point the conversation turns to demonstrating a desire to change. The process continues with weekly meetings with the bishop, who shares applicable scripture and spiritual advice. "Every week, I would tell him about my life and how things were going," said Deanna. "I had a really good experience with the whole process. My bishop was the sweetest man ever. He made me feel so comfortable and was so respectful about everything." Deanna said all the church leaders treated her and Travis with love and respect.

Deanna's bishop did not physically take away her Temple Recommend, although he did advise her not to attend her temple until he deemed her temple-worthy. Travis, on the other hand, did have his Temple Recommend taken away. Neither was allowed to participate in sacraments in their churches, either. Deanna went through a ten-month repentance process, working with the bishop all the while. Finally, she was able to go back to temple, but Travis's bishop wouldn't allow him back for a year. The two vowed to their bishops that they would not have sex again with anyone until they were with a marriage partner. In the meantime, they ended their relationship.

The story behind their breakup seems to differ depending on whom you talk to. Clearly, the rigors of repentance had to have impacted their romantic relationship in some form. According to Deanna, she came to the realization that Travis was never going to marry her and chose to end it, though they were able to segue into a loving friendship. Friends say that when it came to Deanna, Travis also had issues with commitment. One even suggested to him that he seek counseling, believing that because of his upbringing, he felt vulnerable and afraid to let people love him. Others say the many years of rarely interrupted chastity had left Travis, now a man in his late twenties, with a desire for a new experience. A male friend said that while Travis often spoke of his deep yearning to get married, he also repeatedly referred to himself as having a highly sexed nature. Though quite pretty, Deanna didn't exude the arm-candy sexiness that friends say Travis had begun to daydream about.

Part of it was that Travis was living in a house full of single guys, all of whom were handsome, in great physical shape, and always seemed to be dating hot young women. While Travis was the alpha male, the one with the successful career, the big house, and the shiny BMW in the driveway, he envied their ability to get the bombshell girls. He thought that part of the problem was his weight. Travis grew determined to get healthy and into great physical shape. He began an exercise regimen that consisted of long workout sessions and strenuous hikes and bicycles rides, while also eating more fruits and vegetables. He was even juicing and—after viewing a documentary on the horrors of factory farming—had cut back on meat.

Before long, his self-improvement campaign paid off. He had shed pounds and was looking buffed. His natural good looks supercharged his efforts. For the first time in his life, Travis was turning heads. He began to get attention from girls he used to consider out of his league. His reputation as a beloved dork had ended and what emerged was a handsome motivational speaker who felt he just might become the next Tony Robbins.

After Deanna, Travis dated an attractive young woman named Esther. Not much is known about Travis's relationship with Esther, except that they were together for a period of a few months.

In May of 2005, Travis opened his home to a stunning female friend named Elisha Schabel. Elisha and her husband were heading toward a divorce, and she needed a temporary place to stay. At the time, Travis had eight male renters, so there wasn't a free bedroom for Elisha. But wanting to help her, he invited her to share his large master bedroom. Elisha said that Travis expressed an interest in dating her, but she was not interested in a romantic relationship, and Travis was completely respectful. For the month of May, she slept in Travis's bed with him, but the two remained chaste.

"A lot of times he's like, 'Come sleep in my bed . . . Come stay with me. I'll even sleep on the floor,' said Elisha. And I'm like, 'I'm not going to make you sleep on the floor in your own room.' And so we would actually make a pillow barricade, just to keep us, keep him a man of his word. And keep each other honest. At the time, he had a jungle-themed bedroom and a huge stuffed animal lion that we put on top [of the pillows]. So, it was like this huge barricade. And every night he's like, 'Oh, Elisha we don't have to do this.' And I'm like 'yes we do. Just to keep safe.' But we would talk over the barricade every night. And, for like a few days or I don't even know how long I ended up sleeping in that bed." Elisha said Travis never crossed the line and respected her boundaries, literally and figuratively.

That same year, Travis got a black pug. He had always loved pugs, because those were the dogs his beloved grandmother favored. He named his Napoleon. He treated the dog like his child, teaching him lots of commands and tricks. He brought Napoleon with him on road trips as often as he could. Even after the end of Travis and Deanna's relationship, Deanna held on to a key to Travis's house so she could take care of Napoleon while Travis was traveling. And Travis would be traveling a lot.

CHAPTER 7

DEDUCTIVE REASONING

In the days following the medical examiner's findings, Detective Flores hit the phones, reaching out to Travis's friends and business associates with the hopes of getting a clearer picture of the victim and his relationship with his former girlfriend, Jodi Arias. His initial interviews with those close to Travis suggested that Jodi was a likely suspect, and his lengthy phone call with her that past Tuesday had raised his antennae considerably.

On Monday, June 16, one of Detective Flores's first orders of business was to follow up on a phone message left by Travis's friend Clancy Talbot. Clancy, who lived in Salt Lake City, said she had seen Jodi Arias at a PPL seminar there on June 5. Jodi had been in the company of a man named Ryan Burns, who was also affiliated with PPL.

Clancy explained that according to Ryan, Jodi had left California on Tuesday, June 3, but hadn't arrived in Salt Lake City until Thursday, June 5. Ryan also told her that he had lost contact with Jodi for more than twenty-four hours during the drive, which Clancy found alarming because of the possibilities in the timeline. She knew the trip from Northern California to Salt Lake City was typically about ten hours, but Jodi had been traveling for nearly two days. Ryan told her that Jodi had claimed she had gotten lost and had parked on the shoulder of the road to sleep for a while. Clancy said she'd heard that other people at the conference had tried to call Jodi while she was en route, but had also been unable to reach her, as her phone was apparently shut off.

Clancy wondered if Jodi had taken a detour to see Travis in Mesa. Jodi had been very clingy, very *Fatal Attraction* since the two had broken up, Clancy said. She added that when Jodi finally arrived at the conference, she was no longer a platinum blonde, but was now a brunette. As Jodi tried to give her a big hug, Clancy pulled out of it. Jodi was also acting "a little odd," but Clancy assumed it was because she was probably tired after the long drive. Of course, at the time that Jodi showed up a day late in Utah, nobody had any idea that Travis was sitting dead in his shower in Arizona.

It wasn't until Travis's body was discovered in Mesa four days later that Clancy and others began reconsidering Jodi's story and finding it curious that she was off the radar for so long around the very time that Travis was killed. Clancy had had dinner with Jodi, Ryan, and about twenty friends at Chili's on the night of June 5. Jodi had Band-Aids on fingers on both of her hands.

"What did you do to your hands?" one of the friends asked.

"I'm a bartender, I cut my fingers," Jodi replied.

Clancy was skeptical. The story didn't make any sense. Why would a bartender have so many cuts on so many fingers? The injuries didn't seem to bother Jodi. She was acting like everything was totally fine, laughing at people's jokes, not complaining about her cuts. Everybody was going to go four-wheeling the next day. Ryan invited Jodi to join them. Jodi usually loved the PPL side adventure trips, so everybody was surprised when she said she couldn't make it because she had to work. Normally she would find somebody to cover for her.

At the end of the call, Clancy provided the detective with Ryan's phone number. Detective Flores thanked her, and the two hung up. Flores knew he wanted to talk to Ryan Burns, but he had other calls to make first. He also wanted to hear Jodi Arias tell her version of the Salt Lake City events once he had gathered enough information from other sources.

For now, Detective Flores wanted to talk to Travis's most recent girlfriend, Lisa Andrews. Her name had been mentioned by Travis's roommate, Zach Billings, who had indicated Lisa had broken off her relationship with Travis that past February, in part because of Jodi. In a phone call with Detective Flores, Lisa Andrews confirmed her discomfort with Jodi Arias. She recalled a night from the previous December. Travis had been visiting with her at her house, when there was a knock at the front door. She went to answer it, but no one was there. It wasn't until Travis went to his car later that night to go home that he realized all four of his tires had been slashed. It was unsettling, but they both dismissed it as a random act of vandalism.

When the same thing happened the following night, the two could no longer ignore it. There was the same unexpected knock on the door, with no one there when they answered. This time Travis immediately raced to his car, only to find his tires slashed again. Lisa said they called the Mesa police, but after waiting several hours for an officer to arrive, he had to leave before they could file a report. Frightened, Lisa asked Travis to spend the night, which he did. She said they did not have sex; she just didn't want to be home alone.

Lisa said the next day she received an angry email from

a "John Doe," which she had saved. Filled with hostility, it mentioned her relationship with Travis. *"You shameful whore. Your Heavenly Father must be ashamed of the whoredoms you have committed with that insidious man. If you let him stay in your bed one more time or even sleep under the same roof as him, you will be giving the appearance of evil."* There were a number of religious references, with the email signing off: *"Be thou clean, sin no more. Heavenly Father loves you and wants you to make the right choices. I know you are strong enough to choose the right. Your Father in Heaven is pulling for you. Don't ignore the promptings you receive, because they are vital to your spiritual well-being."*

Lisa said that she and Travis suspected that Jodi had sent the email and slashed the tires, but they had never been able to prove it. Detective Flores asked Lisa if she could think of anyone other than Jodi who might want to harm Travis. No one came to mind, although Lisa did provide Flores with the name of one of Travis's former roommates. She recalled that he and Travis did not see eye to eye, and that he had moved out suddenly in the middle of the night the previous December. Still, she didn't believe he had a reason to hurt Travis. In her opinion, Jodi was a much more likely candidate.

Detective Flores wanted to conduct follow-up interviews with some of the people who had been at the house when Travis's body had been discovered, including Mimi Hall, Dallin Forrest, and Michelle Lowery. They all agreed to come to the station to be interviewed and to give DNA and fingerprint samples, a necessary step to exclude them from any evidence found at the scene.

The detective also called Jodi Arias. When he learned that she was in the area, having traveled from Northern California to Mesa, Arizona, for Travis's memorial service to be held that day, he asked her if she could come to headquarters the following day so he could speak with her in person. He explained that he already had three others coming to provide DNA samples for exclusionary purposes.

"I am leaving tomorrow, but I will try and come by," Jodi told him.

At 6 P.M. on June 17, Mimi, Dallin, Michelle, and Jodi arrived at the Mesa police headquarters building on North Robson. They were there to be fingerprinted and to provide saliva for DNA testing. Jodi was the only one who declined to sit down with the detective for a follow-up interview. She said she had been speaking with a close friend who had convinced her that there were a number of people talking about her involvement in Travis's death, and as a result, she was now uncomfortable speaking to him without first consulting with an attorney.

Travis's friends were equally uncomfortable being at the headquarters with Jodi. Almost all of them were already convinced that she had killed him, and they viewed all of her actions since his death as suspect. They had been offended when four days earlier, on June 13, she had posted a photo gallery on her Myspace page dedicated to Travis. It included twenty-five pictures, most of them with Jodi and Travis posing together in various locations they had visited. She titled the collection "In Loving Memory of Travis." As if that weren't enough, Jodi had been calling some of the friends, trying to find out the latest in the murder investigation, which they found disingenuous. In fact, Travis's friends became outraged when Detective Flores, at one point, told Chris and Sky Hughes that Jodi was no longer a suspect, that she had been cleared. It was a ruse. The police wanted Jodi to think she was not under suspicion, though the group at the station house could not have known that she was still law enforcement's number-one suspect.

Among the evidence the police were amassing on her

was the activity on Travis's telephone. The significance of a voice mail from Jodi wasn't immediately appreciated but soon it would be. At 11:48 P.M. on June 4, Jodi left an upbeat message for Travis in which she apologized for not making it to Mesa and told him that she and her friend Heather were planning to see *Othello* in early July and invited him to join them. Of course what police quickly learned was that the voice mail was a cover, a poorly designed smokescreen that Jodi used to strengthen her alibi. And it might have actually worked, if it hadn't been for the crucial piece of evidence at the scene of the crime.

The first significant break in the case came ten days after Travis's body was discovered, in the form of the memory card found in the digital camera police had discovered in Travis's washing machine. Although the camera had clearly been put through the wash, Michael Melendez, a computer forensics detective with the Mesa Police Department, had been able to recover numerous pictures from it, including some that had been deleted.

The deleted photos included images of Travis, who was naked, standing in various poses in the shower, his muscles toned and well defined. He was reaching his arms up as he soaped his body. The photos were eerily reminiscent of the famous shower scene in the classic Hitchcock movie *Psycho,* except instead of Janet Leigh, it was Travis dripping in water and danger. Astoundingly, it appeared the recovered photos had been taken before, during, and after his murder. One of the last photos of Travis alive showed him staring intently into the camera, his handsome face betraying a subtle anxiety as droplets of water rolled down his cheeks. It was time-stamped June 4, 2008, at 5:29 P.M.

Less than a minute later, at 5:30 P.M., another photo showed Travis sitting on the slippery floor of the small shower stall, an extremely vulnerable position. Forty-four seconds later there's a blurry photo of the bathroom ceiling. It's believed to have been inadvertently snapped as Travis was attacked. About a minute later another photo, taken upside down and apparently by accident, shows Travis lying on his back, with large amounts of blood around his neck and shoulders, the bathroom in the background. Remarkably, the photo also revealed the right pant leg and foot of the killer, who was possibly reaching down to move the body. The murderer was wearing a dark-colored sock or shoe and striped sweatpants, probably blue, with a zipper on the back of the cuff.

The last photo, also upside down, appeared to have been taken by accident as well, and was snapped one minute, sixteen seconds after the previous one. After it was enhanced, that photo revealed the bathroom hallway and baseboard drenched in a dark, bloodlike liquid substance.

Detective Melendez retrieved another six photos that had been taken prior to the shower pictures, time-stamped June 4, 2008, starting at 1:40 P.M. The first showed Jodi Arias posing naked on Travis's bed. There were, in fact, four photos of Jodi posing in the nude, some in extremely provocative and graphic sexual positions, leaving nothing to the imagination. The other two were of Travis, who was also naked in both images, a tube or bottle of KY lubricant next to him. The photos were the smoking gun, irrefutable proof that Jodi was lying when she told Detective Flores she had not seen Travis since early April 2008. Police now had the evidence to prove that she had been the last person to be in contact with Travis Alexander before his death.

Detective Flores sat on this stunning information for nearly three days before he finally spoke to Jodi Arias again. On Saturday, June 21, she had left a message with her telephone number on his cell phone, asking that he call her back when he had the chance. That Tuesday, June 24, the detective returned the call.

"What can I do for you?" he asked when Jodi answered the phone. She told him that, when she had reached out to him four days earlier, she had been having a really bad day. She explained that her car had gotten a flat tire on the way to the airport, so she had missed Travis's funeral in Riverside on June 21. That day, there had been a 9 A.M. family service at the Church of Jesus Christ of Latter-day Saints on Fourth Street, followed by a 10 A.M. funeral service, and a burial at Olivewood Memorial Park, and she had missed them all.

Despite missing the funeral, Jodi had been present on June 16 for a memorial service in Arizona in honor of Travis. Jodi had flown there on the morning of Sunday, June 15, to attend the memorial the following day at Travis's church. Jodi was invited to stay with Dan and Desiree Freeman, who lived with their parents in Gilbert. Dan picked up Jodi at the Phoenix airport after which Jodi, the Freemans, and Aaron Dewey, a Mormon friend in their social circle, attended the regular Sunday service at Travis's church. The next day, Jodi planned to go to the memorial with Aaron. He picked her up at the Freemans and, as they headed to the church with some extra time, Jodi had a special request. She asked Aaron to drive by Travis's house because she wanted to see it. Though the house was still locked and sealed, the crime scene tape had been taken down. Aaron and Jodi sat outside and talked, before walking around the front yard. Aaron detected nothing unusual in their conversation.

At the memorial, the crowd numbered at least five hundred friends, co-workers, and church members. The distraught and grieving group gathered to share memories of Travis. The memorial program included a verse Travis wrote in a blog less than two weeks before he died: "The Gold from Within." Aaron sat with Jodi during the service. He said that she sat with her head down, displaying no emotion and no tears. "People commented after about that, saying things like, 'She loved him, he was brutally killed, and she has no tears. What's up with that?'"

After the service, Jodi was "kind of bubbly, going around talking to people and catching up." She had also arranged to have three to four binders of photos of Travis, including some with her in them, displayed on a table at the service. She invited those in attendance to find photos with special meaning, remove them from the plastic sleeve, and write a message on the back. Her intent, according to Aaron, was to give the photos to Travis's family. Needless to say, many people were dumbstruck to see Jodi there. To them she was the first suspect on a list of one. How dare she show her face among them and pretend to grieve his death? She worked the crowd, hugging Travis's friends, acting as though she was making her first trip to Arizona since early April. Travis's friend Taylor Searle was completely unnerved when Jodi approached him for a hug and a chat, recalling how his mind began to race. "My mind tells me that I should not be talking to you right now because you're the one that did this. But I'm also confused because you're here so I don't want to be a complete jackass if it turns out it wasn't you. So, I'm gonna be pleasant with you, but I don't wanna talk to you. Those are the kind of things going through my mind, just throwing me off, like, Hey! 'cause I didn't know what was going on: why was she there?" In what Travis's friends regarded as a positively diabolical move, Jodi also sent a large bouquet of irises to Travis's grandmother Mum Mum expressing sympathy. Horrified, Mum Mum immediately threw them in the trash.

Perhaps because of the awkward reception she had received at the memorial service, Jodi had deliberately missed Travis's actual funeral in Riverside. Yet here she was again talking to Flores on the phone, appearing to be helpful and asking if there had been any new leads in the case. She even apologized to the detective for having declined to speak to him during her visit to the station the day after the memorial.

Jodi explained that she might be traveling to Tucson, Arizona, in the coming weeks and could stop by headquarters to meet with him then, on the way through. She also offered to give a statement over the phone, if the detective preferred, but she couldn't give it that instant. They agreed on a call at 10 A.M. the following day. Just as they were about to hang up, Detective Flores blurted out a question. "Did you send Travis an email about coming down to visit him?"

Jodi admitted she had written him an email a week or so before his murder, but as he had not responded, she assumed he was probably in California. She also knew that he was traveling to Cancún, Mexico, and said she had been planning to stay at his house and visit with friends while he was away. Travis had an "open-door" policy, and according to Jodi, he let her stay there in exchange for taking care of his pug when he was out of town. Ultimately, Jodi said finances had prevented her from going to Mesa, so she had traveled to Southern California and Utah instead.

Before the call ended, Jodi had a practical question for the detective: "How will I get the belongings that I left at Travis's house?" she wanted to know. She had left a few items of clothing there and was wondering how she could get them back. Given the grisly nature of Travis's murder, Detective Flores thought this concern was odd. The detective would learn soon enough just how unusual a woman Jodi Arias really was.

The following morning, Detective Flores dialed Jodi's cell phone at the appointed time. He started his questioning with the basics of how she and Travis had met and when they had first started dating.

"We met in September," Jodi began; "the following weekend he invited me to church, and the following Wednesday he gave me *The Book of Mormon* and I started reading it. I got baptized on November 26 . . ."

She didn't dwell much on nine of the first ten months they had been together, but moved forward to describe the end of the relationship. "Travis has kind of a commitment phobia, I guess you could say," she offered. She said that the ironic part was breaking up "around the same time" she had moved to Mesa in June 2007. Besides commitment issues, the problem had been trust.

"I have been in relationships before where the other guy wasn't faithful and there is just this like distinctive gut feeling that you just have," Jodi explained. "I had this feeling with Travis, and I gently asked him about it. He got really upset and he was like, 'no there is nothing there, don't worry about it.' " She told the detective that she was aware Travis had been texting a lot of girls, but Travis had written it off as being flirtatious but innocent. Jodi described an incident the previous June, when Travis had been napping and she had taken his phone to snoop. "There were tons of girls that I had never heard of. I knew he knew a lot of people from the business, which didn't bother me, but . . . There were plenty of plans, like where do you want to meet, what is the best place to make out in?"

She said she confronted him, and they broke up, because she did not feel he could be monogamous. She said they each associated with a different ward in Mesa, hers being the University Sixth Ward, and Travis's being the Desert Ridge Ward, but she spent some time at his. Still, they both knew they weren't on a path to marriage, despite the romantic and intimate sides of their relationship.

Detective Flores told Jodi that some of the people he talked to had some very unpleasant stuff to say about her.

"You seem like a pleasant person, and they were saying that you were kind of obsessive after the breakup, and things like that. What was going on to make them think that?"

"The only thing I can think of, and I realize that because I was at his house a lot, um, but I didn't go to his house unless I was invited over, or if he knew that I was coming over." She went on to describe a system she and Travis had to alert each other of a pending visit. "He would send me text messages late at night like 'Hey, I'm getting sleepy . . .' And that was like, that became my cue or code word for coming over. 'I'm going to sleep now, sneak into my room and wake me up' kind of thing. That would happen a lot." When Detective Flores asked if that meant there was still a sexual relationship going on, Jodi said that there was.

The detective knew that Jodi had no idea that photos of Travis and her naked in his bedroom had been recovered from Travis's camera with the time stamp that proved that she was with him right before he was murdered. He played dumb when he started a line of questioning about the camera. He asked her if she remembered anything about it, like when it had been purchased or what brand it was. Jodi said she remembered Travis had asked her for some advice, knowing she was a photographer. She thought he had purchased it in April or May, and she had advised against anything Kodak, but did not know his ultimate choice. The detective wondered if she knew any reason why anyone would want to destroy it, without revealing where it had been found, and Jodi said "no."

Detective Flores wanted to know where Jodi had been the day Travis was killed. Jodi told him on Monday, June 2, 2008, she left Northern California for Salt Lake City, Utah, where a Pre-Paid Legal conference was taking place that Wednesday and Thursday. She first drove to the airport in Redding, California, where she rented a car rather than drive her mechanically unreliable vehicle. Once her car was rented, she went to Monterey, California, five hours off course to Salt Lake City, to hang out with friends for the night.

The next day, Tuesday, June 3, she drove farther south to Los Angeles, five more hours out of her way. She was going to visit Darryl's sister, who had a new baby. "I'm a photographer, and she just recently had a baby, and I'm trying to build up my portfolio," she claimed. The new mother wasn't around when she got there, and at that point, she said, she headed northeast to Salt Lake City, eleven hours away.

The detective asked her if she had spoken to Travis along the way. "I did talk to him Tuesday night . . . It was brief though, um . . . like that was a matter of two minutes. It wasn't really an in-depth conversation." Jodi told the detective she was just leaving a Starbucks in Pasadena, just outside Los Angeles, and called Travis to see if he was in the area.

"Do you know what time that was?"

"Ten o'clock? . . . It was late, kind of a late evening. I mean for us that's not late."

Detective Flores wondered about the purpose of the call.

"Um," Jodi said. "I was just calling to check in, say hey. I was calling people, because I was on the road, just bored."

"Oh, so you were on the road at that time?"

"It was real brief, um. He was nice and cordial, but he was acting like he had hurt feelings."

"The reason I ask is we're trying to figure out when [the murder] actually occurred," Detective Flores explained. "And people are saying they lost contact with him maybe, you know, Tuesday or Wednesday, people aren't sure."

"I talked to him last Tuesday, and I'm sure I called Wednesday. I know I called him again from the road twice," Jodi recalled. "I did send him text messages. I know I sent him a picture."

Jodi claimed her long drive to Salt Lake City took her through Boulder City and Las Vegas, Nevada. When she said she had pulled over to sleep in her car, Detective Flores asked her how she kept safe, wanting to raise the issue of a weapon. He baited her by sympathetically telling her that she might be safer if she traveled with some protection, even saying Arizona was a place where you didn't have to register a weapon like you did in California.

"I've actually looked into handguns, because I have lists of things I'm really scared of . . . I'm trying to overcome, and that's one of them," Jodi said. "I'm looking into that, because handguns are expensive. You know, it's not really in my price range right now."

Jodi wanted the detective to know she had a new man, Ryan Burns, who met her when she got to Salt Lake City. He also worked for PPL, and she had gone to the conference to meet him. She was implying that her interest in pursuing Travis, described by those who had talked to Flores as her "obsession," was now done.

When the call was over, Detective Flores started doing the timeline math, and Jodi's story wasn't adding up. She claimed that driving from Yreka to Salt Lake City via Los Angeles and Las Vegas had taken her forty-eight hours. Mapping her route, including a ten-hour rest stop, he concluded her trip would have taken a maximum of twenty-nine hours. Adding Mesa to the route would add a few hours, but there were still ten to eleven hours of additional time to spare.

He called Ryan Burns that afternoon to see what he could corroborate. Ryan confirmed that he knew Jodi Arias. He had met her in Oklahoma at a PPL seminar a couple of months earlier. The trip to Utah had been in the works for about two weeks. Ryan said Jodi called him on Tuesday, June 3, and told him that she had left the Monterey area at around 11 P.M., and she would meet him on Wednesday, June 4. She never told him she was going via Los Angeles. She said she had forgotten her cell phone charger, so the phone was turned off to save battery power for most of the drive. It was 11 P.M. on Wednesday, the day they were supposed to meet, when she finally called him. She had driven in the wrong direction, gotten lost, and then had run out of gas. She said she was currently one hundred miles from Las Vegas, according to the sign she had just passed. When she finally showed up, it was 11 A.M. on Thursday, June 5.

Ryan didn't notice anything particularly unusual about her behavior. She hung out with him at the seminar, and then a group of more than a dozen PPL folks went to dinner at Chili's. Jodi dined with Ryan and his friends, laughing and chatting. Afterward, they went to his place and watched a movie. She fell asleep for a while, and then left Salt Lake City between 2 A.M. or 3 A.M. Ryan couldn't describe the car, but thought it was a white Ford Focus rental. The next time he heard from Jodi, it was by text, early in the next week. She told him that Travis had died. He knew about Travis, but only because Jodi had mentioned him several times.

Ryan said a lot of mutual friends of his and Jodi's in Utah were pointing fingers at her, saying she was responsible for his death. He said he had heard that Travis had been shot with a .25-caliber handgun and that he had also been stabbed. Detective Flores thanked him for his time, saying he would be in touch again soon.

In the coming days, forensic results would give Detective Flores and his team the proof they were looking for. A senior print analyst at the Mesa police identification unit had been able to identify the latent print that had been left in the blood on the bathroom wall. She had individualized the latent print to Jodi Arias's left palm print. It was further evidence that Jodi had been present at the time of Travis's murder. Jodi had left the print when she touched the wall with her left hand.

Members of the Mesa Crime Lab had also turned up something significant. The blood in the palm print indicated it was a mixture of DNA from two individuals, Travis Alexander and Jodi Arias. A long hair found in the same hallway, stuck to the wall in blood, was also identified as Jodi's. Detective Flores had his killer.

CHAPTER 8

—————

AT FIRST SIGHT

Jodi was obsessed with Travis Alexander almost from the day they'd met: September 13, 2006. That initial meeting took place at the MGM Grand Hotel & Casino in Las Vegas, the third-largest hotel in the world, with more than five thousand rooms, five outdoor pools, artificial rivers and waterfalls, and nineteen restaurants. It was at one of these restaurants, the Rainforest Cafe, that Jodi encountered Travis for the first time.

The two were in Las Vegas to attend the Pre-Paid Legal Services convention. Travis and Jodi were on opposite ends of the PPL organization. Travis had joined Pre-Paid Legal Services in 2001, when he was about twenty-four, and since then he had parlayed his role in the firm into something well beyond that of a mere salesman, becoming one of PPL's most sought-after motivational speakers. He was such a successful salesman that by early 2006, he had already become an executive director by achieving at least seventy-five sales in one month, including sales made by those under him. He was now earning close to the hundred-thousand-dollar mark, which was the level at which salespeople were awarded a special ring for executives known as "Ring Earners." As an executive director at the Vegas convention, Travis had access to all the executive perks, things such as special banquets, front-row seats to popular presentations, and other VIP treatments. The conventions were ways for him to network and to troll the crowd of newcomers for fresh recruits.

By comparison, Jodi was a relative newcomer, who'd only just begun working with PPL a few months earlier, in March 2006. Jodi first heard about the opportunities at Pre-Paid Legal from a stranger who had come into the restaurant where she worked as a waitress. Her job at California Pizza Kitchen in Palm Desert was one of several she was juggling in an attempt to make her monthly bills. She and the stranger got into a casual conversation, so it kind of surprised her when he asked her where she saw herself in five years. He let her know that he was going to retire soon, having made enough money at a company called Pre-Paid Legal Services to do so at a young age. Jodi did not object when he handed her some printed material and a promotional DVD. The DVD sat in her house gathering dust for six months, when one day she came across it while cleaning. She was going to throw it away but decided to watch it first. She popped it into her machine. The message seemed like providence. Here, possibly, was the answer to her mounting problems.

Jodi got so excited about the potential financial windfall that she signed up online and was soon contacted by one of the company's salespeople, who signed Jodi up as an independent associate. At the time, Jodi had been struggling, working several jobs just to make ends meet, but because PPL's associates work from home, Jodi didn't have to give up her other jobs in order to make money. After she signed up with PPL, she heard about the company's semi-annual convention in September. Apparently it was a great way to pick up tips on how to profit with the multilevel marketing firm, so when September came, Jodi traveled to Las Vegas with her sponsor/mentor and another Pre-Paid Legal associate to attend her first convention. She had been searching for something financially stable to lock on to and maybe this convention would provide the key. Jodi had just finished lunch and was standing with a group of people near the gorilla bench at the entrance to the Rainforest Café when Travis walked right up to her and introduced himself with an extended hand.

"Hi, I'm Travis," he greeted her. He was dressed in a dapper business suit and well-polished shoes. His short brown hair was combed back off his face, his features were chiseled, his green eyes were light and cheerful, and his smile was bold.

"Hi, I'm Jodi," was the response from the beautiful, demure blonde. Her dimples enhanced a smile befitting a model and her voice was soft, but confident.

Though Jodi later claimed there wasn't really any initial magnetic attraction between the two, what followed led many to believe there must have been a potent spark, a palpable heat, from the get-go. Jodi insisted that, at first, his was just another of the many names she had to remember given the hundreds of people she was meeting that weekend. Still, there was clearly something that drew the two into conversation.

Travis joined Jodi and her friends for a stroll through the casino and before long, the two found themselves wandering away from the group. By the time they had reached the hotel's lobby, where a larger-than-life gold lion statue sat in a raised pedestal surrounded by fresh flowers, they'd discovered their common interests.

That night, Jodi was out for dinner at a Las Vegas Applebee's when Travis called the cell phone of one of her friends. He wanted to invite Jodi to be his guest at the executive directors' banquet, taking place at the MGM that very evening. The upscale dinner was reserved exclusively for the firm's top performers and their guests. Although Jodi knew that being asked was an honor, she initially turned down the invitation because she didn't have any "dress up" clothes, and it was starting in an hour. Her friend implored her to reconsider, telling her it would be a good experience and would get her more excited about the company.

Jodi stopped at a Kohl's department store, where she grabbed a few things off the rack, but she ended up calling Travis back to tell him she had had no luck finding something suitable. Travis was disappointed. He and his friends had been sitting around a table at the hotel waiting to hear from Jodi. Everyone was really excited for him. They knew he really liked her. He had even indicated that Jodi "could be the one." He described her as "sweet" and "super cool." He said the two had lots to talk about, and he was hoping she would be able to accompany him to the banquet that night. Everyone knew she was out looking for a dress, so when Travis's cell phone rang, all eyes were on Travis.

"She can't find a dress," he said with a look of disappointment.

"Oh, what size is she?" his friend Sky Hughes asked. Sky was the wife of Travis's original PPL contact, Chris Hughes. The two were among Travis's closest friends.

"About your size," Travis replied.

"Well, if she needs one, I have one upstairs that she can borrow."

A statuesque brunette, Sky had packed two dresses for the convention, so she offered Travis her black one with the white floral pattern. It wasn't particularly fancy, but it would fit the bill. Sky gave Travis the key to her room and told him where he could find it. When Jodi returned to the hotel, she met Travis upstairs and changed in the bathroom, while

Travis waited. Jodi emerged looking gorgeous that Thursday evening. She was stunning to begin with, and even though the borrowed dress was nothing special, it fit her to a tee.

At the banquet, Travis stood out in a black suit with bold white stripes, a reflection of his extroverted, larger-than-life personality. His outfit was punctuated with a black bow tie, giving him a look that telegraphed confidence. Travis's colorful suits were well known to his friends, and he always wore them with style and assurance. Before dinner was served, there was a period of time for mingling, and Travis used the opportunity to introduce his group to Jodi.

"Hey, everybody, this is Jodi," Travis said with a big smile. "Jodi, this is everybody."

Several of Travis's friends were surprised to see him with a woman this overtly sexy. Jodi was five feet six and a hundred and fifteen pounds, with an almost perfect body, and though nobody knew it then, she'd had breast implant surgery to enhance her cup size. Travis, too, had recently undergone a makeover of sorts. He had long struggled with his weight, and friends say he'd felt frustrated when trying to attract the bombshell women that some of his buddies seemed to wrangle. But he'd been working out furiously and losing weight, bringing out the natural attractiveness of his even features and making him more confident around potentially available women.

This confidence was important because Travis was certainly ready to settle down. With his thirtieth birthday around the bend, he was affectionately considered the "old man" in his Young Singles Adult Ward. He was more eager than most to find a mate and settle down, as his advancing age would soon necessitate him moving to a more age-appropriate group, the Family Ward, where he'd be surrounded by married couples and older singles.

Despite his bachelorhood, Travis was a star at Pre-Paid

Legal, and his motivational talks were legendary. He wasn't speaking at the executive directors' banquet, but plenty of other people were. Jodi listened to the various speeches, and when the speakers talked about not worrying about money, it spoke to her. People were sharing details of their lifestyles and throwing around numbers. They spoke about how they no longer struggled, no longer worried about money. Instead, they were concerned with things of a higher nature, like how to use their incomes to better society. Travis's friends who were there that night said that Jodi was socially appropriate, learning about the other people in attendance and asking good questions. She talked about herself, but not to the point of obnoxiousness. Jodi recalled that Travis spoke of his own success with the firm, as if he was hoping to impress her with the possibilities. At some point in the evening, it became clear to Jodi that his interest in her went beyond a professional relationship.

There was definitely a potent chemistry brewing, but Jodi said she didn't want to start anything romantic because, according to her, she was a "one guy at a time" kind of person, and the timing wasn't right. She liked Travis and had essentially agreed to be his date at the banquet, but she insisted she could not act on her interest because she had a boyfriend back in Palm Desert. Travis was disappointed, but acted appropriately.

Jodi and Travis spent much of the rest of the five-day conference in each other's company. The following evening, the two shared a bench in the casino, where they talked into the wee hours of the morning. Jodi said that at one point, Travis leaned in close as if he wanted to kiss her, but when she reminded him of her boyfriend, he restrained himself.

On Sunday, the last day of the conference, the two met for breakfast alone. Afterward, Jodi accompanied Travis to the front desk, where he checked out of the hotel and got in a taxi for the airport. She gave him her telephone number, hoping he would call. He reached out the very next day.

Travis may have thought he was pursuing Jodi. But in reality, Jodi was already pulling the strings. Her history showed she liked to vine-swing by having another man ready to grab on to before she let go of the last. With Travis waiting in the wings, Jodi returned to Palm Desert and her relationship with Darryl, which she knew would not last much longer. For his part, Travis was amazed that this gorgeous stranger was showing interest in him. But Travis had seen just one side of Jodi Arias. Another side, far darker, was soon to emerge.

CHAPTER 9

REALITY CHECK

On July 9, 2008, exactly one month after Travis Alexander's body was found, a grand jury in Maricopa County indicted Jodi Ann Arias on one count of first-degree murder under two theories: premeditated murder, and felony murder, which is when the murder occurs during the course of a felony. Here, the grand jury said it was a burglary. The definition of second-degree burglary is entering or remaining unlawfully in a residence with the intent to commit any theft or felony therein. In Jodi's case, she had caused the death of another person. The indictment charged that on or about the fourth day of June 2008, Jodi "intending or knowing that her conduct would cause death, with premeditation caused the death of TRAVIS V. ALEXANDER." The state of Arizona further alleged that because a .25-caliber handgun was used, the offense was classified as a "dangerous felony."

Jodi had no knowledge of the indictment. At that moment, she was celebrating her twenty-eighth birthday back in Yreka, California. She had reluctantly moved back to her high school stomping grounds after leaving Mesa in April, in part because her mother, who had been worried about her, had invited her back. Sandy knew about Jodi's financial troubles and was hoping to get her back on track. Jodi moved into the home of her grandparents, Carlton and Caroline Allen, on Pine Street. Right away, she found a job bartending at the Purple Plum, a casual restaurant on East Miner Street in the center of town.

On July 14, Detective Flores and two other investigators from the Mesa Police Department, Danny McBride and Tom Denning, flew to Yreka to arrest Jodi on charges of first-degree murder. Besides the arrest warrant, Flores carried two search warrants, one to be executed on Jodi's parents' house, and another on her grandparents' house. At 9 P.M., the three men from the Mesa Police Department met with members of the Siskiyou County Sheriff's Office to discuss their plan. Detectives from the Yreka police department had been trying to find Jodi. Everyone was given a description of Jodi's car, so that they could locate her and put her under surveillance, but they were unsuccessful in finding the vehicle. Siskiyou County Detective Nathan Mendes reported that he had Jodi under surveillance at her grandparents' and that she appeared to be packing. He could see her inside the house. This concerned them, because it looked as though she might be preparing to flee.

Within an hour Detective Flores and his team joined Detective Mendes at the home under surveillance. The Mesa officers left around midnight, but when they returned the next morning, they noticed a white Chevrolet Cobalt parked in front of the house that had not been there the night before. They discovered that it was a rental car, picked up at 7:50 that morning at a Hertz location in Yreka. Jodi's car was in Medford, Oregon, after having been repossessed by the bank. They could see that the rental car in the driveway had boxes in the backseat marked "JODI," making them more convinced than ever that Jodi was on the move.

During a briefing on how to proceed, the three law enforcement agencies—Yreka police, who had now joined them, the Siskiyou County sheriff's deputies, and Mesa police—devised a plan. The Yreka police officer J. Potter would approach the house under the guise of following up on a burglary that had occurred at the Pine Street address on May 28, exactly one week before Travis was murdered. At that time, Jodi's grandfather had summoned police to his house around 3:40 P.M. to report a break-in. Police arrived to find a broken doorjamb at the entrance to the home. There had been a rash of burglaries in that area recently, but this one had a few odd things about it. The TV appeared to have been moved, but only the DVD player had been taken. Mr. Allen had an extensive gun collection, which he kept in an unlocked cabinet; however, only one of his nine firearms was missing, a .25-caliber handgun. When Jodi had arrived home twenty minutes later, she was asked to inventory her property, and she reported only thirty dollars missing. That day, she had told police her only other valuable, her laptop, was safe, probably because she had it well hidden in a basket of laundry. But the gun Jodi's grandpa had reported stolen that day was never found, and the fact that it was the same caliber as the weapon that had been used on Travis was not lost on the officers.

Just after 9:30 A.M., Officer Potter knocked on Carlton and Caroline Allen's front door, saying he was following up on the open burglary case. At that point, he executed both the arrest warrant and the search warrant. Jodi was removed from the house in handcuffs and was walked down the street to a car where Detective Flores was waiting for her.

While Jodi might not have been surprised by this turn of events, her grandfather was so blindsided by the arrest that he became upset and angry, telling detectives they were wrong about his granddaughter, who he could prove had an airtight alibi. He insisted Jodi had been working at the Purple Plum when Travis had been murdered, and he demanded her immediate release, even going so far as to say he would sue the Mesa Police Department for the false allegations. At that, he asked to leave the residence, and when given permission, he went to the Purple Plum to retrieve Jodi's timesheet. He returned with a sealed white envelope, which he pushed at Detective McBride.

"I have the proof," he announced, shaking the envelope confidently. "After you and I look at this, you are going to let my granddaughter go." He opened it to reveal three photocopied pages of material. The first showed the payroll dates at the Purple Plum, and the second page showed the dates Jodi had worked during the month of May. The third sheet, the one Jodi's grandfather was counting on, unfortunately showed that her last day of work before she quit had been May 31—five days before Travis's death.

It took a moment for Jodi's grandfather to absorb that what he thought was Jodi's alibi was worthless. He apologized for his error, saying he was only trying to help her. He had honestly thought she was at work that day. The officer concurred that he would have probably done the same thing for a member of his family.

Meanwhile, the search of the residence was under way. Items of interest that the police took away were Jodi's personal journals and a box of receipts that detailed Jodi's trip to Utah during the month of June. Several receipts covered locations in California, Nevada, and Utah that police could use to map out her route around the time of Travis's death. There were no receipts, however, that would corroborate her being in Arizona.

Meanwhile, in the rental car, police executed another search warrant and found evidence that suggested Jodi was planning to leave town. They speculated that she had gotten word about the indictment and that they were closing in on her, because the rental car was indeed packed with boxes of books and Jodi's clothing in suitcases, much as the surveillance team had observed. Hidden among the clothes were two knives and ammunition for a 9 mm handgun, but no gun was found. A few weeks later, however, police received a call from someone at Hertz rental car at San Francisco International Airport. While the white Chevy Cobalt that Jodi had rented was being serviced and cleaned, a 9 mm gun had been discovered hidden in the wheel well. It was not the gun used in Travis's murder, but it did match the ammo found in the car during the execution of the search warrant. Later, Jodi would claim she bought the gun because she had been planning to drive to Monterey to kill herself, not wanting to commit suicide in her hometown near her family. This would not be the last time Jodi would explain away suspicious behavior by saying she was driven by thoughts of suicide.

While the search took place at Jodi's grandparents' house, a simultaneous search of Jodi's parents' house was also under way. It turned up nothing of interest in relation to the case. Both of Jodi's parents volunteered to go to the Yreka Police Department to be interviewed by Detective Flores about their daughter.

Upon arrival at the station, Sandy Arias was completely shaken up by the arrest. Clutching a tissue and fighting tears, she told the detective she thought she was going to puke. The physical similarities between Jodi and her mom were striking—both possessing high cheekbones and pretty brown eyes. In front of the detective, Sandy was having a hard time composing herself. She said she had been happy to have Jodi back near her again after so many years in Monterey, Palm Desert, and Mesa, but she confessed that she and her daughter did not have a good relationship. Jodi appeared to have mental problems, happy one minute and crying inconsolably a couple of hours later. A friend had even used the word *bipolar* to describe Jodi, although it was not a professional opinion.

Sandy knew about Jodi's recent trip to Salt Lake City via Monterey and said her daughter seemed fine when she got back. She said Jodi had learned about Travis's death a couple of days later and cried for three or four days, while refusing to discuss it. When Sandy finally spoke to her daughter, she asked Jodi if she had gone to Arizona, and Jodi swore she had not. Her mother had no reason not to believe her. In fact, after Jodi came back from Travis's memorial service, Sandy said they seemed to get along better than they ever had. Jodi would come over and hang out with the family and be on her computer. "Maybe this death has made her see that life is short," Sandy lamented. "It's changing her. The last few weeks, I talked to her more than I had ever talked to her at eighteen."

Sandy paused to speculate on things she imagined Jodi might complain about concerning her childhood. "You get this fantasy in your head that you had a rotten childhood," she said, seeming to want to set the record straight. "The only time we searched her room was once. She was in eighth grade. She was growing pot. I couldn't find my Tupperware container, and she had it on the roof growing pot." After that, she said, Jodi didn't want to be near her. Even when Jodi lived in Monterey, she didn't want her mother to visit for fear she'd snoop through her stuff. Sandy also reflected on how smart Jodi was, saying how Jodi read a lot of books and often wished that her mom could be more intellectual.

Sandy said she knew Jodi was anxious about being questioned regarding the murder, and it may have scared her because she bought a gun. She also mentioned that prior to learning about Travis's death, Jodi had been anticipating a visit from him, his first to Yreka. The two were planning to visit Crater Lake National Park, in Oregon, mentioned in Patricia Schultz's *1,000 Places to See Before You Die*. In fact, it was supposed to be that very weekend coming up. At that, she paused to contemplate. "Maybe she did do it, but I can't imagine her doing it," she muttered softly.

The hardest part of the interview was revealing just how much evidence had been amassed against her daughter, such as the fingerprints, the DNA, and the hair. In spite of it all, Sandy was still incredulous, in disbelief that her daughter could kill and then return home as if everything were normal. She elaborated on Jodi's talk of suicide and a late-night call from a friend of Jodi's years earlier, who said she needed psychiatric help.

Crying off and on throughout the interview, Sandy's mind began to skip. She mentioned Travis's family and how much pain they must be in. She admitted that her daughter was having financial problems. "She's really in debt. She bought a house with her other boyfriend. [She had] house payments, she maxed out credit cards trying to pay her part of it, she thought she could dig herself out. We brought her up here, we tried to get her back on track," Sandy explained, sobbing.

Most of all, Sandy wanted to know what would happen to Jodi next.

"She's booked in the county jail," Detective Flores answered. "The court in Phoenix will ask for an extradition. She could fight it or go along with it. It's usually a moot point. It's going to happen anyway, unless California has more serious charges."

"What happens if she's found guilty?" Sandy asked.

"She'll be sentenced."

"For the rest of her life?"

"She has to be found guilty first."

Next, the detective interviewed Jodi's father, William "Bill" Arias. He looked older than his years, most likely because of his poor health. He had had both kidneys replaced years earlier, as a consequence of a motorcycle accident and subsequent kidney cancer. His thinning hair was combed over to one side. He was wearing thick frameless glasses and a pink button-down shirt. Bill said that Jodi and he were not very close.

"My wife talked to her more. We didn't get along good. She's a strange person . . . She was strange, real friendly, sometimes she'd be in a rage, screaming at my wife. All I could tell you, she had financial problems. Broke up with her boyfriend. I've never even seen a picture of Travis."

Bill also recalled the time right before and after Jodi learned Travis had died. "She [had been] acting so normal. He was found on Monday, the 9th. That weekend, she bawled her eyes out. She came over to the house and said Travis was murdered." In the days leading up to her arrest, Jodi had been preparing to leave Yreka for a few days. Bill had helped her rent a car, but he had a lot of questions for her. Why had she quit her job? Why was she leaving town if she wasn't guilty? It was her last chance to tell him what was going on. Jodi didn't open up at all, even though they talked for an hour and a half. Instead, she used the excuse that she didn't want to tell him anything, for his own good, to avoid his becoming involved in any way. She kept repeating that she was leaving town for Monterey for a few days because she didn't want to be a part of it, which left her father with more questions than answers.

He, too, mentioned how Jodi's relationship with him and his wife had become strained after the discovery of Jodi's marijuana plant on the roof of the house. "After that, something turned in her head, and she hasn't been honest with us since then. She had a house in Palm Desert. We told her we want to come visit her. She didn't want us to stay in her house, because she was afraid we would snoop." Jodi's father said that when she was in Palm Desert, she was crazy for a year. She'd call up crying hysterically, needing money. As for her subsequent stint in Arizona, Bill knew his daughter had also become very upset when she saw Travis with another woman in his house, referring to an August 2007 incident when Jodi was peeping in Travis's living room window and saw him with another woman. She called her father shortly afterward in tears.

Bill explained to Detective Flores that, when his daughter finally moved back to Yreka from Arizona, she brought all of her stuff in a rented U-Haul. Bill said Jodi decided to live with her maternal grandparents, because his house rules were harder to abide by. "We have rules and regulations. She stays up [all night] and sleeps all day," he said.

"She work as a bartender still?" Detective Flores asked.

"She was," Bill replied. "She got hysterical and quit her job."

Detective Flores wanted to know about the rented car. Bill said they had rented it, because Jodi's car was screwing up, maybe because she hadn't checked the oil. He had helped her load some of her stuff into the rental.

"Did she have access to a firearm?" the detective asked next.

"She just got a gun," Bill explained. "I asked her, 'what do you need a gun for?' She said she wanted to feel safe."

Detective Flores repeated to Bill the things he had told his wife, that Jodi was being booked and being seen by a judge. Bill cut him off with a late thought about Jodi's mental condition. "I told her one time, have you ever thought of yourself as being bipolar? She cried . . . then I told her, 'I'm just kidding.' "

"Does she seem to be obsessive?" Detective Flores asked.

Bill didn't answer. "She was gonna stay in town and work . . . she said she was gonna get a job and straighten her life out."

─────⟫⟫⟫ ⟪⟪⟪─────

CHAPTER 10

FLIRTING
WITH DANGER

Jodi Arias once said that aspects of her sexual relationship with Travis Alexander made her feel like a "used piece of toilet paper." Travis Alexander also referred to their intimate relationship as demeaning to him, once complaining to Jodi that he felt like nothing more than "a dildo with a heartbeat." But the story of how their sexual affair became so toxic depended on who was telling it, and in the end, only one of them was alive to talk.

When Jodi Arias finally began telling authorities the tale of her romance with Travis, she had been arrested, and her own photography had irrefutably placed her at Travis's home at the time of the murder. Sensing her life was on the line, she began spinning an intricate, X-rated tale of their affair that enraged Travis's family and friends, as it painted both him and their relationship in a very different light. From the start, Jodi's version of events and her portrayal of Travis's behavior seemed suspect to those who knew them both, and while everyone around them acknowledged Jodi and Travis had sex, questions still remained about what kind of sex it really was and who was actually the one doing the seducing.

There is little doubt that the two had sexual chemistry. What has been less explored is the crucial role that timing played in Travis and Jodi's relationship. Each was at a critical juncture in their personal life when they first met at the convention in Las Vegas in September 2006. Both Jodi and Travis had a heightened desire to find a mate and marry. For Travis, his age was a key factor in his rush to find a wife. He was a single man approaching the big 3-O. Even being over twenty-five and still single was viewed as an oddity in the Mormon Church, where marriage and family were paramount. Being in your thirties and single was viewed as a problem.

In every one of Travis's prior relationships, he had brought up the possibility of marriage early on. He had asked Linda Ballard to marry him, but she had turned him down. Then, for a time, it had seemed Deanna was the right woman. She wanted to get married, but this time it was Travis who had the commitment phobia. Meanwhile, as he was getting older, the median age of the available Mormon women was getting younger. Early on in his relationship with Linda Ballard, which had begun when she was nineteen, the age difference between them had been an issue, and many of the women in their teens and early twenties in his Desert Ridge Ward likely viewed Travis as too old for them. Everybody knew that Travis was in search of a wife, but each time he returned to the Young Singles Ward, he found himself that much older than the available pool of single women.

When Travis met Jodi in Las Vegas, he was only ten months shy of his thirtieth birthday. The Family Ward loomed at the end of his thirtieth year, and if that wasn't ominous enough, he already knew pretty much every eligible Mormon prospect in his Mesa world and was coming up empty.

Jodi arrived in Las Vegas with a crisis in her personal life as well. She had been twenty-two when she first started dating Darryl Brewer, and although she knew then that he was not interested in remarrying, she was young enough not to care. Four years later, she wanted a more committed relationship, if not with Darryl, then with someone who would marry her. At twenty-six, her biological clock was ticking, and she wanted to start a family.

Jodi and Travis's first meeting in Las Vegas had created a connection that had promise, and both thought their luck had turned. Travis went back to Mesa with Jodi heavily on his mind, while Jodi went back to Palm Desert, hoping that Travis would call. Her wish came true the very next day. It soon became a nightly ritual that Travis would phone Jodi at 8 P.M., right around the time she was getting home from her job at the restaurant.

According to Jodi, the things Travis said to her got her thinking. He was a motivational speaker, so he had a talent for making people look at their lives and begin to implement positive changes. He advised Jodi not to settle for mediocrity, and was most likely referring to her dead-end relationship with Darryl. He was a firm believer in going after what you wanted and making things happen, and he wholeheartedly encouraged Jodi to do the same. He also jokingly teased that dating a man of Darryl's age was akin to dating her grandfather. She deserved better. Travis also talked about how important marriage and family were, and he expressed an interest in her. Jodi may have even thought, *Travis is it, he will ask me to marry him,* although he never expressed himself like that.

The phone calls quickly became more, and within days Travis invited Jodi to join him at Chris and Sky Hughes's home in Murrieta, California, the very first weekend after they had met. Jodi didn't hesitate in accepting and was so delighted with the budding relationship that she took the bold step of ending her relationship with Darryl. Just four days after returning home from the convention, she told Darryl, the man she'd been dating for four years, that it was over. It appeared Jodi had her sights set on marrying Travis with no more encouragement than his weekend invitation.

Jodi sat Darryl down at the kitchen table and told him their relationship was going nowhere. She knew he didn't want to get married, and she no longer wanted to have sex, as she was saving herself for her future husband. What she didn't say was that she also wanted to be free to pursue her interest in Travis. Despite the abrupt nature of things, the breakup was amicable. They owned the house together, and they agreed they could continue sharing it for the time being, but they would sleep in separate bedrooms.

Her obligation to Darryl removed, Jodi happily accepted the invitation from Travis to join him for the weekend party at the Hugheses' house in Murrieta, only an hour and a half from Palm Desert. Chris and Sky Hughes were the "it" couple, the Angelina Jolie/Brad Pitt of the local Mormon world. They were tall and attractive, imposing yet charming, and everyone wanted to be in their circle. Jodi arrived in Murrieta hours before Travis showed up, easily fitting in with the crowd. She'd met some of them briefly at the convention and knew Sky from when she borrowed her dress for the PPL banquet dinner.

According to Sky, Jodi behaved quite normally throughout the afternoon. She was dressed conservatively and appeared comfortable socially—shaking hands with everybody she met, carrying on interesting, intelligent conversations, making eye contact with confidence, and impressing everyone present with her friendliness, grace, and charm.

Nobody said anything about her being improper or out of place; she was totally normal, another guest at a beautiful weekend get-together.

Travis arrived by 9 P.M. He brought a few G-rated movies with him. Adhering to the Mormon faith, he never dabbled in anything rated R. He even had a filter on his home DVD player that would block any content above a PG rating. He never cursed, but used substitute words that were acceptable replacements, with *Mother-freaker* being a perfect example. Travis's movies provided the focus for the rest of the evening. Everyone thoroughly enjoyed them, joking, laughing, having good clean fun. When they were over, all the guests went home, except for Jodi and Travis.

That night, Jodi was given her own bedroom by her hosts; however, the details of the night grew fuzzy after that. In Jodi's version of events, Travis came to see her in her bedroom after everyone else had gone to sleep. It was a rendezvous they had planned earlier in the night, and Jodi was expecting his arrival. In her telling, Travis came on hot and heavy right away, although she admittedly didn't resist. They were French-kissing and lying side by side on the bed. Travis began to remove her clothes, which Jodi said made her feel apprehensive, but she didn't want to hurt his feelings or spoil the mood, so she didn't say no. She felt the two had chemistry, and she didn't want to snuff it out. Jodi recalled that Travis was wearing his temple garments, the Mormon church's symbolic protection from the evils of the world, under his sweatpants. Before long, the temple garments were discarded in a joint effort, and according to Jodi, Travis then performed oral sex on her. She then reciprocated, with him ejaculating in her mouth. When the two awoke early the next morning, Jodi claimed they were both naked, and that eventually Travis got dressed and left the bedroom.

While no one doubted that Travis went to Jodi's room that

night, the story seemed bizarre to a lot of Travis's friends. Sky Hughes said it was a lie, and based her opinion on a conversation she had with Travis in the kitchen the following morning. She was in the kitchen when Travis came downstairs with a huge smile on his face and what Sky described as an "I'm cool" walk.

"Oh gosh, what did you do?" Sky asked.

"I left her wanting," was Travis's sly response.

"What's that supposed to mean?" Sky asked.

"Well," Travis responded, "I went in there, we were talking and we started kissing and it got a little more heated. And I said, 'I want you to know that I respect you, and I don't want you to regret anything and let's move slowly.'"

And then, Travis told Sky, he left the room, which was what he thought was so funny. Sky took that to mean no sexual activity beyond kissing had occurred. Still, while it's hard to know whether or not Travis's words to Sky were the whole story, it seemed pretty clear that an intense make-out session had occurred. Others noted that Jodi's story seemed odd in another respect: the idea that a man would aggressively insist on performing cunnilingus on a woman he'd just met didn't ring true to many people. Ultimately it was anybody's guess how far things went, but something had happened, as Travis boasted that Jodi "wanted the T-Dogg."

As Sky and Travis chatted that Sunday morning, Jodi and Chris eventually joined them in the kitchen. The four were going to go to the LDS church for the Sunday morning service, even though Jodi wasn't a Mormon. On the way to the service, Travis rode with Jodi in her car, and on the way back Sky rode with them. During the return trip, Sky found a binder of Jodi's drawings in the backseat. There were drawings of butterflies, and of lots of people. One was of her sister, and another was of Darryl. Travis asked to see the picture, and complimented her talent. The party ended soon after church. Travis walked Jodi to her car, kissed her goodbye, and she drove off for Palm Desert.

The following Wednesday, Jodi and Travis met at a Starbucks near her home. Travis was driving back to Mesa from California and wanted to meet Jodi to give her The Book of Mormon. He was interested in having her learn about the religion that meant so much to him. Jodi couldn't invite him to come to her house, because Darryl still lived there, so they agreed to meet at a Starbucks. Over a caffeine-free chai tea, Travis gave her the sacred book, and the two spoke about the Word of Wisdom, Mormon doctrine that bans the consumption of caffeine and alcohol.

According to Jodi, Travis also told her he was horny, and they decided to act on it, driving separately to a local park. There, Travis got into her car and she said she performed oral sex on him. When it was over, Jodi recalled that Travis readjusted the car visor he had pulled down and then put his pants back on. Jodi recalled that he refused to kiss her afterward, saying it was gross. He kissed her on the cheek and left.

Jodi later said she felt "maybe just a little deflated." She was also a little disappointed in herself, having never been intimate that quickly before. She later said she got a voice mail from Travis, in which he expressed misgivings about the experience.

Travis's friends believed Jodi twisted her tale to make Travis the sexual aggressor when in reality, they believed, it was actually the other way around. While by all accounts Travis had been a virgin well into his twenties, Jodi had lost her virginity as a teenager and had been sexually active ever since. Josh Denne, a good-looking friend of Travis's, said he met Jodi around the very time Travis did and couldn't help but notice she gave off a very sexual vibe. Josh said, "She would just put out that *Look, I'm available . . . how ya doin'? I'm interested* type of energy about her."

Josh, who was single at the time, said he realized he didn't ask for Jodi's number because, while he thought she was attractive, her nonverbal cues made him uncomfortable. "The energy that I got from her, it's almost like a stripper-type of energy," Josh recalled. "She had that look like, *Hey . . . you know, I'm willin' to do whatever.*" Josh said Travis was "a babe in the woods" sexually. He had never been exposed to women who used sex as a tool, so he was likely blind to what Josh was picking up on. On the other hand, Travis was the one who first approached Jodi in the casino, so whatever vibe he was getting from her, he had liked it enough to spend the rest of the weekend with her, and then invite her to the exclusive banquet to show her off to his friends.

Not long after the weekend at the Hugheses' house, Jodi began getting visits from Mormon missionaries. They came for "discussions," the Mormon way of introducing potential newcomers to the church, on average twice a week. Jodi and Travis had only met a few weeks earlier, but already Travis wanted her to become a member of the Mormon church, and Jodi was willing. This way they could carry forward with their relationship. Jodi had no objection to the visits from the missionaries; in fact, she enjoyed them.

Meanwhile, Travis and Jodi spoke on the phone for hours every night. The calls now typically occurred after 11 P.M. and sometimes as late as 3 A.M. Jodi described them as long heart-to-heart conversations, during which the two talked about everything from Travis's dog, Napoleon, to religion to spirituality to her interest in the arts and photography. Jodi felt the two were really connecting.

After a month of telephone talk, the two met again in person. It was October, and the plan was for a romantic interlude in Ehrenberg, Arizona, a spot chosen because it was approximately equidistant between their two houses. Travis had even rented a motel room in town for the rendezvous.

Jodi said they were physical from the moment she walked through the door, that they started passionately kissing, and soon they were both naked on the bed, doing the "Provo push"—the equivalent of grinding, something Mormons aren't supposed to do. According to Jodi, the rest of the weekend was spent in mutual oral sex, watching television, eating at Sizzler, and going to a movie, far more casual than the romantic kind of tryst she had in mind.

Travis also shared scripture from *The Book of Mormon* with Jodi. She said he taught her about the church's Law of Chastity: vaginal sex was off-limits, but everything else— oral and anal sex—was okay. Jodi later spelled out what she saw as Travis's interpretation of the Mormon code, saying, "It seemed like Travis kind of had a Bill Clinton version of sex, where oral and anal sex were also sex to me, but not for him." Travis's friends wondered how anyone would be so gullible as to believe that their deeply conservative religion would condone oral and anal sex, especially someone getting regular visits from Mormon missionaries, who were eager to answer every question. In *The Book of Mormon,* it said plain as day, do not "touch the private, sacred parts of another person's body, with or without clothing" unless you're married. Travis's buddies scoffed at the suggestion that their friend, who never so much as cursed, would try to pull that whopper over on a girl he'd just started dating.

According to one of Jodi's accounts, despite the sex that weekend, she didn't feel they were very connected with each other. To her, they had seemed to be much more in tune with each other on the phone calls. Other accounts of hers had her having a really glorious time, so a lot of the highlights and low points of the story depended on her frame of mind. However, that being said, their lack of romance left her disappointed. It could have been an eye-opener for her that Travis might not be the prince of her dreams. It could also have been an indication of what was going on in Travis's head. If Jodi's description of the weekend is even true, being intimate in a hotel room, whether they were doing nothing or everything, was likely creating a lot of guilt and angst for Travis. Perhaps there was a part of him that was trying to discern if Jodi was the girl for him. The next morning, the two had breakfast at a neighboring truck stop, but there wasn't a lot of conversation. After the meal, they went their separate ways, she back to Palm Desert, and he to Phoenix for a PPL meeting.

Jodi started to replay the weekend in her mind when she didn't hear from Travis for two days. She had called and texted him, but he hadn't responded. She started to feel a little used, so she was happy to get the voice mail from him later that week. His message was kind and reassuring, and everything seemed to get back on track. The two started talking again on the phone every night, usually about both spiritual and sexual things.

According to Jodi, on November 11, 2006, Travis sent her a photo of his erect penis via cell phone. Jodi was in a restaurant when her phone beeped, announcing that a picture had arrived. She had never received a photo on her new phone, and thought Travis must be sending her a file. After seeing the photo, she slammed her phone closed immediately, being in a public place with the waitress approaching. Some people doubt this photo is of Travis's penis, although the prosecutor did not dispute it later at Jodi's murder trial. Based on the two fingers in the photo, which don't resemble Travis's, some suspect Jodi used a penis photo she already had and claimed it was Travis's. Jodi explained that the two had been text-flirting for hours before the photos arrived, with each trying to top the last one's comments.

Two weeks later, on November 26, 2006, Jodi was baptized into the Church of Jesus Christ of Latter-day Saints. She hadn't been approved for baptism right away, because she was still cohabitating with Darryl Brewer. During her pre-baptism interview, the branch president asked if she was obeying the Law of Chastity. "Based on a technical sense, yes," she replied. She had been invited to become a member by the missionaries. She found the Mormon acceptance of all faiths in the world extremely appealing and in line with the faith she already had. She loved their strong emphasis on family and marriage. Her only objection was their rule against caffeine, as she typically enjoyed a cup of coffee every morning, but she could live with that.

At Jodi's request, Travis, who was an elder in the Church, agreed to perform the ceremony. Jodi even invited her ex Darryl Brewer, but he didn't attend, nor did her family. Jodi said that even if her family could have teleported, they wouldn't have come. The baptism took place at the LDS church in Palm Desert. Travis was already in the baptismal font when Jodi arrived in her white baggy jumpsuit, the traditional baptismal outfit. He said a blessing, she dipped into the water, and she came back up. She described the emotion afterward as a very peaceful feeling. After the ceremony, the two went back to her house, began to kiss, and got intimate again.

The way Jodi remembered it, she and Travis were in her bedroom kissing when Travis spun her around, bent her over, unzipped his pants, and began having anal sex with her. Jodi said she endured it as long as she could but that, eventually, it was so painful she had to stop him, after which he ejaculated on her back. At the end of her spiritual day, Jodi said she ended up feeling like "used toilet paper."

Sky Hughes was at the baptism that day and said it was an awkward ceremony, with not many people in attendance. But, more than that, she doubted Jodi's recollection was accurate. She seemed to recall Travis going back to her house after the ritual, contradicting Jodi's version. Sky noted that Jodi's vivid juxtaposition of religious and sexual rites seemed designed to inspire anger against Travis and sympathy for her. Jodi's absurd anecdote wasn't just about anal sex; it was anal sex after a baptism, a sacred ceremony. Indeed, Jodi was no stranger to anal sex. She and Darryl had done it once or twice, something Darryl later acknowledged.

The next month, Darryl moved out of the house in Palm Desert and back to Monterey, where his ex-wife, with whom he shared custody of their son, had relocated. He was done and ready to leave. The final piece of Jodi and Darryl's breakup seemed to go without incident, and they remained on friendly terms.

Jodi would continue to live in the Palm Desert house as long as she was financially able. Already, she had missed her half of several mortgage payments, and Darryl had been carrying the full financial load. This was the first time since they had taken ownership of the property that Jodi had failed to meet her financial obligations. Her goal of turning her job with PPL into a full-time career was not happening as quickly as she had hoped. While she was realizing some income from the company, sometimes between $1,000 and $1,300 a month, it was hardly enough to cover all her household bills. When Darryl tried talking to her about it, she would tell him not to discuss anything negative. Since reading *The Secret,* Jodi had been trying to employ the power of positive thinking to change reality by making only positive statements.

Yet she continued to connect with Travis. That Christmas

season, Jodi went to Arizona for a corporate event that was taking place in Phoenix. Travis was putting up about thirty people at his place so he told her that because of the guest load, he had no room for her. One of the friends invited to stay there, a curvy blonde named Clancy Talbot, said she overheard Travis on the phone with Jodi explaining to her that there was no room for her to stay. He ended the call by saying he would see her at the event the next day. Several hours later, Jodi appeared at the house uninvited. Her unexpected arrival was particularly awkward, because Travis's ex-girlfriend Deanna was one of the invited guests, and there were still tender feelings between them. Clancy said Jodi announced herself to the room as Travis's girlfriend right in the middle of a motivational presentation Travis was giving, and that he tried to make light of it. "He says 'wait . . . no. We've gone on a couple of dates, but we're not like hitched or anything.' He tried to be nice to her, but at the same time make sure everyone knew . . . that she was not his girlfriend," Clancy recalled.

Jodi spent the night anyway. Her recollection of the evening had Travis joking quietly to her that he wanted oral sex, but he didn't want to be affectionate with her in front of Deanna. She claimed he had even told her that Deanna was "emotionally unstable," so she tried to steer clear of her. Jodi said Travis was hypervigilant about any public display of affection. Even after Deanna left, they slept on separate couches. After lights were out and the house was quiet, she reached for his hand, and he sat up abruptly to see if anyone was awake.

Clancy's account was a complete contradiction to that. She said that she had come downstairs during the night to find Jodi asleep under the Christmas tree. Travis had a portable wrought-iron gate so that Napoleon, his dog, could not get to the tree, and Jodi was sound asleep in the secured area behind the gate, curled up under the tree. Clancy said she and some of the others were really put off by Jodi's odd behavior. "It just gave me a stomachache. It just gave me the creeps . . . a yucky feeling, like something's not right."

CHAPTER 11

JODI SPINS

Picking out the strangest moments in Jodi Arias's July 15 police interview is difficult, but everyone seems to have his or her personal favorite—the headstand against the wall, the slow, seductive backbend, the low lilting rendition of Dido's song "Here with Me," the stuffing of sheets of paper down into her pants, or the trifling self-criticism as she ponders her appearance while in the interrogation room. It had been just a few hours since she'd been formally arrested for the savage murder of the love of her life, yet in the windowless room, Jodi didn't appear concerned with her accused crime. "You should have at least done your makeup, Jodi, gosh," she says during a moment alone, as if she is waiting in the wings in the final moments before taking the stage and is not pleased with what she sees.

Dressed in white pants, a formfitting gray V-neck shirt, and a pair of flip-flops, Jodi appeared lifeless as the cameras in the tiny interrogation room began to roll. She sat completely motionless, her head lying on the round table in the small room, her hair neatly combed but falling wherever it may in her pose. There was no option of pushing it back out of the way—her hands were handcuffed behind her back, and therefore unavailable for primping. She alternated between sitting at the table and sitting on the floor, back pressed against the wall and legs extended straight out. At one point, Jodi whispered to herself, "It's cold in here," but little other action took place until five minutes in, when Detective Flores entered the room.

The detective, in dark blue pants and a lighter blue dress shirt without a tie, hid his fatigue well. As he extended his hands toward her handcuffs to unlock them, he offered her anything she needed to help with her comfort, from a bottle of water to more heat in the small, chilly room. He warmly reintroduced himself as the detective on Travis's case, and Jodi politely told him she remembered him well.

After the niceties were complete, he got right to work. "I know exactly when it happened, when he was killed," he told Jodi in a matter-of-fact, nonaggressive manner. Jodi was completely without hysteria or confusion, listening with an affect so flat that the only way to know she was hearing anything was by her occasional "okay" or "uh hunh" to a statement. "I know a lot of details, and just recently we found quite a bit of evidence that I'll discuss with you. The main thing I'm looking for, though, is answers on why certain things happened and why they went so far." He explained that many of the details were known only to the killer, not even to Travis's family, and Jodi offered her total cooperation. He then read her her Miranda rights. After she acknowledged that she understood them and agreed to talk, the questioning began.

"Let's start with this: what have you been up to since Travis's death?" the detective asked; hopefully, fewer confrontational questions like this would produce fewer defensive responses and make the interview that much more productive than going straight into the crime scene. Jodi talked about both her jobs, PPL and the Mexican restaurant in Yreka, but added that she had been in a daze for the last few weeks. She deviated almost immediately to Travis's Facebook page and the flood of memorial entries that had been posted since his death. She called her own entry and its "my dear Travis" sentimental tone "immature," so she had taken it down. In reality, Travis's friends had been aghast by its over-the-top nature, with dozens of pictures of the couple in happier times. Even after Travis's brutal murder, she had the nerve to enshrine him like her saint, although she had most likely butchered him. It was a postmortem stalking in the most tasteless manner, with Travis, even in death, unable to shake her or defend himself.

At that point, the detective brought up the murder. "You know . . . everybody is saying, I don't understand what happened to Travis, but you need to look at Jodi. That's one of the reasons I started looking at you a little bit closer and over the last month or so, I've gotten into Travis's lives, talked to his friends, his family. I got a really good understanding of who he is now, and I got a very good understanding of your relationship with him. And I'm kind of just putting the two together . . . obviously, you weren't boyfriend and girlfriend anymore."

Jodi was slightly tongue-tied. When it became clear that she was conflicted about spilling information on the sex life of a man who had committed to chastity, the detective helped her out. "Well, I'm sure if Travis could speak right now, he wouldn't care what people thought about him. 'Cause they knew who he was." Flores went on to describe his view of their relationship, based only on what he learned by probing Travis's side, and his analysis was spot-on. "Well, the way Travis thought by, you know, getting into his head, and everything he's written, his journals, and everything I found out about him, he truly had feelings for you. And for some reason he felt that the relationship between you and him was somewhat unhealthy. But he couldn't stop it. And I assume it's probably maybe the same way you felt about him . . ."

Jodi agreed that their relationship was unhealthy. Even though Arizona was the "Mormon land of opportunity," following Travis there after their breakup led to more sex, but less spirituality. She described signals that she would get from Travis to leave her residence and come to his home for a rendezvous. "My nightlife was about him . . . He would text me, *I'm getting sleepy dot dot dot . . . zzz,* and that was his code to, like 'come on over' kind of thing . . . the coast is clear. I lived five minutes away, maybe ten depending, and it was just too convenient and too easy, and it was fun, and we had fun. We were together. So, it wasn't healthy, and I totally agree with that."

Jodi said she moved back to Yreka for three reasons: she needed to regroup financially, with her money situation described as being "in dire straits"; she wanted to be with her family in Yreka, especially urgent because of her father's poor health; and she wanted to put physical distance between Travis and her. The nine months she had lived in Mesa had done nothing to promote a meaningful relationship between them. She made it clear that she had also been in intimate relationships with other men in her life, that her interpretation of Christianity and the Bible had always been true to the Ten Commandments, which did not say, "Thou shalt not fornicate." When she converted to Mormonism, she had grown to understand the importance of chastity.

While it may be laughably unreasonable to buy into her lifestyle as chaste, Travis had been a Mormon a lot longer than she had, so following his lead to the outer limits of chastity was not wholeheartedly absurd. She admitted to feeling guilty when she and Travis were doing things that would make a streetwalker blush. But, somehow, instant sexual gratification seemed to prevail.

Jodi provided a lot of fodder for psychologists. She moved to Travis's town only after they decided not to keep dating. The sex was hotter after the split. Big emotional moments came mostly on the phone. When Detective Flores asked Jodi if she and Travis ever seriously talked about getting married, Jodi said he had proposed to her in a telephone conversation. "Once we broke up, he brought it up, he actually proposed to me. That was really hard because we were on the phone and it was just like, none of that stuff should be done on the phone anyway, but I was hundreds of miles away, and I told him that I loved him. We didn't say 'I love you' during our relationship, but we said it afterward. It was weird." Skeptics would later say this conversation between Travis and Jodi never took place, but aside from Jodi Arias being a pathological liar, she would not be the first to look back and romanticize a toxic relationship that was driven by lust.

Jodi provided the detective with a timeline. She did not dispute the fact that she and Travis were only official for five months, all of it long-distance, and that she had moved to Mesa within weeks of breaking up. She dismissed the hint from Detective Flores that this was kind of stalker behavior, saying she had found a roommate in Mesa back when she and Travis were still an item. Because she had to leave Palm Desert anyway, she was following through with a plan that was already in place. She said there were plenty of advantages for Travis, too, when she settled in his town, and in her telling, he'd even hired her to clean his house, knowing she could use the money so he wasn't at all upset. Flores listened and let her go on. He'd likely already talked to people close to Travis who'd told the detective they'd heard him arguing on the phone with Jodi about her move to Mesa.

During the course of the investigation, Detective Flores had also learned about Travis's more recent relationships, and he brought those names into the conversation with Jodi. He asked her if she knew anything about Mimi Hall or Lisa Andrews, and she said she knew about them, had been shown Mimi's picture on Facebook, and had been very happy for her ex. As far as jealousy was concerned, she said she was fully aware that Travis had a reputation for being a flirt. She went on to say that when she first started meeting Travis at the Hugheses' house, Sky had often called her "Deanna" by mistake, referring to Travis's ex-girlfriend. Jodi went on to describe how Travis treated her differently depending on the situation and whom he was with and how that hurt her.

Detective Flores seized the moment to sum up the situation between them, as he was more capable of seeing it objectively. "He liked you, he loved you," the detective said sincerely. "He wanted to be with you, but he was reluctant to make a commitment . . . and he truly didn't think you were marriage material. And I don't know why not. You're a wonderful girl . . . and I don't see how you guys couldn't have made it, you know?"

Jodi offered accounts of jealous moments between them that created arguments. In the stories she chose, more often than not Travis was the jealous one. Detective Flores knew Jodi's own possessiveness and jealousy was likely a motivation for the murder. He wanted to hear what Jodi had to say about Travis's plans to go to Cancún with another woman. The working theory was that Jodi, enraged about Travis's pending vacation to Mexico with another woman, had gone there with an ultimatum: take *me* or else pay the price.

"So, you know, moving over to his trip to Cancún . . . ," he started. Jodi agreed she knew about it, although she threw the detective a curveball when it came to the timing. "When did you first find out about that . . . that he was going with Mimi?"

"I found out about that at his memorial services on Monday," she replied.

"You didn't know he was going to Cancún?" Flores asked, not believing that she had just recently learned that news. "You didn't know he was taking Mimi?"

"I think that's awesome, actually," Jodi answered, as if the vacation were about to take place, and she couldn't be happier for the two.

"Yeah, well, unfortunately . . . ," Detective Flores said, hinting at the obvious. Instead, he revealed to Jodi that Mimi had told Travis she just wanted to be platonic friends, which had left him heartbroken. Jodi took responsibility for being part of the reason she and Travis were having trouble forging ahead in new relationships, the gist of which was they had compromised each other spiritually. These things being said in an interrogation room setting made their sincerity suspect. But, still, the detective wanted to know what kept Jodi so drawn to Travis. "What kept you with him? I don't understand," he asked again. "Why did you continue to go back to him? You know what he wants. You know that it's not healthy, but yet you continue to go back, and it brings us to the point where we are now."

He brought up discussions he had had with friends of Travis who thought Jodi was being obsessive. "They are saying that you had become obsessive with him to the point where you would go into his house when he wasn't there, or when you weren't invited, and he would say . . . 'I don't want her here.' "

Jodi again had justification, if indeed Travis had been complaining. She said they had an open-door policy, which had advantages for both parties, as she often took care of his dog, Napoleon, when he was away. She also said they both understood that they had to keep their sexual trysts completely under wraps, implying that people with no knowledge of the situation might mistake her visits to Travis's bedroom as completely unwanted and unsolicited because Travis was putting on a hypocritical façade.

Detective Flores returned his line of questioning to Jodi's road trip from Yreka to Salt Lake City at the time of Travis's death. "The first week of June, you took a trip to Salt Lake City; remember that trip we talked about?" he inquired. "You had gone to Redding and rented a car." She recalled the make and model, a white Ford Focus, and she had driven it straight to Santa Cruz, then Monterey for the night before heading to Los Angeles. "Instead of going to Utah, you went straight down to the Los Angeles area?" the detective asked, not lost on him that such a route was completely the wrong direction. Jodi said she had a photography gig there, so the detour was worth it. But from there, her tale of the next twenty-four hours was filled with information that would never be able to be confirmed . . . the photography assignment never panned out because of missed phone calls; the route to Salt Lake City was unfamiliar, so she had gotten lost; the nap in her car along the shoulder of a lonely road may have lasted several hours, as she described herself as a heavy sleeper . . . the list went on and on.

"Did you actually cross over into Arizona?" asked Flores, offering Jodi a large map.

"I crossed over twice I think," answered Jodi pensively. "If my map is wrong, 'cause the 93 goes north, and I hit the 15 again, and then I hit here, and then I hit Arizona, and then I hit here . . . Somehow, I got north on the 93." She then tried to make all those locations fit in with the days of the week that she was on the road. Detective Flores let her finish, all while doing his own math.

"It would still leave eighteen-some-odd hours for something else, okay?" he finally said. "This is what people are focusing on, this trip that you took. 'Cause they're saying, 'she left, she didn't get there until Thursday,' and Wednesday, that's when Travis was killed."

"I did not go near his house," Jodi objected.

Flores laid out his own timeline. "I do believe that you had time to come to visit Travis," he said without raising his voice. "I truly believe it. Did you have the opportunity? Yes, you were traveling alone. There are no other witnesses. Your phone just happened to turn off from here to here . . ." Detective Flores used the map to show where Jodi's phone had mysteriously turned off, exactly when and where her plan deviated from his version. "You need to be honest with me, Jodi."

"I was not at Travis's house," she insisted. "I was not."

Next came the bombshell. "You were at Travis's house, and you guys had a sexual encounter, for which there's pictures," he announced. "And I know you know there are pictures because I have them. I will show them to you, okay? So, what I'm asking you is for you to be honest with me. I know you were there."

With that, Jodi's story was a bust. The detective gave her doses of all the evidence they had, all pointing to her. Even then, she continued to play dumbfounded, saying she would never hurt him. She went so far as to ask to see the pictures, perhaps figuring she could talk her way out of them by saying they happened at a different time. The bloody palm print, identified as coming from her hand, was certainly going to be harder to explain. So was the fact that her hair was stuck in the dried blood and therefore had likely only arrived at the scene when the murder took place.

"Jodi, Jodi, this is over," Detective Flores said, releasing his detainee from the agony of having to keep creating possible explanations. "This is absolutely over. You need to tell me the truth." He brought the gun stolen from her grandfather's house into the scenario, noting it was the same caliber as the one used to shoot Travis. He recapped the fact that her DNA was mixed in with Travis's blood, something that was an impossibility if she was not present at the time of the murder. Still, she resisted.

"I was not at Travis's house on Wednesday, the fourth," she said emphatically.

"The motive is there, the jealousy issue . . . ," Detective Flores began. When Jodi said most of the jealousy problems lay with Travis, he challenged her. "That's not what everybody else says. They know he was jealous, but they think you were absolutely obsessed. *Obsessed* was the word that they used. That's the word I hear from everybody. Fatal attraction. I don't know how many times I've heard that. 'Look at Jodi. Jodi had to have done this.' "

He told her that they had no other suspects and that detectives were currently at her grandparents' house looking for the gun. He asked her if she had a pair of sweatpants with zippers and stripes around the backside. Only after she answered affirmatively did he tell her the image of such a pair of pants had been captured, probably by accident, in one of the photographs on Travis's camera. "You were there, and you did this. It happened. There's no doubt in my mind . . ."

Detective Flores left for five minutes and returned with a blue binder containing the photographs recovered from the camera in the washing machine. After flipping through the binder, he stopped on a photo and placed the open binder on the table in front of Jodi.

"Do you remember him?" he began.

"Yeah," said Jodi. "Is he naked? In the shower?" She perpetuated her lie by saying Travis would never go for something like that.

"Soon after you and him had sex on his bed," Detective Flores continued, not buying in.

After a short pause, Jodi stumbled, "It couldn't have been soon after."

"Umm? An hour or so?"

"The last time I had sex . . ."

"Two hours?" Detective Flores was determined.

". . . in his bed was in April."

Flores wasn't buying it. He continued to thumb through the photographs in the binder, and as he flipped from page to page, he appeared to be deliberately stalling, saying one was too gruesome or another was not appropriate. Finally, he made his choice and pushed the binder to Jodi. The photo was apparently one of the photos of Jodi naked taken before Travis was killed, and Flores covered up part of her exposed body in the photo with a piece of paper, perhaps out of respect. Before she had too long to process the photo of herself, he took the binder back.

"Let's just say I've seen all of you, and I've seen all of Travis," he offered, in case she might decide to become embarrassed. "But the one that sticks in my mind of Travis . . . is on the autopsy table."

He leafed through some more until another image struck him. As he was shifting the binder, he admitted that he wasn't sure if he should share the photo with her, emphasizing that this was "just one of the photos that was taken by accident." She didn't react, and he placed the image in front of her, pointing to part of it.

"That's your foot, Jodi," Detective Flores said. "And these are your pants." Jodi studied it intently without showing much emotion, as the detective explained how the color of the pant leg had been changed by the enhancement on the print. Gesturing toward the photo again, Flores added, "And that's Travis."

Jodi was quiet for a moment before finally speaking. "This is his bathroom. That is not my foot!"

Putting her head into her hands, her long brown hair spilled out of her fingers. She fell into a long litany of excuses why those couldn't be her pants, everything from the zippers being wrong, to there being too many stripes and too few zippers. Paging through the rest of the photos, Flores pointed out the time stamps on the images of her, proving irrefutably that she was there that day. He showed her some of the crime scene photos, too, in particular the one of the bloody palm print, explaining that there was no way that her palm print could have been made in the blood if she hadn't been at the crime scene.

Changing tactics, Flores put the binder away and moved his seat closer to Jodi, looking her in the eye. "There is no doubt in my mind that you did this—none," he said, explaining how there was nothing she could say that would change his mind. "I will not believe you," he said plainly.

Still, Jodi remained adamant that there was no reason she would want to hurt him. When she started worrying about things her parents might think, he again had a suggestion. "I wouldn't be worrying about your reputation right now," he said. "I'd be worrying about the rest of your life."

Despite all of this clear-cut, irrefutable evidence, Jodi continued to grasp on to her lies. They'd been on the tip of her tongue for so long perhaps it was just impossible for her to avoid them. Her denials came so naturally, with no apparent hesitation in her voice. This didn't seem like someone who was deliberating whether or not to tell the truth. This seemed like someone who had already made up her mind that the truth would not be spoken. When confronted with this binder full of irrefutable evidence, it would have been the perfect opportunity for her to confess; instead she doubled down on her lies, refusing to turn back and holding on to her story that she was not there.

Ultimately, Jodi still wasn't willing to take responsibility for the murder except for saying she should have been there, and maybe that would have changed the course of time and the murder would never have happened. Maybe whoever killed him wouldn't have stabbed him over and over again, wouldn't have sliced his throat from ear to ear, and never put a bullet in his head to finish him off. Maybe the shower pictures of Travis and the photos of Jodi nude, posed on Travis's bed like Eduard Manet's famous Olympia, were erroneously time-stamped. Maybe she didn't own pants like the ones worn by the killer, and the bloody palm print was wrongly attributed to her. She said unequivocally that she was incapable of killing Travis. In her own words, she couldn't even hurt a spider.

Detective Flores spent hours trying to convince Jodi to confess, but he made little headway. As he entertained her denials and excuses, he countered each one with overwhelming evidence to the contrary. Finally, he surrendered. All they had left to discuss was what was going to happen next. The detective told Jodi she would be taken across the street to the county jail, where she would be processed and brought before a judge within twenty-four hours. He informed her that the bond was already set at $2 million, and eventually she would be extradited and brought back to Arizona to await trial. At that point, Jodi worried about how the story would play on the evening news and exactly what the Alexander family was going to find out. The detective said they didn't provide much to the news media, but since everything was part of the public record, and because a grand jury had indicted her, her arrest making the national networks was certainly a possibility. As far as the Alexander family, he spoke to them every day.

Flores promised Jodi that someone would be in to handcuff her and escort her out of the interrogation room within a framework of five to fifty minutes, no promises how soon beyond that, only that it would be sometime after he had talked to his associates. Handcuffs were mandatory, a requirement for someone accused of murder or of writing a bad check, he told Jodi, nothing to do with that person's potential for violence. Her obligatory one phone call could be made as soon as she reached the county jail. With that, he left the room.

Whether Jodi was aware the cameras were still rolling or not, the next few minutes were captured on video. Jodi, alone in the room, strolled over to a far wall, got down on both knees, placed her head between her knees, flipped her legs up and over, and assumed a headstand position against the wall. When she was back on her feet, she gazed around and criticized her makeup. She started to sing softly to herself, and was just at the "O night, divine" part of the popular Christmas carol "O Holy Night" when an officer could be seen entering the room.

"Here are your shoes. Why don't you go ahead and put those on . . .

"Step right there and just turn around. Put your hands behind your back . . ."

With that, the officer led Jodi, cuffed and mellow, out into the hall.

CHAPTER 12

THE CHAMELEON

Even though they'd been fooling around with each other since the fall of 2006, it wasn't until February 2007—five months after they'd met—that Jodi and Travis came out as an official couple.

Years later, it was still not entirely clear why it took so long for Jodi and Travis to make their relationship public, but it most likely had something to do with Travis's reservations. Because of his weight loss and his success at PPL, Travis was no longer struggling to get the attention of beautiful women—women, like Jodi, who had previously been out of his league. As a result, friends seemed to think that, for those first several months after they met, Travis was flattered by Jodi's attention, but more interested in casually dating her, so he could keep his options open for other women. In addition, there remained a lingering closeness between Travis and his ex-girlfriend Deanna that was hard to ignore. They'd been broken up for nearly a year, but Travis and Deanna spoke often, and despite Travis's insistence that his friendship with Deanna involved nothing physical anymore, his emotional connection to her was palpable to everyone. Meanwhile, Jodi was apparently growing impatient and pressing for more—more than Travis was initially willing to give.

Another barrier to making their relationship official could have been the physical distance between them. Travis and Jodi didn't see each other that often, so the doubts about the relationship being based on love were always confounded by the imperative of a sexual reconnection after a long absence. For Jodi especially, the emotional muddle of it all may have left her feeling lost and desperate. Travis may very well have used the word *marriage* in casual conversation—Mormons say it a lot, nothing strange about that—but Travis probably didn't realize how seriously Jodi would interpret those casual references. She was a woman extremely anxious for a man to want to be with her for the rest of his life. She had never dated a Mormon, and she quickly jumped to false conclusions, in no way based on reality.

Early on, part of how Travis expressed his ambivalence toward Jodi was by encouraging her to date other men. She took him up on it and went on two dates, one a platonic lunch date with a guy named John Dixon and another, an outing with someone named Abe Abdelhadi. Abe was older and interested in her, saying in an interview that he thought she was hot. He made a first-base sexual advance, followed by a comment about her undergarments. He reached toward her panty line to feel if she was wearing a thong.

"These aren't magic underwear," he joked, to which Jodi replied, "but there is magic in them," not exactly the reaction of an insecure wallflower.

He hoped that her reply was a come-on, and called her the next day for another date. She didn't call him back right away, and when she finally reached him, she told him she was getting back together with her ex. Abe and Jodi stayed in touch on the phone, but all Jodi did was talk about Travis to the point where it seemed almost obsessive, Abe said. According to Jodi, she felt like she was cheating on Travis, even though he had been the one to recommend it. Jodi said Travis couldn't ignore the dates, and even wanted to know about them after the fact, almost testing his own level of jealousy. He wasn't angry, but he was upset, and his mood changed, according to Jodi.

While it remains a mystery what changed in Travis and encouraged him to make their relationship official, one possibility stemmed from Jodi's budding friendship with Chris and Sky Hughes, two people whom Travis held in high esteem. After that first weekend that Jodi spent at their house, Chris and Sky had gotten to know Jodi better, and they initially liked what they saw. Sky began to see how deeply Jodi cared for Travis, but it also became increasingly apparent to her that Travis was not treating Jodi well.

During one conversation with Sky, Jodi voiced her frustration with Travis's lack of commitment, complaining that Travis took her for granted. She also told Sky about Travis pushing her to date other men and how he frequently wouldn't call her until late at night. Despite all this, Jodi confided in Sky that she'd experienced "a vision" that she was going to marry him. Bolstered by tips she had learned from *The Secret,* Jodi was certain that through the power of positive thinking she could manifest Travis Alexander as her knight in shining armor. Once he rescued her, he would transport her to a new life of financial security, marriage, children, and social status. Yet the reality that Jodi was confronted with fell far short of this vision; instead of becoming the wife of a brilliant motivational speaker, she was getting sexual trysts at a motel and breakfast at a truck stop.

Though she would come to regret it later, explaining she was actually manipulated by Jodi, Sky was moved by her appeal, and in response, she sent a difficult, impassioned email to Travis, scolding him for how he was treating Jodi. In the email, Sky elaborated on how much she liked Jodi, even going so far as to say she would love for the two of them to get married. To Sky, the root of Travis's indecisive behavior toward Jodi was his relationship with Deanna—he was interested in having an emotional relationship with Deanna and a physical one with Jodi. Sky encouraged him to confront whatever feelings he still had for Deanna because it wasn't fair to string Jodi along if he still had feelings for Deanna.

Understandably, Travis's reply was defensive. He responded that Jodi worked late and he called Jodi after she got off her shift, because he wanted to let her know he was thinking about her, despite the late hour. He denied being a jerk and insisted he adored Jodi, expressing concern that Sky had jeopardized his relationship with her.

It's difficult to say what the impact of this testy exchange was on Travis; however, he did put a lot of weight on the opinions of both Chris and Sky. Though Sky had been critical of Travis's behavior, her email could have influenced him in more ways than one. Sky had given Jodi her seal of approval. Since Travis idolized Chris and Sky, it's easy to see how this endorsement of Jodi could have motivated him to take things with Jodi to the next level.

Ultimately, it wouldn't matter what Travis's rationale was; a month later he and Jodi were officially an item.

The first "real" date began with a trip to Travis's house during the first weekend of February. The visit was cozy and comfortable, with Travis and Jodi watching a movie, hanging out, reading books, and sitting in an oversized chair next to the bed. Travis seemed eager to show off his hot new woman to the world. He started calling her on a more regular basis, and the two would see each other about twice a month. This distance was one of the biggest challenges, with Travis almost three hundred miles from Jodi's house in Palm Desert. Another problem was Jodi's worsening financial crisis—in fact her Palm Desert house went into foreclosure the very month her relationship with Travis became official.

For Valentine's Day, Jodi said Travis sent her a gift package, which included chocolates, a gray T-shirt with the words "Travis Alexander's" printed across the chest, a pair of pink shorts that said "Travis'," and a package of boys' Spider-Man underwear. The significance of the personalized gifts was the apostrophe at the end of Travis's name. The possessive form broadly hinted that Jodi was Travis's possession or sexual property. The boys' Spider-Man underwear wasn't completely weird. At the time, boys-cut briefs were trending at Victoria's Secret. However, being for boys, Jodi described them as too tight, but she said Travis really wanted her to wear them, so she would adjust them as needed to make them comfortable. Even if she felt silly, she claimed Travis told her they made her look hot. Whether Travis actually gave her the personalized T-shirt would ultimately become a subject of heated debate. A photo of the T-shirt was taken by Jodi on July 12, 2008, more than a month after Travis was murdered and the very time police were closing in, and there were no pictures of her wearing it before that. No images of the Spiderman underwear have ever surfaced.

Despite the suspect nature of the supposed Valentine's Day gift, one thing seemed indisputable: Jodi and Travis had a relationship that was super sexually charged. Because extramarital sex is a sin in the Mormon world, there was a great deal of speculation about who was to blame for the fact that they were breaking their religious vows. Because Jodi had not been a Mormon when she met Travis, she wasn't initially restricted by the Law of Chastity. Also of note was the fact that Travis had already been censured by the church for his sexual behavior with Deanna, after he admittedly lost his virginity. However, many of Travis's friends said Jodi gradually became like a drug to him, and he progressed into an addiction that he felt powerless to resist. The two had a sexual chemistry that may have melted any willpower either of them had. The attraction was mutual and the sex consensual.

Jodi's account of events had Travis and her engaging in vaginal sex for the first time in May 2007. She said she had fallen asleep in his bedroom and woke up to find him already penetrating her. "I wore cotton shorts and they were gone, and my shirt was pulled up pretty high," Jodi explained. She said she was on her stomach, and he was on top of her. When he began to quicken his pace, she maneuvered herself out from beneath him, at which point she said he pushed her head down under the covers to perform fellatio on him. Jodi said Travis complained that the torment of "blue balls" and a "sustained erection" needed release.

Skeptics found her story doubtful. The idea that Jodi would not have woken up while Travis pulled off her shorts, pulled up her shirt, and inserted his penis inside her struck most as absurd. Even though Jodi did not describe the incident as an unwanted and aggressive act of rape, she often seemed determined to portray herself as a meek, submissive woman who often just endured sex because Travis liked it, and she wanted to please him.

Jodi claimed she thought that the relationship would be more blessed if she and Travis were less sexual. Even when she took some of the responsibility, it was in a passive manner. "I was partially responsible, fell asleep next to him, in his bed. It wasn't entirely his fault, maybe it seemed invited," she said about the vaginal intercourse. She also blamed it on her "cute shorts," saying they might have been enticing.

Travis's friends said that Travis gave them a completely different portrait of Jodi. She was not simply placating Travis with sex; according to Travis, Jodi was a woman with a voracious sexual appetite. One of Travis's best friends, Taylor Searle, said Travis revealed to him that Jodi was a sexual dynamo who could achieve numerous orgasms in a row.

Taylor said, "We were driving one day and he was talking about Jodi and was describing how she was a nymphomaniac. He was explaining that Jodi had gotten herself off eight times in one day. It might have been nine or it might have been thirteen. It was a high number. But he was just using that as an illustration of how over-the-top she was. He was like, 'She's crazy. She's a nymphomaniac.' And we were like, 'Whoa!' And he was just explaining just how big of a nympho she was." While Travis was clearly bragging and might have exaggerated, others said they saw Jodi behave in a sexually aggressive manner in their presence. One of Travis's friends, Shaun Alexander (no relation), recalled Jodi's sexually aggressive behavior the first time he met her. Shaun said he was talking to Travis at an LDS wedding reception in the spring of 2007 and watched as Jodi came up from behind and began sucking on his ear, seductively wrapping her arms around him. Shaun was flabbergasted, given that they were in a church, but Travis did not seem surprised.

According to his friends, Travis was oblivious to her inappropriate, even weird behavior, failing to see the danger signs others picked up on. Because Travis had been trying for years to land a bombshell like Jodi, her sex appeal insulated him from the true nature of her character, so much so that, in the words of Shaun Alexander, Travis "failed to see a lot of the red flags that everybody else could see."

But it wasn't just about Jodi's good looks or her overtly

sexual nature; Travis also found himself drawn in by Jodi's neediness. Shaun Alexander saw shades of Travis's difficult upbringing in his relationship with Jodi, explaining that "Travis felt a constant need to pay it forward to somebody. He really wanted to help everybody else." As Shaun saw it, Travis himself had been rescued from his tough life, and so he in turn wanted to try to rescue Jodi from hers. She was a wounded bird that he was going to save—and she was attractive.

"She fit both bills," Shaun said as he remembered Travis's infatuation. "She was good-looking, but also somebody who's damaged emotionally that he could help."

This combination of vulnerability and sexuality proved exceptionally potent for Travis, and once they were together he struggled to determine where her neediness ended and her manipulation began.

One person who was no longer blind to Jodi's behavior was Sky Hughes. It had only been a few months since Sky had reached out to Travis on Jodi's behalf, but already she was second-guessing her decision to help bring the two of them together. As Travis's relationship with Jodi progressed, Sky as well as her husband Chris became concerned about Jodi Arias.

For one thing, Sky felt increasingly uncomfortable with what she saw as Jodi's calculated attempts to make Travis jealous. Sky got the impression that Jodi wanted Travis to think that other men were pursuing her, so that Travis would know he had competition and commit to marrying her before she got away. Sky said one time, at a hotel, Jodi kept walking past an open door where a group of men were involved in a business meeting. "She goes down to where the door's open, flips her hair, primps in front of the mirrors and walks back and she does it like a couple of times," Sky recalled. "And I'm like 'What's she doing?' This is bizarre. And she's like, 'Oh my gosh, that guy won't leave me alone. I think he's going to talk to me . . . If he talks to me, tell him I'm Travis Alexander's girlfriend.' So a guy comes out, talks to her, and she looks at me and I say, 'Oh, she has a boyfriend.' And, then after he leaves she says, 'Why didn't you tell him I am Travis Alexander's girlfriend?' Why would it matter? It was just really weird. She was so possessed . . . If he left the room, she would ask, 'Where's Travis? Where's Travis? Where'd Travis go?' It was disturbing."

The more time Sky spent around Jodi, the more suspect she became of how Jodi conducted herself. During the first couple of months of their relationship, Travis and Jodi often used the Hugheses' home for a rendezvous point, since it was somewhat convenient to each of them. In that time, Sky had plenty of opportunity to observe Jodi, and she'd grown concerned by the obsessive and downright strange behavior she'd witnessed.

Jodi seemed to be growing more and more suspicious of Travis and jealous of other women. On one occasion, Sky and Chris caught Jodi listening at the guest room door while Travis talked on the phone to Deanna. They had also found her lingering outside the bathroom, waiting for Travis to emerge. When they surprised her, she threw her hands up in the air and told them she was just about to knock. What really disturbed them, though, was Jodi's admission that, not only had she found emails from other women to Travis, but she had taken the liberty of forwarding them to her own account, presumably so she could have more time to read and scrutinize them.

Finally, one night in April 2007, when Jodi and Travis were staying with them, Chris and Sky confronted Travis. That night Jodi was angry with Travis for not looking her in the eyes, so she announced she was going to bed early. At that point Chris and Sky told Travis they needed to talk.

"So, we're upstairs talking for a long time," Sky recounted. "And, I just got this cold, weird, yucky feeling like I was being watched. And I mouthed to Travis.' 'She's out there, outside of our door.' And Travis whispered, 'No way.' And I'm like, 'Yeah, she's out there.' So, we changed the subject—I don't know how long but not for very long—and then she knocks. And Travis goes to the door and opens it and Jodi says, 'Is everything okay?' and Travis says, 'Oh yeah, we're just talking about some things,' and she says, 'Is everything okay?' and he says, 'Yeah, it's fine.' And she says, 'Are you going to bed anytime soon?' and he says, 'Yeah, I'll come down and say good night before I go to bed.' She said okay. So she went downstairs. Travis looks down. She goes in her room and shuts the door."

Forty minutes later, Sky thought Jodi was eavesdropping again.

"She's out there," she repeated. When Travis ripped open the door, Jodi was standing there. "The look on her face and the feeling Chris and I got is something I've never had before or since," said Sky. "It was like pure evil. And it's not hindsight. Just the darkest, yuckiest, scariest feeling that I've ever had."

Sky said that night she and her husband were actually frightened for their children. "Chris and I were talking and we're like, 'Do we need to get our kids, is she going to burn our house down?' And we're like, 'How did we get in this situation where there is this girl in our house that we are afraid of?' We don't know, is she going to harm us? Is she going to harm our children? . . . And I said, 'I don't want her here. I don't want her here ever again. We're done with her. You need to tell Travis in the morning that she's no longer welcome here.'"

While the discovery of Jodi's eavesdropping was unsettling, Travis wasn't as freaked out as Chris and Sky were, and their decision to ban Jodi from the house caught him off guard. According to Sky, when Chris finally told Travis why Jodi was no longer welcome at their home, Travis was quite upset. "He was really hurt," Sky said. "He didn't understand. He kept saying Jodi was a really sweet person, but he was totally duped by her. I told Travis, 'You're not seeing what we see. There's something wrong with her.'"

Though they'd initially welcomed Jodi into their home, all of that goodwill was gone. Through small glimpses, Chris and Sky had come to see what Travis could not: that there was something unsettling and even frightening about Jodi's behavior, something that could not be trusted. Travis respected both Sky's and Chris's opinions immensely, but now that Travis knew his friends disapproved of Jodi, his relationship with them was awkward for months afterward.

However, their words may not have fallen on deaf ears completely. Perhaps in part because of Sky and Chris's intervention with Travis, two months later Jodi and Travis were done . . . but not really. Some would say their relationship just went underground.

CHAPTER 13

THE NINJAS

The following day, Jodi was brought back to the same interrogation room to resume the interview that had left Detective Flores so frustrated the day before. Jodi's resolve to maintain her innocence, despite the overwhelming proof of her guilt, was not entirely unusual in this interrogation process. Often, the shock of being cornered and captured brings on denial, especially in someone like Jodi, who had assumed she was too clever to be caught. More time to think about it often leads to a softer stance and a willingness to talk the next day.

The cameras for the July 16 interview again began to roll with Jodi alone. This day, she was wearing a jail-issued orange jumpsuit, her brown hair hanging neatly down across the front of her shoulders. Although she looked comfortable and relaxed, seated with her cuffed hands resting in her lap, she occasionally showed signs of nerves, cracking her neck and rubbing her eyes. When no one else came into the room for several minutes, she began to sing the final verse of Bette Midler's love song "The Rose." "Just remember in the winter / Far beneath the bitter snows . . . Lies the seed that . . ." Her a cappella rendition trailed off as sounds of someone arriving could be heard in the hallway behind the closed door.

That day, Jodi's first interviewer was Detective Rachel Blaney of the Siskiyou County Sheriff's Office. Part of the hope was that a female officer might make Jodi more comfortable, especially in light of the sexual content of so much of this case. Blaney removed Jodi's handcuffs, then spent the next several hours with her, trying to convince her that revealing her point of view at this early stage in the process could work in her favor later on. If Jodi remained unwilling to offer her version of what happened, then the portrait of her would be painted solely by the prosecution and would remain one-sided unless and until she decided to talk.

The clock ticked away with very little to no headway. Jodi seemed less inclined to engage with this female cop, perhaps thinking that the subtle flirtations she relied on with men would be wasted on her. Again and again, Blaney reminded Jodi that the explanation of what her breaking point was, of what made her snap, could potentially better her situation in the long run. Detective Blaney played off her vanity. "You appear to be a cold-blooded killer," she reminded Jodi about the current state of affairs, "and the media is going to feed off of that. Do you want to be out there like O. J. Simpson? Because nobody felt sorry for him. Nobody respected him, even though he maintained his innocence." Occasionally, Jodi appeared ready to talk, but then she'd clam up again. Her moments of emotion usually came when she was reminded that her family was part of this now, too, by virtue of her actions. At times, Jodi appeared to sob when she acknowledged the pain the Alexander family was in, although skeptics would say she was faking it.

"Grasping the reality of the situation" was what both Detective Blaney and Detective Flores had in mind for Jodi. But they were in for a surprise during the next part of the interview. When Detective Flores took over the questioning, what Jodi told him was far more ludicrous than what had come before. He came back to the table at Jodi's request, as he had been in touch with Travis's family as recently as that morning, and she wanted him to update her on their well-being.

The interview continued at its snail's pace for what seemed like an eternity. Jodi's posturing and body language was markedly different with Detective Flores than with her female interviewer, and she grew much more talkative and attentive with Flores. With Detective Blaney, she had mostly sat with her feet planted firmly on the floor. Now she often pulled her feet up to the seat of her chair and wrapped her arms around her knees, sitting the way you would if you were relaxing by a campfire.

Detective Flores knew what he was doing. He was trained to create an atmosphere of trust and ease, so Jodi didn't stand much of a chance of manipulating him. There was nothing wrong with patience and pacing. The guilty party was across the table from him, so making her comfortable was more important than rushing her. He had been in this career long enough to know that most people accused of crimes, no matter how heinous, want to be liked and understood before they do much confessing. He allowed Jodi to ramble on about the beautiful things she remembered about Travis and their months together, and never suggested she speed it up. In fact, at times Jodi seemed so relaxed, it was as though she didn't even realize she was under arrest for the murder of the man she was so fondly recalling.

Eventually, when the opportunity seemed best, Detective Flores turned the interview back to the crime scene. He began by asking her if Travis had known she was arriving that night, "So, he knew you were coming . . . he was expecting you?"

"I feel really powerless in here," Jodi replied, a brutally honest statement in a sea of lies.

"You think his roommates were there? Were their cars there? You would have had to have seen their cars." Jodi said the cars were a hard predictor of who was home, because sometimes the roommates used the garage, so when she rolled in around 3 A.M., she didn't pay much attention. (Perhaps by mistake, perhaps intentionally, Jodi had shaved one and a half hours off her road trip as she recounted the day. The evidence would later show that Jodi arrived at approximately 4:30 A.M.) "That makes sense," observed Flores. "You're pretty sneaky. You go up there, and his roommates didn't even know you were there."

Jodi said Travis was awake and watching YouTube videos when she got there. She had great memory of the details: "It wasn't anything profane or bad or vulgar. It was just like people dancing, but they had boxes of foil on their head. It was weird, like robotic." Her memory of other events from that night became increasingly odd as a timeline unfolded.

"What went wrong?" Detective Flores asked, looking for Jodi's snapping point. "Did he say something to you? Were you angry about something? What was it?" He referred to the photos with Travis alive, which had no indications of tension between Jodi and Travis. "The last one we have is him sitting in the shower. And that's when I think it happened. He was sitting down, looking up at you. What did you do? What happened, Jodi?"

Jodi's anxiety kicked in, now that she was fully back in the reality that she was the only suspect. She started vigorously pulling her hair between her fingers as she stared at the wall high above the detective's head.

"You have to tell me," the detective continued, pausing long enough to not seem impatient. Jodi put her head into her hands and began to cry. Flores brought up the possibility that there was premeditation, based on her bringing a gun to the house. "I don't believe you planned it, but then I don't understand why you took a gun with you," he said quietly but deliberately.

"I didn't," answered Jodi, just as deliberately.

"Where was that gun from then? Where did you get it? If you didn't take it, did he have one in the house? Did you get it there in Arizona?"

Jodi maintained that the weapon wasn't hers. "I didn't ever have it actually in my possession," she said barely audibly.

"Then who had it?" asked Flores. The detective was probably hoping that Jodi would see that her story didn't make sense. After the question was asked, Jodi sat there silently. It was a long, pregnant pause. Finally, with almost timidity, she said she was going to come clean.

"I didn't tell you . . . I can tell you everything I know or I remember . . ."

"What happened after that last picture was taken?" the detective pressed. "If you want me to believe that somebody else was there, you have to show me."

The fabrication started slowly, with a cryptic "I didn't actually see it. I heard it first." But it picked up energy as it went along. Jodi said she hadn't been able to talk about the "real" perps initially because they had threatened to hurt her family. She had to improvise the story as she went. She showed either remarkably quick thinking, or painfully amateur floundering, depending on your perspective, as she spilled her on-the-spot story to the detective. She said she was present when the murder occurred, but didn't actually see it with her own eyes, so she didn't know what the intruders had done at first. She asked to look at the pictures from the crime scene, presumably to help her memory, but more probably to help her craft her story. Her request was denied.

As she elaborated, her story grew stranger, with her trying to justify her reluctance to talk. "They know where I live. Or they know where my parents are. I don't know if they know where my grandparents are, but they got my address, they know where my family is." It was remarkable how quickly she covered every possible address in Yreka, in case the invaders had put out a carte blanche "take no prisoners" when it came to their threat to do harm to her family.

"You're saying someone followed you all the way to Arizona from here?" Detective Flores asked incredulously.

"No, I don't think . . . I think I was an element of surprise for them."

"So they *didn't* expect you?"

Jodi was definitely faltering, but she carried forth. She said they argued about if they wanted to kill her or not. "For what reason?" Detective Flores asked in apparent shock over the outrageousness of her story. Jodi answered with a theatrical flair, "Because I'm a witness."

"A witness of what?" Flores pressed.

"Him, of Travis . . . but I didn't really witness it. I didn't see much," Jodi sighed.

She didn't know why they had wanted to get rid of Travis. She didn't recognize them, so she didn't know if they were local.

Detective Flores couldn't hold back. "You need to make this believable, because to me it's not believable right now," he interjected. "I am listening, and it doesn't make any sense to me. People don't just go in somewhere and kill someone for no reason and let a witness go. That just doesn't happen." He needed the details.

Jodi played with her hair a bit, pulling it behind her head and combing it with her fingers. Eventually she pulled her feet back up onto the seat of the chair, with her knees bent. "They were white Americans from what I could tell. They had . . . ummm . . . wummm . . . what do you call those things? Beanies, but they cover your whole face. They have holes for your nose, mouth, and eyes . . . Ski masks! They were black, or dark blue or something."

At this point, she took the story back to the few hours before the murder. Jodi said she and Travis had sex a couple of times in the afternoon, once in his bed and once in his office; they fussed with his computer, trying to figure out a virus that was creating problems on his hard drive; they fed Napoleon; and then Travis went upstairs to shower and shave. Jodi said she had begun taking pictures of him shaving for his Myspace page, even though he was a rather reluctant model at first. Jodi says, that fateful afternoon, she convinced a hesitant Travis to pose in the shower so she could take some photos based on a Calvin Klein ad that she admired. That was when all hell broke loose.

Jodi tried to describe the events of the murder. Travis was inside the shower stall, and she was crouched down outside the door snapping the pictures of him. Suddenly she heard a loud ring and Travis began screaming, and then she thought she got knocked out, but only briefly. She next saw two people near Travis, while he was holding his head. Because "he was on all fours" Jodi rested her head on his back and was begging him to tell her if he was okay. He told her to go get help, but the two masked intruders were still there.

"One was a guy, and one was a girl. I couldn't tell that at first. But I could just see one was a girl, and I assumed the other was a guy because of their build and their voices. I don't remember what they were wearing . . . like maybe jeans . . . One was in all black, and one was in jeans."

"Did they say anything?" Flores asked. "What words did you hear?"

Jodi said the girl wanted to kill her, but the guy just wanted to finish off Travis. She said Travis was screaming the whole time, but not like a girl, more like he was in pain because he had been shot. Mortally wounded, he was lying on the floor of the shower, not writhing, just screaming in agony.

The male came after her next. She used the crime scene photos Detective Flores displayed for her to indicate with her finger where the action took place, and her pointer finger went to Travis's bedroom closet, where the male confronted her. "He stopped me and he didn't touch me. He just held the gun to my head and was like 'You don't go anywhere.' He told me to stay there and not to move." She was helpless to contact 911—Travis's phone was downstairs, and hers was dead.

Jodi still wanted to save Travis. In the face of extreme danger, she sprang from the closet and jumped the female assailant, who was slightly taller than Jodi. She had been hovering over Travis, and Jodi pushed her aside. "Travis was bleeding everywhere because he had been shot at this time . . . He wasn't talking, but I could tell he was breathing."

Flores wanted to know who was armed. Jodi wasn't sure. "I thought she was the one with the gun. Maybe she had the gun. He had the gun. Maybe there were two guns. I don't know." She maintained that the female was Travis's shooter, but everything was fast and muddled, as she had been knocked out herself that brief amount of time. When the assailants left the room, she tried to stand Travis up, but he was weakening. They came back to find her supporting him and trying to help him walk, and there was a brief discussion between them about killing her as well. "They had an argument back and forth, and she wanted to kill me and he didn't. He said, 'That's not what we're here for . . .' It was obvious they were there for [Travis]."

A small struggle ensued, but Jodi was not a fighter by nature. "I'm not a person who knows about self-defense. I took some classes eight years ago, but I've never been consistent with it . . . I just knew I had to hold on to her hand because she had a knife." After the struggle, the pair decided to spare Jodi her life. They told her not to move as the man rifled through her purse. His last act before making her flee the house was removing the small amount of cash she had in her wallet. That was when he found her car registration, and the story came full circle. "You must be that bitch from California!" The threat to do her family bodily harm if she ever told what happened to Travis was real now that the killers had her registration and her home address. They told her to leave, which she was reluctant to do with Travis still alive. But they were in control, and she left.

Detective Flores wondered if Jodi had seen any cars outside, or thought of going to a neighbor's. "I was really scared; I was freaked out of my mind," she told him without emotion. He asked her if she had been injured, and she showed him some healed slice wounds on her left fingers. He questioned her again about who might have wanted to hurt Travis.

In the end, he told her he didn't believe her. "I came in here hoping you would tell me the truth, and this is not the truth, Jodi," he sighed. "This does not make any sense, to have two people come in, first two white males and later you change it—"

"No, I don't think I ever said white males," Jodi interrupted.

"Yes, you did."

"When?"

"At the beginning of this story, and then you change it to 'Oh, one was female.' That doesn't make any sense to me." He also suggested that the scenario of letting Jodi go was absurd. "The fact that they left you alive and let you go? That never happens. Why would anyone do that? Why would somebody risk the chance of getting caught and just let you run out the front door while they're upstairs in his house, knowing you could just run across the street and tell somebody? It just doesn't make sense." He didn't show particular exasperation as he discounted the masked intruder story. "There is a reason that you did this, and you just refuse to tell me why. Maybe because you *are* just cold and calculated . . ."

In creating an alternative killer/killers, Jodi was not particularly unique in the phenomenon of blaming someone else. Her masked intruder story, morphed into the "ninja story" in the press, would become particularly infamous, more for her steadfast devotion to it in the face of it being totally ludicrous than anything else. Nonetheless, she showed that she was willing to take a lie as far as she could, eventually holding on to this story—one that she'd made up on the spot with Detective Flores—for the next two years.

On September 5, 2008, Jodi was extradited to Mesa, Arizona, to face charges of first-degree murder in the death of Travis Alexander. Her new home would be Maricopa County's Estrella Women's Jail in Phoenix. The dormitory-style jail on Durango Street was relatively new, having been built in 1991, and housed about one thousand inmates. As part of the booking process, Jodi was required to pose for a mug shot, which she did with great camera comfort, tilting her head and coyly smiling. The resulting picture could easily be mistaken for a yearbook photo, save for the orange jumpsuit. She was given a seven-by-eleven-foot room with a locked door in the maximum-security wing of the facility. The cell was fitted with a stainless steel toilet, a vanity/shelf bolted securely to the wall, a rusty stool, and bunk beds, two slabs jutting out from the rear wall. Though it was a far cry from Travis's sleigh bed with the expensive mattress, Jodi accustomed herself to her little bunk, with its thin, ill-fitting mattress and ugly pink linens, to sleep in. She managed to use her small space to maximum efficiency, storing court documents, art supplies, and miscellaneous other things, including her spare white and gray striped uniform, as all the inmates wore.

She received two daily meals, with a nutritionally adequate standard of 2,600 total calories. The first meal was a "sack," served between 6 and 8 A.M. It typically contained a protein like peanut butter, two pieces of fruit, two rolls, and a dessert, cookies being the usual offering. The second meal was served between 6 and 8 P.M. This was typically a hot meal, a stew or a casserole, accompanied by mashed potatoes and fruit.

Six days after her arrival in Arizona, Jodi entered a plea of "not guilty" at her arraignment at Maricopa Superior Court in downtown Phoenix. A two million dollar bond was set. Just days before her arraignment, Jodi sat down for an exclusive interview with Jim Walsh, a reporter with the *Arizona Republic*. This would be her first jailhouse interview in Arizona. In response to questions, she maintained her innocence, but declined to address the DNA evidence that tied her to the crime.

"God knows I'm innocent. I know I'm innocent. One day, when I am before God, I will not be held accountable by God for Travis's death," she proclaimed. "I would never hurt him. He was my friend." Jodi used the opportunity to perpetuate the theory/lie she had started during her interrogation, that two intruders had killed him. She claimed that Travis's physical strength alone dictated that more than one person had been responsible for his death.

On the day of her arraignment, Jodi scheduled a press conference from jail with several local news stations, including KTVK and at least one national network. Even captive, she had the ability to make herself look like a prison-stripes women's wear model, appearing totally put together and composed. Jodi called the murder story far more complex than what was being portrayed, using the word *multifaceted* to describe it. "I need to be honest, it is very compelling, but none of it proves that I committed murder." A question from the background asked how she was managing to stay so calm. "Through my faith and through the knowledge of my own innocence" was her quick answer, without so much as a pause to think about it.

The public was intrigued with the murder, and the coverage in the media began to balloon. It had all the makings of a media sensation. According to the "National Data on Intimate Partner Violence" for the complete year 2007, there were more than two thousand "intimate homicides," or homicides involving people who were either in or had been in an intimate relationship. In 25 percent of intimate murders in 2007—more than five hundred in all—the victim was the male partner or ex-partner. What propelled the Jodi and Travis doomed relationship into such a disproportionate headline grabber, beyond the "ex-girlfriend murders ex-boyfriend" scenario? Travis and Jodi were a couple that appeared to be ideal—good-looking, smart, savvy, personable, sensible, religious—appealing in every way. Added to that was a relationship undercurrent that most of us can relate to on some level—insecurity, jealousy, flirting, and desire. Then add the forbidden love, the raunchy sex, the stalking, and the web of lies, with a twist of Mormonism, and the press could not resist. The fact that the murder was so brutal, bloody, and partially documented in accidental photos added to the fascination of the red-hot story, and crime junkies could not get enough.

As if the raw materials for the case weren't incendiary

enough, Jodi herself kept fanning the flames by venturing further into the media circuit for a jailhouse sit-down with a correspondent from the nationally syndicated TV show *Inside Edition*. The interview took place in a holding cell, and Jodi was allowed to wear street clothes. She showed up looking pretty and composed in a blue three-button top and dark-colored pants. Her long brown hair was neatly combed and parted to one side, her eyebrows were perfectly tweezed, and her makeup was flawlessly applied. Responding to questions, she insisted she had not been involved in Travis's murder, although she did admit to being in the house at the time of the attack. This was the first time that Jodi paraded her ninja theory to the public. "I don't know who they were," she said matter-of-factly. "I couldn't pick them out in a police lineup. They came into the home and attacked us both."

Jodi claimed that the last time she saw Travis, he was on all fours on the bathroom floor with the female assailant lording over him with a knife. She said blood was dripping from his arm, although she hadn't seen the woman actually stab him. She said she'd tried to rescue Travis during a brief moment when the assailant had left the bathroom. "I grabbed his arm and said, 'Come on, come on, come on,' and he said, he couldn't," she explained. "I am not proud that I just left my friend there to be slaughtered at the hands of two other people. I am not proud of that at all."

Jodi claimed her responsibility in Travis's death lay in the fact that she had been too afraid to call anyone on his behalf, a bystander who maybe could have helped. But that had been her only crime, as she had not killed him. "I know that I am innocent," she said emphatically. "God knows I am innocent, Travis knows I am innocent, and no jury is going to convict me. And you can mark my words on that."

On October 8, 2008, not long after her public campaigns on her own behalf, Jodi learned that the Maricopa

County Attorney's Office had filed a "notice of intent" to seek the death penalty, accusing her of committing first-degree murder "in an especially cruel, heinous or depraved manner." If convicted, she was facing execution by lethal injection.

In order to seek the ultimate sanction of death, the state was required to prove at least one "aggravating circumstance" that qualified a particular murder for the death penalty. In Arizona, the law sets out fourteen aggravators, which include scenarios such as the killing of a police officer or a witness, killing for monetary gain, and killing in an especially cruel, heinous, or depraved manner. Since Travis was stabbed and sliced more than two dozen times and shot in the head, the state concluded that he suffered physical and mental anguish, and was conscious long enough to know that he was going to die. That qualified the murder to be considered for the aggravating circumstance of especially cruel, heinous, and depraved.

Nearly a year later, in August 2009, Maricopa County Superior Judge Sally Duncan conducted a probable cause hearing to determine if there was enough evidence for the aggravating circumstances to go to the jury. Perhaps surprising to some, she found that the murder of Travis was not heinous or depraved, but that it was especially cruel. Hence the jury would only consider "especially cruel," a third of the statutory circumstance, when determining whether or not the death penalty was appropriate.

However, even with the stakes so high, Jodi did not back down from her crazy story. If anything, Jodi's talking so much was only working against her, but she seemed to like the spotlight. She had already conducted another television interview, this one with probably more national exposure than anything she had done to date. She was interviewed by CBS News' much-respected *48 Hours*, where one hour was devoted to her interview alone, interrupted by minimal backstory. Her derring-do with the masked murderers deviated from prior stories, however. In this one, Jodi added a detail so brand-new, anyone who knew the case closely picked up on it immediately. She told her interviewer, correspondent Maureen Maher, that the male intruder who had been threatening her had actually pulled the trigger while he had the gun pointed at her head, but it had not gone off. Never before had Jodi said Travis's murderer had initially tried to kill her, too. Jodi had to have been a legal team's worst nightmare. The more she blabbered, the more she dug her own grave. She kept making the state's case easier and easier each time she felt the pull of the stage lights. All her various stories, with more and more inconsistencies added each time she tried to promote herself, were becoming embarrassing.

After a furiously fast first few months following Travis's death, Jodi's path to trial slowed to a crawl, as the arduous pretrial filings for both sides took years. This was partly due to the death penalty aspect to the case; however, that alone was not enough to justify the delay. In fact, the real delays came from Jodi's defense team, who in 2010—after nearly two years of sticking by Jodi's story of the masked intruders—made it clear through court filings that Jodi's account of June 4, 2008, was about to change.

This shift in Jodi's version of events began rather obscurely with a disclosure of some letters. On June 1, 2010, as part of the defense's obligations to share evidence with the prosecution—a process known as "discovery"—Jodi's attorneys disclosed to the state copies of ten handwritten letters, letters they claimed were written by Travis between November 2006 and May 27, 2008—basically the time Jodi and

Travis knew each other. In these letters, which have never been widely published and which would later be the subject of an explosive forgery controversy, the writer describes his fantasies, as well as his feelings for Jodi, and in one admits an attraction for boys. For a defense that up until this point had been focused on a tale of masked intruders, these allegations against Travis's character were pretty explosive stuff, and it was not initially clear what purpose these letters could serve. On June 10, the state filed a motion to preclude the letters, arguing that they were hearsay and not relevant evidence in the case. The state also argued a week later at a court hearing for the original letters, but Jodi claimed she had received her copies of the letters electronically from a third party, and procuring the originals was impossible. As it turned out, the letters were just the beginning, a precursor to a shift in defense strategy that no one saw coming.

Four days later, the case exploded after Jodi's attorneys stunned everyone by filing a "notice of intent" that Jodi would assert self-defense at trial. With this filing, Jodi had finally admitted that her story about masked intruders had been fabricated. The defense abandoned the "alternative killer/reasonable doubt" strategy and went full-blown "Jodi was being attacked by Travis when she managed to defend herself." The defense would now lay out its case with what they said was past evidence of Travis's abusive behavior, using the letters as evidence to support these allegations. Since these letters would now be relevant to Jodi's newfound claims of abuse, the defense continued its fight to have the letters introduced at trial. The prosecution dug in its heels. "The fact that the defendant now apparently regrets certain acts that she consensually engaged in with Mr. Alexander does not elevate those acts to abuse or domestic violence," it contended, and also added the letters might have the effect of tainting the victim's character, which did not justify his murder. Ultimately, the court ruled with the prosecution, that the letters could not be admitted at trial.

Although the letters couldn't be used at trial, they were still a controversial issue. Outside the courtroom, there was much speculation that Jodi had actually forged the letters, and at a hearing, the state had presented evidence that challenged their authenticity, leading the defense to withdraw its request to use the letters. This withdrawal was significant as it meant that the letters were officially out of the case, at least for now. Despite the court ruling not to admit them, the defense could still revisit the issue during the trial and could potentially use them depending on how other evidence came in.

The letters never came into evidence, and the theory that they were forged gained credence in the court of public opinion, as it seemed plausible that Jodi forged them during her two years in jail. Sorting through all the communications in this case was monumental, between journals and written letters and the Internet. Some estimates were that Jodi and Travis exchanged something like eighty thousand messages, including emails, texts, and IM's from the time they met until his death.

With the emails and the text messages that the court was allowing, the outlines of Jodi's defense were beginning to take shape. Like the letters, many of the emails and text messages were of a sexual nature, and part of Jodi's self-defense claim would clearly be tied to a strategy of character assassination. In an attempt to prove that Travis was an abuser and that Jodi would have needed to defend herself from him, she would reveal the most intimate details of their sexual relationship. In the process, Jodi was all too willing to shatter the perception of Travis as a chaste Mormon churchgoer. However, the question remained: would anyone believe a word she had to say?

Still, no trial date was in sight. Jodi had been in jail more than three years, and had moved through three different defensive positions—one, that she had never been in Mesa the night Travis was butchered, in fact, hadn't seen him since the day she left town in April 2008; two, that a male/female team dressed in ski masks came upon them in the bathroom and the bloodbath began; and three, that Travis had come at her, and she needed to defend herself or lose her life. Changing the defense from "innocent because she did not do it" to "she did it, but in an act of self-defense" took time and added years onto the pretrial. The defense most likely spent months and months preparing for the first defense, filing the motions and preparing for court on those grounds. When the story was changed, most of those preparations had to be abandoned, and it was back to the drawing board. Because either of the stories was going to be exceptionally challenging to defend, the work preparing for trial was extraordinary. The back-and-forth in an incredible number of evidentiary hearings was lengthy and heated.

Jodi's time in jail was not entirely wasted with waiting and more waiting. In December 2010, with a splendid rendition of "O Holy Night" in the jail's *American Idol*–like competition, aptly called Inmate Idol, a Christmas carol talent contest, Jodi came in first place and won a dinner for all the inmates in her pod.

Finally, in June 2011, three years after Travis's murder and one year after Jodi's bombshell revelation that she was going to use a self-defense tack, Jodi's defense team put on the table that its client would be willing to enter into a plea bargain. She would plead guilty to second-degree murder in exchange for a term of years. In 2011, second-degree murder carried a sentence of as little as ten years and as much as twenty-two years. The prosecution had absolutely no interest in accepting an offer to plead guilty to a lesser crime, as it felt it had more than enough evidence to prove that the murder was premeditated. This case would go to trial.

Further delays followed, though, with changes to the legal team. At one point, Jodi even defended herself. It was short-lived, from August 8 to August 15, 2011. She had told Judge Sherry Stephens she no longer needed counsel, and Stephens granted her request. Still, Victoria Washington, a Maricopa County public defender and Kirk Nurmi, who had left the public defender's office earlier that year and was now in private practice, were being paid by the state of Arizona to defend Jodi, and they would remain as advisors. However, Jodi soon learned that, though she often considered herself the smartest person in the room, she was no legal match for her adversary in her own capital murder case. (Even Jodi understood she was in no way skilled enough to be her own advocate.) She then wanted to return to her original team of defenders. When one of them, Victoria Washington, petitioned to withdraw from the case later that year, the court granted permission, and the trial was delayed yet again. Jennifer Willmott then joined Kirk Nurmi. The two became the team that would handle the trial.

After rejecting the plea, the case continued on track. On December 10, 2012, four and a half years after the murder of Travis Alexander, the jury selection for the *State of Arizona v. Jodi Ann Arias* case began. The media was ready to capture it, every step of the way.

CHAPTER 14

BETWEEN LOVE
AND MADNESS

In the aftermath of the eavesdropping at the Hugheses' house, it became harder for Travis to ignore some of the signs that Jodi's jealousy was beginning to take over their relationship. Indeed, the eavesdropping that weekend was just one of many questionable snooping tactics that Jodi seemed to be using, and whether it was listening in person or digitally through his email, she seemed to be growing more suspicious of him. While Travis said his text exchanges with other women and his phone calls with Deanna were harmless, Jodi didn't feel the same way, and her distrust of Travis had her playing amateur detective at every turn.

As Jodi's paranoia grew, it became harder for her to contain, and later, in April 2007, a couple of weeks after the eavesdropping incident, Jodi revealed her true colors to another member of Travis's inner circle. Travis and Jodi were attending a Pre-Paid Legal convention at Cox Convention Center in downtown Oklahoma City with a large group of friends. Busy networking, Travis paid little attention to her, and she became more insecure, complaining that he was treating her like just another conventiongoer, not his girl-friend, and that he had a tendency to treat her more affec-tionately when no one else was looking. It was as though he was comfortable with her being the companion in his bed, but not in his everyday life, she complained. This attitude toward Jodi was something that had also been noticed by some of Travis's friends, who said that he seemed less af-fectionate toward her whenever they were in a group. Dan Freeman observed that the smaller the group, the cozier he was to her. But others disputed that and even produced a videotape that got a lot of airplay on national news showing Travis hugging Jodi as she cradled up against him, while he spoke to a sizable group of people. Travis's friends asked rhetorically, if Travis was hiding his relationship with Jodi, *why* was the Internet awash with photos of them hugging?

Suffice it to say at the convention and at the convention's executive banquet, Jodi was unhappy and lonely. Travis was ostensibly ignoring her, and seeing him chatting in a group that included the vivacious but happily married Clancy Talbot didn't help Jodi's mood. Clancy had had a couple of glasses of wine and stumbled, grabbing on to Travis's arm for support. The two were laughing and enjoying the embar-rassing moment, but Jodi took deep offense, calling a friend and crying hysterically that Travis was flirting with another woman. She was already suspicious of Clancy, having spied email exchanges between the two that she considered "flir-tatious."

Clancy said she was flabbergasted when the following day, Jodi followed her into the ladies' room and confronted her. As Clancy recalled recently, Jodi "comes in and says, 'I just want you to know Travis and I are an item now. We're a couple. We're together. And I'm not upset with you as much as I am with him. I'm mostly upset with him.' And she's shaking and she's angry . . . and she kept saying it over and over." Clancy said she felt intimidated as Jodi tried to block the exit door. "I couldn't leave, and she was standing really close to my face. She was talking and while she's talking, she's really angry and shaking. And she just kept saying over and over that I just want you to know that Travis and I are boyfriend and girlfriend. We're a couple. We're an item. We are together." Clancy stared back at Jodi, before brushing past her. "I just thought *you are so crazy*. And, then, I left."

In addition to Jodi's distrust of Travis and other women, her finances may have fueled some of her insecure behavior. Because of the foreclosure on her home back in February, she knew that she would soon be forced to find a new house. With that, there was likely a new urgency in her interest to move things forward with Travis, but it looked less and less like Travis was going to swoop in and offer her a place to live anytime soon.

Finally it got to the point where Jodi had to do something for herself, and in April she called the Ventana Inn in Carmel to inquire about being rehired. When she learned there was an opening, she packed up her belongings and headed north for Big Sur. She found a room in a historic house off Highway 101 in Monterey that her ex-boyfriend Matt was sharing with other roommates.

According to Jodi, Travis was not jealous that she was going to be under the same roof as Matt. However, he did have his jealous moments at other times. One time, Travis and Jodi were planning a trip. The idea was to rendezvous in Anaheim and go to Disneyland. Before Jodi took to the road, she wanted to shower, but the water had been turned off at the Ventana Inn. She showered at a friend's house instead. The friend was a male, and when Travis called her to find out if she had left yet, she told him where she was. She said he started yelling at her, saying she had put herself at risk, that she should have showered later. When she arrived in Anaheim just before sunset, Travis was still angry. Jodi claimed it didn't lead to a fight, but that Travis wouldn't let it go.

Although Monterey was farther from him, Jodi and Travis continued to date, traveling frequently and visiting Mormon holy sites in Illinois and Missouri. They also took suggestions from *1,000 Places to See Before You Die,* visiting Niagara Falls and the Finger Lakes in New York State, and the Rock and Roll Hall of Fame in Cleveland, Ohio. Apparently, Jodi's dire financial straits didn't deter her from splurging on vacations.

Still, traveling couldn't mask the tension that was growing between them. That June, Travis and Jodi went on a short trip to Sedona, Arizona, and the Grand Canyon with the brother/sister duo named Daniel and Desiree Freeman. According to the Freemans, Travis and Jodi's relationship showed signs of strain. Travis pretended to be ditching Jodi when she got out of the car to take a photograph, something that didn't sit well with her. They screamed at each other about the childish behavior on one side, and the lack of ability to take a joke on the other. Again, if one were to look at the photos from these scenic pit stops, some of them posted on Myspace pages for anyone to browse, one would more than likely see an extremely handsome couple enjoying each other as much as the sights behind them.

Not long after the trip to the Grand Canyon, Travis and Jodi traveled to Daniels Summit Lodge outside Heber City, Utah, where they were meeting friends, including Clancy Talbot and her husband, Chad. The setting was the epitome of romantic, high in the Rocky Mountains on the edge of Uinta National Forest, and a gem of a wilderness destination. The rustic log cabin lodge was known for its amenities, everything from snowmobiling to horseback riding to a full-service day spa. Still, the jealousy issues traveled with them.

When Jodi was convinced Travis was flirting with Clancy and other women, she once again became rabidly insecure. In her eyes, the love of her life was unquestionably pulling away. She was one hundred percent sure he was cheating on her, and she confronted him.

According to Jodi, Travis became angry when she made her accusations. To her, his anger was an indication of his guilt, not innocence, because she had clearly touched a nerve. Either way, the entire relationship was becoming extremely toxic, with little to sustain it except jealousy and sex. After the lodge, the two went to the home of one of Travis's friends in Park City. Travis fell asleep on the couch with his cell phone between the couch cushions. Jodi saw it and eased it from its location, snuck into the bathroom, and read the text messages.

There were no names by Travis's texts, only phone numbers, but based on what she claimed she uncovered, she concluded her instinct was correct: Travis was being unfaithful. Though it was unclear if he'd done anything physically, in the text messages she saw a trail of verbal bread crumbs that showed he had been coming on to other women in ways that were not innocent. She thought his behavior was emotional two-timing, even if nothing physical had occurred.

In retrospect, it's hard to say how much of this was in Jodi's head, how much she fabricated outright, and how much legitimate reason she had for suspicion. While Jodi was obviously prone to paranoia, Travis did like to flirt. Even his close friends said that Travis was flirtatious by nature, laughing that he would flirt with an eighty-year-old woman if given the chance. It's easy to see how this tendency could be misunderstood, especially in Jodi's eyes.

In addition, Travis's personal history may have been playing a role. For one thing, he didn't have the best role models for a healthy relationship. Emotionally unavailable, his mother had never offered him affection, and her idea of human contact was to rage after her kids if they woke her from her comatose slumber. While Travis's grandmother had been a great role model, unfortunately her benevolence came after many difficult years with his mother. Furthermore, as Sky Hughes had mentioned before Jodi and Travis had started dating officially, Travis still shared a connection with his ex-girlfriend Deanna that went beyond mere friendship, and even though Travis did not see a future with Deanna as his wife, understandably that would have bothered Jodi.

But just as Travis knew that Deanna was not the right partner for him, he was also increasingly aware that Jodi was not right for him, either, and these texts may have been a reflection of that. The connection between Travis and Jodi was wearing thin, and sadly, the sex seemed to be the only remaining common denominator. Jodi elicited Travis's reckless forbidden passion, which was what he craved about her. Unfortunately for her it was also what he loathed, as it came with more and more guilt each time. She was the vehicle of his moral corruption, and over time, the sexual fire sale that she offered him didn't increase her value in his eyes—if anything, it brought her worth to an all-time low.

Whether it was because of his upbringing, Deanna, or Jodi's skills in the bedroom, Travis clearly had a difficult time deciding what he was going to do about Jodi. The flirtatious texts with other women that Jodi had discovered by snooping while he was sleeping reflected his ambivalence about Jodi, but they also demonstrated another reality for Travis: if he was going to move on from Jodi, he had to do it soon. The fact that Travis was getting older meant that there was a different urgency for him. Because it was highly unusual for an eligible man in the Mormon church to still be a bachelor at the age of thirty, Travis found himself in a conundrum—he wanted to find the right balance of sexuality and personality in a future wife, but he was running out of time. There seemed to be a pattern with Travis's women—the ones *he* wanted *didn't* want him, and the ones who *did* want him, *he* didn't want. As his friend Dave Hall put it, "I think he just didn't have enough experience and freedom to find out the different types of love there were, and he just wasn't quite ready to settle down."

For Jodi, there did not appear to be any ambivalence. In Travis, she saw a man who had everything. He had the home with five bedrooms, plenty of room for children. He had the career, the six-figure income, and the upward mobility. He loved to travel and to read. He had religion, and he had a great group of friends, something Jodi both lacked and envied. He was only missing a wife, and she was more than willing to fill in that missing piece. Unfortunately, Travis needed to feel the same way, and the more desperate Jodi became to keep him, the more uncertain he was about her, which led him to start looking for other potential women. It was a dangerous cycle, and now that Jodi had the text messages, she had to wallow in self-pity and righteous indignation.

As angry as she was, she put the phone back where she found it and sat on the information. She and Travis were scheduled to fly together to Rochester, New York, on June 18, for their vacation to Niagara Falls, the Finger Lakes, and the Sacred Grove of Palmyra. The trip was already paid for and was nonrefundable, and she wasn't about to cancel it. She would finally be alone with Travis without the Mormon women she considered to be her competition.

The trip went off as planned. Jodi and Travis paid a visit to the Sacred Grove of Palmyra, the site where Mormons believe Joseph Smith Jr. received his first vision while praying in the grove of trees on his family's farm. According to Mormon history, two heavenly beings appeared before him, the Father and Jesus Christ, and they offered him spiritual guidance. At the sacred site, Jodi and Travis snuggled close to take a "selfie," a portrait snapped by one of them holding the camera. They next went to Niagara Falls. The photo of them on the Canadian side shows two people appearing to be very happy and content in each other's arms, beaming while a distant waterfall cascades behind them. The reality was, this was the last time they would be together as an official couple. They would terminate the relationship within two weeks.

Jodi said while the two were acting like a couple, it was all a pretense. She now was convinced that Travis was cheating on her, but she just needed to get through the week without letting on that she was hurt. Her version had her biding time until they were back at their respective homes. The reality was probably closer to neither party was happy with the state of things, and save for being sexually addicted to each other, the official relationship was about to be over as fast as it had begun.

On June 29, 2007, Jodi says, she broke up with Travis over the phone but that he called her back the next day to apologize. He was at the Hugheses' house, but he wanted to say he was sorry for how things worked out, and he promised to change. The two even joked about marriage and children, before the conversation then turned sexual in nature. They did not reconcile, but left it open that they could possibly get back together again in the future.

However, it wasn't long before the regular late-night calls resumed. The sex picked up again just as quickly.

Less than a month after the breakup, Jodi moved to Mesa. She hadn't been making the kind of money she had hoped at the Ventana Inn, and when considering her options, she liked Mesa best. Travis had painted his town as a great LDS community, and her friend Rachel had offered to let her live in her house there until she got her footing. Soon Jodi was exactly where she shouldn't have been, had she had even a morsel of self-respect.

Travis may not have wanted her to come to Mesa. A close friend overheard Travis talking to Jodi on the phone. Even though he didn't hear both sides of the conversation, he clearly heard Travis telling Jodi that he didn't want her to live in Mesa and put down roots so near him. Jodi's relationship history with Bobby was now repeating itself with Travis. In both cases, her story didn't pass the smell test. Both times Jodi used espionage and claimed she discovered cheating via emails or texts. Both times she claimed to be the one who was dissatisfied in the relationship. But, both times, Jodi followed the ex a considerable distance, across state lines, and proceeded to repeatedly initiate contact, in some cases uninvited. Many suspected the truth was more likely that Jodi was rejected by both men and, each time, refused to take no for an answer and followed them to try to win back the relationship with sexual favors. When that failed to achieve the desired result, then she turned vengeful.

Rachel's place did not work out for very long. Jodi was only there for two and a half weeks when Rachel and her boyfriend eloped and needed the house back for the two of them. Jodi found her next accommodation from a church website called LDShousing.net. She found a room in a house in Gilbert, about ten minutes from Travis's house but in a different LDS ward. Jodi insisted separate wards were exactly what she had in mind, not wanting to be obligated to run into her ex if they weren't getting along. She didn't want to have him treat her poorly or outright ignore her in front of their mutual friends.

Travis didn't want Jodi in his ward, either, but for different reasons. He was already in the process of moving on. In July 2007, not even two weeks after the official breakup with Jodi, he was dating a fellow church member by the name of Lisa Andrews. Lisa was exactly the kind of nice Mormon girl that Travis was convinced he wanted. At only nineteen, she wasn't in quite the same hurry to get married that Travis was, but it didn't take long for him to raise the topic of marriage. Lisa told him she was in no way ready to make such a commitment. Once again, Travis was in his all-too-typical dilemma: the one who wanted him was waving her arms madly and screaming "marry me," while he was offering up his devotion to someone who was probably going to say no.

Meanwhile, Jodi was settling into Mesa life. She got a job at a P. F. Chang's restaurant, and according to Jodi, when Travis offered to pay her to clean his house, she accepted, needing the supplemental income. He was going to pay her $12.50 an hour for sixteen hours a week, giving her an additional $200 weekly. It is unclear if Travis ever paid Jodi, as some of his friends said that it was Jodi who had offered to clean his house for free. One of his friends recalled how on one occasion Travis told him that no matter what Travis did, he couldn't get rid of Jodi, explaining how she'd even offered to clean his house for free just to be around him. Another friend, Sky Hughes, said Travis was often too busy to see Jodi, which was why she offered to clean—just to be near him.

Regardless of whose idea it was, her cleaning at the house gave the two of them a way to be together legitimately but clandestinely, and they took advantage of the situation often, according to Jodi. Unfortunately, giving Jodi access to his house meant Travis was able to keep his addiction to his guilty pleasure full-blown. The pusher was right there serving him his drug on a silver platter.

It was going to be hard for either one to move on when they were completely enmeshed in each other's business and watching each other's every move. Clancy Talbot was on an out-of-town PPL group trip with Travis around the time that Jodi moved to Mesa. "Every time we'd come back into cell phone service his phone would just go off. And you could tell by the look on his face he was frustrated and it was her. She was calling and texting and texting," she said.

But, when the PPL excursion ended and he got back to Mesa, the sexual feeding frenzy started again and continued for months. Now that the two were in the same town for the first time, the situation couldn't have been messier. It almost became impossible to tell what the dynamics were. For all intents and purposes, each one was using the other at will, be it sexually or manipulatively, and the energy between them was becoming more and more toxic. On one hand, Travis seemed to be having Jodi fulfill his wildest sexual fantasies, and she in turn would later interpret that as her being "used like a doormat." On the other, her own behavior could easily be seen as manipulative—going to bed with Travis to remind him that sexually, it couldn't get better than her, so he'd best marry her. Therefore, she was the one selling herself short for self-serving purposes, no matter how she might describe herself later as the passive player in their sex games. It was always a possibility that Jodi enjoyed the taboo sex more than she was ever willing to admit, their kinky games supercharging her sexual pleasure. A straight shooter would say they were both using each other.

Collateral damage in all this was Travis's relationship with Lisa Andrews. In fact, part of Travis's inability to resist Jodi's body was rooted in the fact that Lisa and Jodi could not have been more different from each other sexually. Lisa was a strong adherent to the Law of Chastity, and she struggled with Travis's apparent lack of commitment to leading a chaste life. Already, she was having Mormon guilt about kissing Travis to the point where he had an erection. She was so naïve about the situation inside his pants, she assumed it was something he could control, not an act of nature. She also thought it was somewhat her fault that she had not done enough to keep his thoughts clean.

It was a difficult situation for Travis. He was torn between the path of chastity with Lisa and the lingering temptation of Jodi. On at least one occasion, Travis spoke to his friend Taylor Searle about it.

"What should I do?" Travis asked Taylor one day. "Should I keep dating Jodi or should I light-speed go pursue someone like Lisa? Jodi is hot, and she is what I want if I'm pursuing my physical desires, or should I give all that up and go date the little Mormon girl and have something that has a possible future?"

According to Taylor, Travis was super-attracted to Jodi, but he didn't think his physical attraction to her was enough to make her an appropriate choice for a wife. Once again, the importance of Travis's age came up. "The reason Travis was asking the question was because he was approaching the age of thirty, which is kind of the significant age in a young Mormon's life, where he all of a sudden feels old, and realizes that he hasn't gotten married yet. So, he was approaching that age and realized that he needed to stop being a playboy who just dated a whole bunch of girls without an eye to the future," Taylor said. Travis raised his dilemma several times with Taylor, showing just how aware and pre-occupied Travis was about the trajectory of his relationship with Jodi. He was torn between dating Jodi, who represented his old life, or dating someone like Lisa, who represented the direction in which he wanted to go.

Unable to sever ties with his past, that September Travis and Jodi went to Havasupai Falls in Arizona, another region of stunning natural beauty near the Grand Canyon. They went with Dan and Desiree Freeman, the brother-and-sister team they had traveled with that past spring. This trip was also not without uncomfortable arguments, at least at the outset. In one antagonistic confrontation, Jodi had filled a backpack with ten pounds' worth of beauty products, everything from lotions to hand sanitizer. Travis and Dan wanted to make it lighter, and as they started taking items out of the bag, Jodi began crying and ran upstairs, with Travis close at her heels. Dan described how the two barely talked to each other at the start of the trip, although within a half hour everyone was joking and happy again.

Of course, lost in all this was the fact that Travis was still dating Lisa. Finally, later that month, Lisa decided that she'd had enough. For a while Travis's communications with other women had been concerning her, as it seemed either Jodi, Deanna, or both were always trying to get in touch with him. What made it worse, though, was that Travis was always responding. The behavior made her very uncomfortable. However, when Lisa learned from one of Travis's former roommates that he had been cheating on her with Jodi, she knew enough was enough, ending things with him less than twenty-four hours after hearing about his infidelities. Lisa had been under the impression the two were exclusive, but Jodi made sure that didn't happen.

A prevailing question might be, why didn't Jodi just walk away? She was a young lady with incredible tenacity, always managing to scramble out of dire circumstances and land on her feet. She was funny, smart, and extremely attractive. She was stylish and easygoing. She was artistic, creative, and clever, and yet she had her sights on one man only. She had been a monogamous person. She didn't have a track record for being a classic black widow, going after rich men to secure their wealth for herself and discarding them in the process. According to Jodi, she didn't want to completely abandon the relationship with Travis, despite how he treated her, because she loved him. However reasonable it would have been to move on and find someone else, she held on to her fantasy that he was her prince, even though he didn't know it yet. Eventually, it got to the point of being delusional.

By mid-fall, the reality of Jodi's place in Travis's life had grown impossible for her to ignore. In October, she and Travis traveled to a balloon festival in New Mexico together, but instead of the trip being a sign of Travis's renewed interest in Jodi, it was merely a precursor to Travis getting back together with Lisa a couple of weeks later. As it turned out, Travis worked his charm, calling and texting Lisa to ask her for another chance, trying to convince her that things between him and Jodi were over. Travis and Lisa began dating again, breaking up once more a few weeks before Christmas. This time the breakup was not because of Jodi, but because Lisa felt that Travis was getting too serious for her. Like their previous breakup, though, it did not last long, and soon Travis and Lisa were back together.

And all the while, Jodi was poking around, making sure Lisa knew that he still had the hots for his ex. She'd come over after a shift at P. F. Chang's bearing to-go containers of the restaurant's honey chicken, claiming she knew it was a favorite of Travis's roommate. One night in January 2008, as she entered the house with her carry-out, there was Travis standing in the kitchen with Lisa. Jodi turned around and ran out the door, but at least she had interfered with their evening together.

As Travis tried to pull away from Jodi emotionally, these unannounced drop-ins became Jodi's signature—and they weren't always through the front door. According to some of Travis's friends, if the front door was locked, she'd come in through his doggie door and sleep on a couch or even jump into his bed naked.

Still, his text messages with Jodi during this time make it clear that, despite his renewed relationship with Lisa, he continued to talk with Jodi about sex. That very month Jodi sent this text to Travis: "Ahhh!! I fell asleep! But to answer your question, yes I want to grind you. And I want to be LOUD. And I want to give you a nice, warm 'mouth hug' too. :)" About a month after walking in on Travis and Lisa in the kitchen, in February 2008 Jodi sent Travis a raunchy text message, saying, "Maybe u could give my ass a much-needed pounding," apparently inviting him to engage in anal sex with her, the very anal sex she would later paint as degrading.

Finally, later in February 2008, Lisa broke off the relationship with Travis for a third and final time. Unlike the previous breakups, this one was more mutual, with both of them acknowledging that there were problems. For one thing, Lisa again thought he was getting too serious about his marriage agenda. Although he had worked for months on issues that upset her—she had blamed him for getting erections during their make-out sessions, she didn't want him to grab her butt in public, and she wanted him to be more supportive of her aspiration to be a teacher—there were still issues, namely, Jodi Arias and his lingering relationship with her.

In Travis's final months with Lisa, Jodi had become a huge problem, and she seemed to be growing more and more unhinged. Travis and Lisa had been in Barnes & Noble one afternoon, and the next day Lisa received an email from an unknown sender that referred to them being in that store. It was clear from the content of the email that the person had been watching them. Travis told Taylor he was sure it had been Jodi. "She must have been outside in the parking lot watching us through the window," Travis reported. He also told Taylor that Jodi had stolen some of his journals from his bedroom. There were no other suspects. For years, he had been keeping journals devotedly, chronicling his journey through life. He hoped to publish them in a self-help memoir titled *Raising You*. The pages that were missing were the dates of his relationship with Jodi. Lisa was not exempt from Jodi's relentless stalking. Someone had hacked into her Facebook and email accounts, and Travis was sure it had been Jodi.

Then, also in December, there was vandalism against Travis's car when his tires were slashed. Even more strange was the fact that, the next day, Jodi called him nonchalantly on his cell phone, and when he told her about his four tires being slashed, she came right over to pick him up for the trip to the mechanic, sort of like the arsonist phoning in about the fire. When Travis's car was ready, Jodi followed him on the freeway only to watch him get off at Lisa Andrews's exit again. Jodi then had the audacity to call him on his phone, saying that she had seen him get off at the "wrong" exit. That night the doorbell rang and the tires had been sliced, again. Travis and Lisa had tried off and on for a year, and their relationship had reached its natural conclusion. At least for the time being, it appeared that Jodi was victorious— Travis Alexander was hers.

If Jodi thought Travis would come running back to her after he broke up with Lisa, she was quite mistaken. He may still have had sex with her, but now his more "innocent" affections moved to Marie "Mimi" Hall. She was foxy and brunette, "smoking hot," he told a friend, and she had confidence that the younger women in the Desert Ridge ward lacked. His friend Taylor said Travis was infatuated with Mimi. "He'd never really even talked to her more than once, but for some reason, he was super-drawn to her, and he really wanted to pursue her." Taylor cited Bambi when he said his friend was so lovestruck, he was "twitterpated," weak in his knees at first glance. "He just had a crush on her right away. He saw pursuing Mimi as pretty much his way of starting over, getting over the Jodi baggage."

Meanwhile, the Jodi baggage was still in the front hall. He was having sex with her, but he had never been more emotionally distant. The sex was becoming more and more outrageous, according to Jodi. Travis was even making a long list of sexual fantasies he wanted to fulfill with her. For him, however, the sex was where the relationship began and ended. The whole thing was so poisonous, it was *almost* lethal.

In early March, Travis invited Mimi out on a date. He was thrilled when she accepted. Two dates later, however, Mimi said she wouldn't mind being friends, but there was no romantic interest on her part. Travis still pursued her anyway, even though she never really reciprocated or showed interest back. He said they started doing nonsexual things together. They started a movie watchers' club, where they and a few others from the church would watch an old movie and then talk about it, like a book club for movies. Travis was disappointed that the relationship had turned platonic, but he was not completely deterred. He may have even been motivated by the fact that Mimi had started seeing someone else, and he loved the challenge of besting a rival to win her over. Dating Mimi would mean he and Jodi could finally be through. Mimi seemed to have the combination of sex appeal and sensibility that he had been searching for. And, being in her late twenties, she was age-appropriate. He had put up with Jodi's antics for the nine months she had been in Mesa, from the tire slashing to the inappropriate phone calls, to her possessiveness and outright stalking. He was done with her stealing his stuff and cornering his female interests.

Luckily for him, Jodi had decided she was leaving town to go back to Yreka, and not a moment too soon. Jodi's mental state was deteriorating. At one point, a friend who cared about her had phoned her mother to let her know he thought Jodi needed help. Sandy Arias also worried about her daughter's nomadic lifestyle and seesawing mood swings. Her daughter would call the house in a great mood, and she and Sandy would chat for a while, but after the call ended, Jodi would unexpectedly call again minutes later, this time crying hysterically. The fast-changing tenor of her calls both confused and upset her mother. Sandy didn't understand what was happening with her daughter and became increasingly anxious, especially after several of Jodi's friends began calling the house, pleading with Sandy to get her daughter some help. Whatever concern the Ariases may have had about Jodi, pundits have debated why her parents didn't try to get her into treatment. Perhaps it was because they were old-fashioned and knew little of mental illness and interventions. They may have also felt a sense of shame that their promising, beautiful, now adult daughter seemed to be in a downward spiral. Whatever the case, her parents watched helplessly as Jodi became more and more uncontrollable. With not much coaxing, Jodi had agreed to move to California to live with her maternal grandparents.

At the news, Taylor said, Travis was jumping for joy. "It was like a big burden was lifted off his shoulders, where he felt like he could actually move on with his life and not have to deal with her," he said. Despite Travis's euphoria, the drug was still in him. Taylor recalled in the midst of his excitement he was still talking to Jodi. "We were driving in his car, and Jodi called him, and he answered it, and he was talking to her. I said, 'Why are you talking to her? I thought you were done with her.' He says, 'I'm done with her, but she really needed help with something, so I'm helping her out.' He just couldn't *not* help somebody, was the feeling I got, like he was in need of saving somebody. He talked to her even though he wanted nothing to do with her, because he didn't want her to be in trouble."

Two weeks before Jodi moved, Sky invited Travis to Murrieta to spend time with Chris and her. He didn't go, saying to Sky something along the lines of "She's leaving town in two weeks; everything will be fine." Soon, it was "She's leaving in one week. I know this is bad; I know she's bad for me." Sky was concerned that Travis had messed up. "Travis was in turmoil over his relationship. He wanted it to end. He wanted Jodi to move home. But, at the same time, he's a guy. Sex is fun, and when a good-looking girl comes over at three in the morning and jumps on you naked and starts rubbing all over you, stuff's going to happen . . . She ensnared and controlled him with sex." His friends worried that when he detoxed from Jodi, he might be in a bad place, and they were there for him.

By this point, Jodi was willing to leave her stuff behind in Mesa and just get herself out of there, but her father talked her into renting a U-Haul and bringing everything with her. Travis sold her his car with the generous offer of letting her make nominal payments of $100 a month to him on a monthly schedule, according to Jodi. He was already getting rid of it and replacing it with a Toyota Prius, pro-actively supporting his newfound environmentalism. Jodi packed her boxes into the U-Haul and hitched the BMW to the back end. Off she drove, behind the wheel of her rented truck only to make it about twenty miles before she blew the transmission on the car she was pulling behind her. She had been towing it in first gear and hadn't raised the two front tires off the ground, so the car was ruined. What a way to go out.

With Jodi gone, Travis thought a lot of his problems had gone with her. He had qualified for an all-expense-paid trip for two to Cancún, Mexico, based on his PPL sales. The winners were going to make the trip the first week of June, and Travis invited Mimi to be his guest. Taylor remembered Travis's excitement when Mimi agreed to go. "He texted me and he's like, 'I just called up Mimi and said, "Hey, I know we're just friends and all, but do you want to go to Cancún?" She said, 'Sure.' He's like, 'I'm so stoked. It's going to be awesome.' " Mimi had to be sure Travis understood it was going to be platonic. She liked the arrangements, where she and Travis would be staying in separate rooms. The flight was scheduled for Tuesday, June 10, Phoenix to Cancún direct.

There has been some discussion that Travis initially invited Jodi to be his guest on the trip and then took her off. One friend said that Travis may have been asking around about how to make a change on an airline ticket for the Mexico trip and he suspected Jodi's name was being changed to Mimi's. But Taylor Searle said he didn't believe that Jodi's name had ever gotten as far as the ticket, even if the two had talked about taking the trip together. In his opinion, "Travis doesn't want to pick anyone from his past, and Mimi is the only thing he has on his plate for the future. She was pretty much the only answer." If Jodi had been invited initially, she had now been officially replaced.

Travis took the two months before the trip to really work on himself. He met with his bishop to try to get himself temple-worthy again. The bishop knew about the sexual behavior with Jodi, so Travis was working on rectifying that. Some of Travis's friends said Jodi had taken it upon herself to confess for both of them about their violating the Law of

Chastity. Others said Travis himself had gone to confess. Either way, Travis was embarrassed and ashamed that his Temple Recommend had been pulled once again. He especially didn't want Mimi to find out.

On church days, Mormon men carry what they call a "temple bag" with them. In it they keep a shirt and tie and other temple garments, which they change into before entering the sacred hall. He wanted Mimi to think that he was temple-worthy, so he invited everyone, including Mimi, to come back to his house after a particular service. According to Taylor, Travis's plan was to leave his temple bag on the kitchen counter, where he knew Mimi would then see it. He could then say, "I was about to go out to the door to the temple with you guys, but I was too late." Taylor said he staged it to hide his shame. Travis desperately wanted to get back in good standing with his faith.

On his new self-improvement campaign, Travis went to the gym regularly and was proud of his weight loss and bodybuilding. He was putting his guilt and his unchaste life behind him. "This year will be the best year of my life," he affirmed in a blog post that April. "This is the year that will eclipse all others. I will earn more, learn more, travel more, serve more, love more, give more and be more than all the other years of my life combined."

In late April 2008, as Travis was celebrating his new self and his metamorphosis, he sent Jodi a text message that showed his detox from his drug of choice was not going as well as he was projecting.

"I am at a night club right now and it helped me to come to the conclusion that you are one of the prettiest girls on the planet," he wrote. The very next day, he texted her: "Send me a naughty picture."

They were a thousand miles apart, but by the sound of his own comments, he was in need of a binge. On May 2,

Travis sent Jodi this text: "There's not a day where I haven't dreamt about driving my shaft long and hard into you," he wrote. "You are the ultimate slut in bed . . . you'll rejoice in being a whore, whose sole purpose in life is to please me any way I desire."

But their dirty pillow talk was not limited to texts and emails. In the early morning hours of May 10, 2008, Jodi and Travis had one of their signature late-night phone calls. Like other late-night calls they'd supposedly had, this one was explicit in nature—a phone sex session between them in which each climaxes—but this time something was different. This time Jodi recorded all the words and sounds of their intimate discussion. While Jodi would go on to claim that Travis was aware of the taping, there was no proof anywhere on the tape itself that this was the case. For Travis, his behavior on the call did not betray any hint of the self-consciousness that one would expect from such an outwardly modest man; indeed his words on the call were as uninhibited as his text messages. It was unclear why after months of sexual discussion between them this call would be singled out, why this call would be the one to remember. Even harder to discern was Jodi's true motivation for recording this conversation. And yet, its larger significance was immediately apparent: now no one could deny just how sexually involved they'd been. Jodi held the proof of the explicit nature of their relationship in the form of Travis's voice. That tape was her "Monica Lewinsky blue dress," the smoking gun that documented some of the acts that had occurred between them. After listening to the charged language from both of them, no one could ever doubt the extent of their sexual relationship.

Perhaps it was that call she was thinking about on Saturday, May 10, when she wrote the final entry on her blog: "I cannot ignore that there is an ever-present yearning and desire that pulses within me. It throbs for gratification and fulfillment," she wrote in a very long entry filled with flowery passionate language.

It was unclear what Travis's interpretation of that was or if he believed it to be for another man. Either way, on the same day Travis was angrily texting Jodi with cryptic comments that hinted of jealousy and resentment: "Why don't you have him come and f—k you in the woods, I can only imagine you are so worried about me reading. You are paranoid because you have no respect for people's privacy and you dare insult me of all people . . . Through your actions you hate more than love by denying me a human right of privacy countless times. You have a lot of freaking nerve. We are all not like you in that aspect." The volatility was hitting the upper ranges of the relationship Richter scale.

Ten days later, Travis posted his last blog entry, "Why I Want to Marry a Gold Digger." The blog talked about how he used to love being single, but now he wanted to find an "eternal companion." He wasn't using the term "gold digger" in a stereotypical sense, but in a metaphorical sense. "I want someone to love me for the Gold that is within me and is willing to dig with me to extract it," he wrote. He continued with great reflection. "I did a little soul searching and realized that I was lonely . . . I realized it was time to adjust my priorities and date with marriage in mind . . . This type of dating to me is like a very long job interview and can be exponentially more mentally taxing. Desperately trying to find out if my date has an axe murderer penned up inside of her, knowing she is wondering the same about me."

Ultimately, sexual phone calls and text messages could not pave over the unmovable issues between them. As May progressed, Travis became increasingly frustrated with Jodi's behavior. On Monday, May 26, Jodi and Travis got into a nasty fight. The following day, Travis called Taylor to tell him about the confrontation with Jodi the night before. He had been on Facebook and had gotten bounced off, a sign that someone else had logged on with his name. He was livid. He logged back on, and there was Jodi. She had hacked in again, but this time he caught her red-handed. "Did you just log in?" he wanted to know. Travis got her to admit it and started unloading on her. "You are the worst thing that ever happened to me," he wrote. He also told her that her grandparents would be ashamed of her. Taylor let him go on. When he settled down, Taylor took a deep breath.

"That's brutal," Taylor said. "You just let her have it. Aren't you afraid that she's going to try to hurt you or something?" Travis said she got the message to stay away from him, and it was over. While he'd told at least one friend he was really afraid of her, others said Travis didn't think Jodi could actually, physically hurt him, especially now that she lived so far away.

Unfortunately, Travis Alexander was wrong. He was wrong about Jodi Arias, wrong about what she was capable of, but mostly he was wrong about just how deep her obsession with him had taken hold.

Much mystery remains about the lives of Travis and Jodi during the first few days of June 2008, but some facts are indisputable. On June 2, Jodi packed an overnight bag with some clothes, a cell phone and charger, and most likely the .25-caliber pistol she had allegedly stolen from her grandfather. She put it all into the car she had rented in Yreka. She drove south to Monterey to borrow two gas cans from her ex, Darryl Brewer, then set off for Mesa via Pasadena. Having the gas cans with her meant that she could get through the state of Arizona without having to stop for gas, but more important, it meant that there would be no evidence of her journey popping up at a gas station. There would be no receipt from an Arizona gas station or security camera footage of her standing by a pump. Along with the gas cans, she calculated an alibi story, which would allow her to go to Mesa and still arrive in Salt Lake City without being suspicious.

At about 4:30 A.M. on June 4, she rolled up in front of Travis's house. Based on the evidence recovered at the scene, the two spent several hours together, much of it in bed. The photographs from the camera in the washing machine show Jodi and Travis quite relaxed and very naked for much of the day. However, just after 5:30 P.M. something changed. Suddenly Travis was on the receiving end of twenty-nine stabs and slashes and a gunshot to the head. Jodi had killed him, and while the extraordinary overkill and excess of the crime pointed to a killer harboring extreme personal rage, the question that remained was why.

PART II

From a young age, Jodi was fixated on art, and it was an outlet to which she would turn for the rest of her life.

August 1, 1997 ~ Pismo Beach
"Best Friends Forever! Jodie & Patrisha!

Jodi's childhood best friend, Patti, explained that Jodi was a good kid when they were friends. She never expected Jodi would become a killer.

Jodi was happiest with her friends in Santa Maria.

From an early age, Jodi was always preoccupied with her appearance, trying to keep herself as perfect as possible.

Jodi's financial troubles began before she and Travis met. Jodi reportedly could not afford to buy her own bridesmaid's dress for her friend's wedding, so the bride's dad bought it for Jodi. But about a year later, Jodi got a mortgage on a house with her then boyfriend Darryl.

Travis with one of his first loves, Linda Ballard, whom he met years before Jodi. He was head over heels in love with Linda and wanted to marry her—even going so far as to buy her a ring. But while she cared for him, she decided he was not the one. (*Courtesy of Linda Ballard Boss*)

Travis with his longtime friend and ex-girlfriend Deanna Reid. When Travis and Jodi met, he and Deanna had been broken up for about a year, but the two still shared an incredibly close connection. Despite Travis and Deanna's mutual Mormon faith, both admitted to having a sexual relationship together. Friends later felt that Travis was still emotionally in love with Deanna when he was dating Jodi. (*Courtesy of Sky Hughes*)

When Deanna and Travis were dating, her job led her to move near Phoenix, and Travis decided it was a good opportunity for him to move as well. He eventually bought a five-bedroom home in Mesa, Arizona. (*Courtesy of Joe Conrad*)

Travis outside his house in Mesa, Arizona. He rented out some of the other bedrooms to men he met through either the Mormon church or his job at Pre-Paid Legal. It was in this house that he was found dead in the bathroom shower. (*Courtesy of David Hall*)

Though Sky Hughes (left, with Deanna Reid) initially supported Travis and Jodi's relationship, she and her husband, Chris, quickly became uncomfortable with Jodi. Sky was one of the first of Travis's friends to voice concerns about Jodi to Travis. (*Courtesy of Beth Karas*)

Chris *(right)* and Sky Hughes initially welcomed Jodi into their home at the start of her relationship with Travis. But they soon revoked their support and banned Jodi from their home, warning Travis there was something very wrong with her. (*Courtesy of Sky Hughes*)

This shot was taken at the Pre-Paid Legal conference in Las Vegas when Jodi and Travis first met. Shortly after Jodi returned home, she broke up with her long-time boyfriend Darryl and began her conversion to Mormonism for Travis. (*Courtesy of Sky Hughes*)

During the five months during which Jodi and Travis openly dated, they remained long-distance, with Jodi often traveling to Mesa to see him. (*Courtesy of Sky Hughes*)

Travis baptized Jodi into the Church of Latter Day Saints. What followed the baptism remains a subject of fierce debate, with Jodi alleging that the two engaged in anal sex, while Travis's friends maintain that he never would have engaged in a sexual act following such a sacred occasion.

This photo of Travis (*left*) and his friend Taylor Searle (*right*) was taken on Travis's personal camera around May 26, 2008, the day of a heated fight between Jodi and Travis. While the exact cause of the fight remains a mystery, many people believe it was that fight that set Jodi's murderous plan in motion. This photo is believed to be from the same camera that took the infamous shots during the murder. (*Courtesy of T. Searle*)

These photos of Travis in the shower were taken by Jodi, and they are the last images of Travis Alexander alive. Documenting Travis's final moments, these images became key evidence in Jodi Arias's murder trial.

This final photo depicts Travis's bloody shoulder being dragged and Jodi's foot in the forefront.

While awaiting her murder trial, Jodi won a singing competition in jail for her rendition of "O Holy Night." (*Courtesy of Maricopa County Sheriff's Office*)

On July 9, 2008, exactly one month after Travis's body was found, Jodi was indicted for his murder. Her mug shot poses caught the public's eye and became infamous. (*Courtesy of Maricopa County Sheriff's Office*)

The Maricopa County courthouse was the epicenter of the national media firestorm during Jodi Arias's murder trial

After Jodi claimed for two years that masked assassins attacked Travis, her lawyers, Kirk Nurmi and Jennifer Willmott, entered a surprise plea of self-defense. (*Courtesy of Joe Conrad*)

During the months of her trial, Jodi was housed in this tiny cell. (*Courtesy of Chris Hrubesh*)

hough Jodi's father's health evented him from being in court ery day, her mother was there ithfully and her family often alked solemnly to the trial to-ther. (*Courtesy of Joe Conrad*)

Of all the things that Travis Alexander's family had to endure during the trial, the eighteen days during which Jodi was on the stand were likely some of the most difficult. In that time, Travis's sister Tanisha—pictured here with her husband—and some of Travis's other siblings had to listen to Jodi's allegations about Travis's sexual behavior. (*Courtesy of Joe Conrad*)

Travis's death crushed his brother Steven, who told the jury during his impact statement that his older brother's death still haunts his dreams. (*Courtesy of Joe Conrad*)

Samantha Alexander, Travis's sister, also made an impact statement about the traumatizing nature of her brother's death and the unspeakable loss they all suffered. (*Courtesy of Joe Conrad*)

Deanna Reid *(top left)*, Lisa Andrews *(top right)*, and Mimi Hall *(center)* all testified to Travis's kindhearted nature in their respective relationships with Travis. While Mimi had only wanted her relationship with Travis to be platonic, the stories that all three told were drastically different than the portrait of Travis that Jodi offered in her testimony.

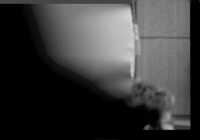

Domestic Violence expert Alyce LaViolette was publicly criticized after speaking in support of Jodi Arias and claiming that Travis committed acts of domestic abuse against her. (*AP Images*)

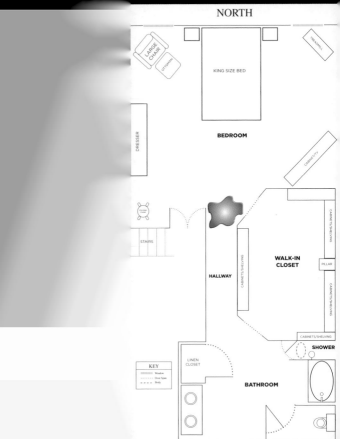

Infuriating many people, Jodi often smiled, giggled, and expressed herself with hand gestures while addressing the jury. (*AP Images*)

Prosecutor Juan Martinez led the powerful case against Jodi Arias. His fiery questioning often led to impassioned arguments between Martinez and the witness in question. (*AP Images*)

Steven, Tanisha, and Samantha Alexander, Travis's younger siblings, were visibly heartbroken throughout the trial. (*Courtesy of HLN*)

As she begged the jury for a chance at life in prison, Jodi fit in one final jab at her victim. Jodi held up the SURVIVOR T-shirt she claimed to have created to raise money for victims of domestic abuse. (*Courtesy of HLN*)

The Arias family appeared worn down while hearing Jodi's explicit testimony throughout the trial. (*Courtesy of HLN*)

Crowds of media and supporters of murder victim Travis Alexander swamped the exterior of the Maricopa County courthouse while awaiting the verdict. (*Courtesy of Joe Conrad*)

Travis's sisters reacted with a mixture of raw emotion and relief to Jodi Arias's guilty verdict. (*Courtesy of HLN*)

CHAPTER 15

JODI'S TRIAL

It had taken four and a half years to get to this point, but the prosecution and the defense were ready. Because of the huge amount of publicity surrounding the trial, both sides were equally worried about being able to seat a fair jury. They began with a pool of three hundred and seventy five potential candidates, from which they needed only eighteen—twelve jurors and six alternates—who had heard so little about the case that they would have no opinion.

Veteran prosecutor Juan Martinez was used to high-profile cases like this. He had never shied away from a challenge during his twenty-five years with the Maricopa County Attorney's Office. In fact, he would be accompanied at the prosecution table by only Detective Flores; no attorney would assist him in handling the witnesses, something that one doesn't typically see in a death penalty case. However, he was the exception, preferring to work alone. Determined, methodical, and highly aggressive in the courtroom, his bulldog style and unwillingness to plea bargain had made him public enemy number one among the local defense attorneys, who despised his relentlessness and tenacity. Not only did he avoid cutting deals, but he usually won anyway.

For such a huge personality, Martinez was small in stature—only five foot four—although when he took on a tough witness, he seemed infinitely taller. He came from very humble beginnings; his parents were Mexican farm workers who came to the United States when he was a young boy, settling in Victorville, California, just north of Los Angeles. Determined to make a better life for himself, Juan learned English and worked hard in school. His hard work paid off when he made it through Arizona State University and Arizona State University Law School. He was licensed to practice law in 1984 and joined the Maricopa County Attorney's Office in 1988. In a short time, he made a name for himself in the legal community. For the last seventeen years, his focus had been prosecuting homicide cases.

The case he was now trying was not his first death penalty case involving a woman. Among the numerous capital cases that he had tried was that of Wendi Andriano, whom he'd sent to death row in 2004. In that case, Andriano had murdered her thirty-three-year-old cancer-stricken, terminally ill husband Joseph Andriano. She had asked male friends of hers to pose as her husband so she could get life insurance on Joseph, then ordered poison to carry out her plot. On the morning of October 8, 2000, she started serving him capsules of sodium azide with his breakfast. Later, she beat him with a bar stool and stabbed him in the neck, then claimed self-defense. Martinez won the death penalty conviction in that case, based on cruelty.

Opposing Martinez on the defense side were Kirk Nurmi and Jennifer Willmott and, like Martinez, both were graduates of Arizona State University Law School. Jodi was unable to pay private attorneys, so both Nurmi and Willmott had been appointed by the court. Nurmi was a huge man with a very gentle voice, kind of the polar opposite of his opponent, Juan Martinez. He specialized in sex crimes and DUIs, but typically defended people accused of being the aggressor rather than the victim. His co-counsel, Jennifer Willmott, was a petite powerhouse prone to wearing well-tailored skirt suits and high heels. A career public defender, she had quickly established herself on the defense side of the law, joining the public defender's office in 1995, the same year she graduated law school. Since then, she'd defended major felonies of all types, including death penalty cases, and was in private practice by the time she joined Arias's defense team.

It took three weeks to seat the eleven men and seven women on the panel. Besides one Hispanic juror, everyone else was non-Hispanic Caucasian. They appeared to range in age from their late twenties to their seventies. A couple of people stood out more than others: One woman had a two-tone bob cut, platinum blond and rosy red, and one older male had lots of tattoos. All eighteen were of equal importance. The ones who were going to be alternates would not be chosen until after closing arguments, right before deliberations. Even then, the alternates might still be switched into the regular panel if someone were to be dismissed. These eighteen were also going to have the power to ask questions of any witness they wished, via the judge, so they were going to play a far greater role than most juries do.

Judge Sherry Stephens would be presiding over the proceedings. She was a slim, put-together woman whose wavy, dirty blond hair brushed the shoulders of her black robe. Often seen peering thoughtfully over her brown framed glasses, she was first elected to the bench in 2001, after serving eleven years as assistant attorney general in the Organized Crime and Fraud section of the Arizona Attorney General's Office. She had attended the same law school as all three attorneys, Arizona State. The Arias case would be the most high profile of her eleven years on the bench.

The trial was going to be taking place in the new Maricopa County Superior Courthouse, which had opened the year before on February 14, 2012, the one hundredth anniversary of Arizona's statehood. The room itself was a windowless courtroom on the fifth floor, with dull, tan paneling, a jury box with two rows of nine thinly upholstered swivel chairs, tables for both the prosecution and defense, the judge's bench with attached witness box, and places for the court clerk and court reporter to do their work. The American flag and flag of the State of Arizona, directly behind Judge Stephens's bench, added the only color.

To get to the fifth floor, everyone had to pack into the available elevators at the east bank, so passionate supporters of both sides and the very few who were neutral would occasionally find themselves face-to-face in the same elevator car, as they rode to and from each session. Despite the painful circumstances, Jodi's family and Travis's family would somehow find the courage to remain cordial. They never spoke, but once in a while would glance at one another during court proceedings when the other wasn't looking. The truth was that both parties were in an unimaginable nightmare of a situation.

The courtroom was filled to capacity on Wednesday, January 2, the day after New Year's. Travis's friends and family dominated the gallery, far outnumbering Jodi's supporters. All seven of his siblings, Gary, Greg, Samantha, Tanisha, Hillary, Allie, and Steven filled the front rows behind Juan Martinez's table. Some brought their spouses with them. Many had traveled a long way to be in Phoenix for the opening remarks. Work schedules and financial restraints would prevent most of them from being in court frequently, but Tanisha, Steven, and Samantha would attend the proceedings nearly every day. Travis's mother had died in 2005, three years before her son was murdered. His father had died in 1997 in a tragic motorcycle accident on Travis's birthday while Travis was on his Mormon mission. The bedrock of the family, his grandmother, had passed away just days before jury selection got under way. Her heart had been broken over Travis's death, and it appeared she had never recovered from it. In a matter of days, Travis's supporters would be wearing blue ribbons in solidarity for their lost friend and brother.

It wouldn't be long before Jodi's side was also wearing ribbons, but theirs would be purple, the symbolic color for victims of domestic violence. On their side of the room, behind the defense table, sat Jodi's mother, Sandy Arias. Like Tanisha, Samantha, and Steven, she would come just about every day for the duration. Sandy often took notes in an open, spiral notebook that had an image of Mickey Mouse on its cover. Sandy's twin sister, Jodi's Aunt Susan, would often be at her side. Jodi's father would attend from time to time, but his failing health kept him closer to home in Yreka. Two of Jodi's four siblings, Joey and Angela, would come to support their sister when they could. Nobody knew that the trial would drag on for months.

By 10 A.M., reporters, local court buffs, and other people piqued by the scandalous nature of the crime filled the remaining seats. With cameras permitted in the courtroom, and the accounts of steamy sex certain to be broadcast to the world, this was a big trial. CNN's sister network HLN would carry the proceedings, often live or with a modest delay, gavel to gavel for most of the trial. As it progressed, voyeurs everywhere would come out of the woodwork, driving halfway across the country for a chance to get inside the court, coordinating their vacations to coincide with key testimony. So great was the public's obsession with the trial that Jodi Arias would even be spoofed in a skit on *Saturday Night Live*.

At precisely 11:01 A.M., Judge Stephens took her seat on the bench. Jodi, dressed in a black shirt, her brown hair in feathered bangs, was already sitting at attention at the right side of the defense table next to her two attorneys when the jury filed in. Within seven minutes of their arrival, the court clerk stood to read the indictment against Jodi.

The moment the clerk had finished, Juan Martinez sprang from his chair and launched into his opening remarks, which gave jurors a taste of the gruesome evidence to come.

"This is not a case of whodunit," he began, his voice booming. "The person 'whodunit,' the person who committed this killing, sits in court today. It's the defendant, Jodi Ann Arias. And the person that she 'done it' to is an individual by the name of Travis Victor Alexander, a former boyfriend of hers, an individual she was in love with, an individual that was a good man, an individual that was one of the greatest blessings in her life. And, this love? Well, she rewarded that love for Travis Victor Alexander by sticking a knife in his chest. . . . *She* slit his throat as a reward for being a good man and in terms of these blessings; *she* knocked the blessings out of him by putting a bullet in his head."

Martinez recapped the relationship between Travis and Jodi, explaining that it had been Travis's misfortune to have ever met Jodi Arias, and described the murder scene in details so graphic that some of Travis's family began weeping. For the past four years, they had tried not to be consumed by the gruesome details of their brother's last moments, but now they were forced to confront them in all their hideousness. Tanisha's eyes burned with indignation as the prosecutor displayed a diagram of Travis's master bedroom suite, the scene of the crime. "Somebody had taken the time to manipulate, stage, change the appearance of the scene," he said, directing the jury's attention to the large poster board at the center of the courtroom and pointing out the many areas in the bathroom where blood was found. "The body was found inside the shower and the killing had obviously taken place somewhere else because there was blood all around. . . . Right there on the sink it's clear that the victim had stood over that and bled. . . . There were some drags marks down that hallway," referring to the hall that led from the bathroom to the bedroom.

Then he moved on to the cover-up. "Whoever had done this killing had also taken the time to wash the body down . . . with this big cup, had taken it and had poured it all over the body so that basically there was almost no blood on the body; it was just bloated from decomposition. Whatever evidence was there is not going to be there anymore because the body had been washed." Martinez explained that the killer had removed the murder weapons (the gun and the knife), had taken a towel and tried to clean the area, and that someone had taken the bedding and run it through the washer and dryer. Martinez talked about the camera found in the washing machine that contained so many of the naked and incriminating photos.

Finally, he talked about the attack itself, which he broke down into three phases. "This was a very violent attack that took some time. . . . There was a stab to the heart area, that was not immediately or rapidly fatal and what that means is: he's stabbed and he still lives, he still can walk, he can still stand, he can still grab, he can still speak."

Prosecutor Martinez was encouraging those listening to visualize the bloodied victim staggering around with a deep chest wound, but he was not done. Moving on to phase two, he explained how Travis's "[t]hroat was slit from ear to ear and that one was rapidly fatal which means it would have killed him very quickly because of the blood loss." The prosecutor emphasized the word *killed* with a clap of his hands. He moved on to the final phase of the attack, the gunshot to Travis's head. "Since that involved the brain . . . according to the medical examiner that one was also rapidly fatal."

After summarizing the three-pronged attack—chest wound, throat slice, gunshot—the prosecutor then doubled back to describe how Travis, as he battled for his life in the moments before he expired, accumulated many defensive wounds. "Mr. Alexander did not die calmly. He fought. . . . The first injury was the one to the heart. And when that was inflicted Mr. Alexander at some point began to fight and what he was able to do was grab the knife but he grabbed the blade of the knife so he has cuts on his hands as he's fighting, presumably for his life." The prosecutor raised his hands and jabbed as if mimicking how a reeling Travis lurched toward the knife only to slice his own hands before staggering to the sink and leaning over it. "Mr. Alexander was able to get up . . . go over to the sink, stand there and bleed."

Sitting at the defense table Jodi Arias hid her head behind her long hair and blew her nose with a tissue as though she might be crying. At times, she seemed to be mumbling to herself. The prosecutor described how Travis was ferociously attacked from behind at the sink, stabbed repeatedly in the back and rear of his head. "Whoever done it, basically followed him around . . . went to finish him off and cut his throat. But, they weren't through with him . . . This individual—the killer—then dragged him . . . and finished the job, as if it needed to be finished." Prosecutor Martinez explained further that by the time Travis was shot in the face he was likely dead, "So, Mr. Alexander probably didn't feel that one." It was a rare moment of understatement.

Shifting from the victim to the accused, Martinez next reiterated the various stories Jodi had told police in the days, months, and years following Travis's murder. There was an odd symmetry. Just as there were three phases to the attack, there were three phases to her lies: One was that she hadn't been there; two was that masked intruders did it, and, finally, self-defense.

To punctuate Jodi's lies, the prosecutor played several snippets from Jodi's jailhouse interview with *Inside Edition*, in which she proclaims her innocence. He then used Jodi's own words to illustrate her arrogance. "No jury is going to convict me . . . and you can mark my words on that."

Martinez implored jurors to "mark her words" and return a guilty verdict.

Jurors were given a ten-minute recess before hearing from Jennifer Willmott, who would give opening remarks for the defense. She appeared poised and self-possessed in a tailored gray jacket and skirt as she crossed the courtroom to address the panel of jurors.

"Jodi Arias killed Travis Alexander. There is no question about it. The million dollar question is: What would have forced her to do it?" Willmott posed this question in a confident voice, suggesting Martinez was wrong about what happened during the final minutes of Travis's life. "Throughout this trial you will hear that Jodi was indeed forced. In just under two minutes we go from the last picture taken of Travis in the shower . . . to the picture of Travis's body. You can see the foot in the front with his head and his shoulders and blood clearly on his shoulders. In just those two minutes, Jodi had to make a choice. She would either live or she would die."

From this, Willmott immediately segued to perhaps the biggest challenge for the defense, Jodi's utter lack of credibility: "Jodi did not always tell the truth about what happened that night. She was scared, scared about what had happened, and scared about what she had done. She had absolutely no experience with police interrogation before and, so, when they talked to her she wasn't always truthful. Her fear and her panic about what had happened led her to tell different stories." Then, Willmott added her own monumental under-statement. "You will learn that what she said, those stories, were not the truth." Travis's family hugged each other for support and glared with visible anger at the defense attorney as she began praising the defendant. "Throughout this trial, you will learn more about Jodi Arias. Much more about Jodi. You will find that she is an articulate, bright young woman who's a very talented artist and photographer. But, most of all, what you'll learn is that Jodi loved Travis. And, so, what would have forced her to have to take Travis's life on that awful day? In order to answer that question, we have to go back to the beginning, back to before she and Travis met," Willmott explained.

Less than one minute into the remarks, Jodi seemed to suddenly cry into her hands, but, then, just as quickly she regained her composure, eventually leading to a debate over whether she was actually shedding tears or faking them. Either way, Jodi's outburst did not distract her lawyer, who continued with her commentary, telling the jurors about Jodi's stable four-year relationship with Darryl Brewer, about her dreams of being an artist and of financial stabil-ity, about the real estate market crash and how Darryl's and her finances had crashed along with it. She next described Jodi's trip to Las Vegas to attend the Pre-Paid Legal Con-vention, where she first met Travis. "Travis spent a lot of time with Jodi wowing her with how important he was," Willmott said, in a not so subtle swipe at the dead man. The defense attorney then described how Travis introduced Jodi to Mormonism, gave her *The Book of Mormon,* began sending missionaries to her house, and convinced her to convert.

Just as the prosecutor did, Willmott displayed photographs, showing jurors several of Jodi and Travis posing together, snuggling and smiling for the camera on some of the trips they had taken. There was another photo from Jodi's baptism, which showed Jodi and Travis dressed in the white baptismal clothes of the Mormon faith. Then, slowly, almost imperceptibly at first, Willmott began to pivot toward Travis's character, taking baby steps toward her full-fledged strategy to blame the victim.

"On the outside, looking in, it really appeared like they were involved in a very loving and healthy relationship. But nothing could be further from the truth. In fact, behind the smiles in these photographs there was a whole other reality for Jodi. A reality that Travis created. Because, in reality, Jodi was Travis's dirty little secret."

Dirty little secret: The catchy phrase was immediately picked up for news headlines. It would become so associated with the trial that, months later when Lifetime network aired a made-for-TV movie on the case, they called it *Dirty Little Secret.* "Despite projecting himself as a good and virginal Mormon man," Willmott continued, "someone who is a Temple member, from the moment he met Jodi he was pushing and pushing her to have a sexual relationship with him." Pacing just a few feet from where the murder victim's family sat sobbing, she accused their dead loved one of hypocrisy, arrogance, rage, and intimidation. "As Travis would explain to Jodi, oral sex really isn't as much of a sin for him as vaginal sex. And so he was able to convince her to give him oral sex. And, later on in their relationship, Travis would tell her that anal sex wasn't as much of a sin as vaginal sex and so he was able to persuade her to allow him to have anal sex with her."

Shock rippled through the courtroom. While those who'd followed the case closely for months knew about the sexual nature of their relationship, many people were caught off guard by these explicit sexual details. It turned out that Jodi's defense was just getting started.

"And so, while he continued this façade of being a good and virginal Mormon man, he was inwardly dealing with his own sexual issues . . . In Jodi, he found somebody who was easily manipulated and controlled, someone who would provide him with that secretive sexual relationship that he needed while, on the outside, he could still pursue the appropriate Mormon woman." Portraying Jodi as a meek, frightened, submissive female eager to obey her abusive dominant male partner, Willmott continued, her flat voice and nasal tone belying the provocative content of her words. "Jodi wanted nothing but to please Travis . . . at some points during their relationship he would tell her you know you really ought to see, date somebody else. But, the moment she would even text another man or talk to another man Travis would instantly degrade her, yell at her, embarrass her, and humiliate her. So, Jodi learned very quickly how to deal with Travis's temper . . . by being humble, compliant, and agreeable." What she left unsaid was why Jodi, if she were so put upon by Travis's behavior, would keep tracking him down to get another dose of it.

Willmott then moved on to paint Travis as a womanizer saying, despite all the sex he and Jodi had, he still pursued other women on the side, which prompted Jodi to break up with him in June 2007. "He begged her for forgiveness . . . Travis sent Jodi a poem that apologized for his behavior . . . Travis showered her with attention, he was nothing but sweet and kind." Making it seem as though Travis cajoled Jodi into moving from California to Mesa after their official breakup, Willmott kept upping the ante.

"You'll hear how Travis degraded Jodi to his friends. . . . You'll hear that he often referred to her as a stalker or claimed that she was crazy. And if she did anything like speak with another man or text another man he would further degrade her by calling her names, names like slut, and whore." However, Willmott's big theme was the sexual secrecy. "The more Travis distanced himself from Jodi to his friends the easier it was for him to keep control of her . . . for his own sexual needs."

From there, she turned to domestic violence, promising to deliver an expert who would explain how "a lot of times domestic violence comes from control through verbal abuse." The defense attorney explained that, because victims are ashamed of what happens to them, and believe it will get worse if they take action, domestic violence often goes unreported. This was designed to address Jodi's failure to ever mention being battered by Travis in either her journals or conversations with friends.

In Willmott's sweeping opening statement, she also accused Travis of having had a possessive nature, citing the T-shirt that Jodi claimed Travis made for her which stated "Travis Alexander's." In her remarks, Willmott spoke about the T-shirt as though it were fact that Travis had made it; yet, once again, Jodi was the only source of that information. Those close to Travis later insisted that he would have written "T-Dogg's" and not "Travis's," saying that Jodi probably had it printed herself.

Willmott had now gotten to the late history of the two. She said by April 2008, "Jodi had had enough because she found out that once again Travis was pursuing other women even though he was having her in his bed." So, she said, Jodi moved from Mesa back to California, settling in her old hometown of Yreka. "Even though she moved, Travis didn't let her go. He continued emailing, texting, and calling. He guilted her about leaving him. And, the thing is, with the type of relationship they were in, the minute Travis was nice to Jodi and caring to Jodi, she fell right back into that relationship with him." As Willmott explained, they weren't even in the same state, but Travis continued to "use Jodi for his own sexual desires through the phone and phone sex."

Jennifer Willmott then dropped the bombshell that would propel this case into a new stratosphere of public interest. "You'll actually hear a recorded phone call . . . between Travis and Jodi that's very explicit," Willmott explained, alluding to the graphic sex tape Jodi had recorded just a couple of weeks before she had killed Travis. "Travis talks about how he's going to Cancún with somebody else. Jodi knew that, and she expresses absolutely no dismay about it whatsoever, and this was just weeks before he dies."

Again, Willmott reverted to her motif that Travis led a double life. "Most importantly, when you hear this call, it's crucial to understand the difference, the difference between the type of person that Travis portrayed himself to be versus the things that he said on this recorded call. Because while he was supposed to be this virginal Mormon man who didn't want to have any type of relationship with Jodi and she just wouldn't leave him alone, in this phone call he talks about his fantasies, his fantasies with Jodi of tying her to a tree and putting it, forgive me, in her ass all the way. That's Travis. And, then, when Jodi pretends to climax during this phone call, Travis tells her that she sounds like a twelve-year-old girl who is having an orgasm for the first time. And then he tells her 'it's so hot.' These comments are not comments of a man who is being relentlessly stalked and who does not want to have any contact with Jodi. These are comments of a man who has a real problem with the comparison to the person he portrays himself to be and who he's supposed to be versus . . . his own private reality and the person who he really was."

Willmott's explanation of what would be on the sex tape caught even the most seasoned trial watchers off guard. While plenty of people knew that Jodi and Travis had broken Mormon laws and had premarital sex, few, if any, were aware of just how graphic the content of the phone sex tape was. From this opening it was clear that their sexual relationship and Travis's apparent hypocrisy over it would be used as evidence to an extent that no one could have predicted.

However, Jodi's defense attorney knew she could not argue that Jodi killed Travis over hypocrisy. "So, what would have forced Jodi? It was Travis's continual abuse. And on June 4 of 2008, it had reached the point of no return and, sadly, Travis left Jodi no other option but to defend herself." Willmott had finally gotten to her version of motive. "On that horrible day, Jodi believed that Travis was going to kill her. He threatened to kill her, and—given her experience with him—she had no reason to not believe him."

The final summary of the defense attorney's thirty-five-minute-long remarks gave jurors a window into Jodi's version of the killing itself. Willmott claimed it was Travis who had beckoned Jodi to Mesa and then, after arriving at Travis's home at about 4 A.M. and sleeping until around noon the next afternoon, Jodi woke up with Travis, and they had sex.

While both sides agreed they had sex, Willmott's narrative couldn't have been more different than what the prosecution laid out. Even the kind of sex they had was in dispute, with the defense alleging that bondage had played a role. "Travis always had wanted to tie Jodi up and he had done it before," Willmott said. "He had tied her up with rope before but the rope he had used had really hurt her. So, this time he was prepared. . . . He had rope that was soft . . . and he was ready. And, so Travis tied Jodi up, tied her to the bed with this rope. He used a knife to cut the rope when it was at the appropriate length. They engaged in sexual activity." Left unsaid, of course, was that this story also conveniently placed a knife at the scene.

Jennifer Willmott then got to the part of the trial that she acknowledged would make most everyone cringe with embarrassment, but especially her client who dropped her head down and sighed because she clearly knew what was coming. Willmott explained that Travis was playing around with his new camera. "These are the photos Travis took of Jodi, very up close." Indeed, the jury would see gynecologic photographs, tight shots of Jodi's vagina and anus. In one Jodi is on all fours and he is aiming the camera at her from behind, very up close. Willmott was getting closer to the killing, but first she described how Jodi and Travis went downstairs and got on the computer. However, there was a problem, because Travis was not able to upload pictures.

"Well, Travis's temper flared and he took the CD and he threw it up against the wall in the den. Jodi went immediately into protective mode . . . 'I'll fix it, don't worry about it.' And, as she was telling him, she knew the one thing that calms his temper the quickest is sex . . . Travis grabbed her and spun her around. Afraid that he was going to hurt her, Jodi was actually relieved when all he did was bend her over the desk, pull her arm up behind her back, pull her pants down and have quick and rough vaginal sex with her, ejaculating all over her back. When Travis was finished, Jodi was allowed to go to the restroom." Travis's family, some with their arms folded, listened silently, their faces contorted with derision and frustration.

Jodi's attorney said the two then went upstairs and Travis, now sexually sated, became charming again, convincing Jodi to take some photographs of his newly buffed physique while he was naked in the shower. Willmott did not address how this claim directly contradicted what Jodi had told Detective Flores about Travis's shyness over being photographed in the nude or her earlier insistence that it was her idea for him to pose in the shower because she had been inspired by a Calvin Klein ad. Willmott said Jodi began taking tasteful, waist-up photos of a dripping wet Travis. "She was snapping picture after picture after picture . . . These pictures are ultimately found and time stamped." She went through the prosecution's most powerful evidence, the photos taken during the killing itself, and tried to spin it. "The next picture is taken when Jodi accidentally drops Travis's camera. You can see it's not an intentional picture 'cause, one, it's blurry and, two, it's of the ceiling . . . Jodi accidentally drops Travis's camera and as that camera was falling that was enough for Travis because he lunged at Jodi in anger, knocking her to the ground in the bathroom where there was a struggle. Jodi's life was in danger . . . In just a minute, from this picture we go to the next picture, where it's Travis's body. He's clearly injured already, in a minute. Now that very brief moment of time, a minute, is not the result of premeditation. It is not the result of a planned out attack."

With that prosecutor Martinez dove in calling, "Objection. Argument."

The judge refereed, "Sustained."

Willmott tried again. "The evidence will show it is not the result . . ."

Martinez interrupted again. "Objection, argument."

The judge hit pause. "Counsel approach."

As the two sides argued at the judge's bench, Jodi's mother sat expressionless, whispering occasionally with her twin sister. Travis's family huddled together. Tanisha, in particular, revealed her anguish through her body language, hanging her head, then looking up and staring at the court-room, as if to ask: *Who is on trial here? My brother?* Soon,

Willmott was back with a very short wrap-up. "In that one minute, had Jodi not chosen to defend herself, she would not be here. Thank you."

With that, opening statements were done. The war between truth and lies had begun.

CHAPTER 16

THE PROSECUTION

The courtroom was pulsing with anticipation as Juan Martinez called his first witness. It was not lost on anyone that the prosecutor chose Mimi Hall as witness number one; after all, she was the woman that Jodi Arias probably considered her biggest rival at the time of Travis's death. It had been Mimi who Travis had invited to Cancún instead of Jodi; Mimi was the one he had a crush on.

As Mimi strode to the stand it was clear why Travis would have been attracted to her. With a slender build, tasteful clothes, good carriage, refined features, and curly brown hair, Mimi Hall had good looks and a classy demeanor. Mimi told the court that she had met Travis during a church service in early 2008. "I gave a talk, and he commented on how well I did." The two went on three dates that couldn't have been more G-rated and wholesome. First, they went to Barnes & Noble where they had some hot chocolate; next to a place to paint pottery; and finally for an afternoon of rock climbing in Tempe. After the third date, Mimi let Travis know she just wanted to be friends. "He understood and thanked me for telling him directly," she recalled. "We continued to see each other at church and had a book and film club. A fun friendship."

"Did he ever berate, scream at you?" Martinez asked.

"No," was her instantaneous reply.

In response to questions about sex before marriage in the Mormon faith, Mimi said it was a serious sin that could be punishable with excommunication. As far as she was concerned, Travis had been a perfect gentleman. "I felt very safe with Travis," she explained. "An awkward hug goodnight was the extent of anything." It couldn't get more Mayberry than that.

"How often did you and Travis speak? Did he ask you to go somewhere?"

Mimi recalled that the two communicated virtually every day via text, phone, or email. "He invited me to go to Cancún," she recounted. "When he first asked, I wanted to think about it. I knew he liked me more than I liked him. There were probably a couple of days between being asked and actually saying yes." Mimi agreed to go to Cancún as a friend, because she would be rooming with another single female on the trip. Mimi said she and Travis had been in contact until the week before they were scheduled to leave for Mexico. Then, it just went silent. "I didn't see him at church on Sunday, so I texted him. He didn't respond. I began to get worried . . . I was scared something might have happened to him because he had a stalker."

Mimi went on to recount the night of Monday, June 9, 2008, when she went to Travis's house to check on him because they were supposed to be leaving for Cancún together the following morning. She explained how she noticed there was a "real bad smell" inside Travis's house, detailing the horrific moment when Travis's roommate, who'd opened Travis's bedroom door with a spare key, ran back out and said, "He's dead." Mimi also revealed that, at Travis's memorial service a week later, the defendant had approached her, introduced herself, and commiserated with her over the tragic events.

Martinez thanked Mimi for her cooperation and turned over the questioning to defense attorney Kirk Nurmi. Mimi was clearly a strong prosecution witness, but defense attorneys always try to use cross-examination of state witnesses to make their own points. Given that Mimi was born into the Mormon faith, the defense attorney's point of focus was how her religion handles sex and sin. He wanted to expound on the LDS view of sex before marriage. He asked Mimi how a person could repent for a sin in the Mormon faith. Mimi said she didn't know the process, as she had never known anyone who had gone through it. When asked about the seriousness of sex before marriage, she said it was the third most serious sin, after murder and adultery.

"Can you describe what temple worthy means?"

"Someone who has gone through a couple of interviews and repents when he makes a mistake. Serving in their calling."

When asked if Travis was temple worthy, Mimi said she didn't know. "I assumed he was since he was an active member. He was also a priesthood holder."

Then, Nurmi asked several questions about Mimi's decision to accompany Travis to Cancún. "Did he tell you he was dating Jodi Arias?" he asked.

"No," Mimi replied.

"He told you he had a stalker?"

"He didn't say a name at all, but said she followed us on a date. I suggested he get a restraining order."

"You said you gave him advice about a restraining order. You said you were scared of this stalker?"

"I'm scared of any stalker," Mimi responded.

"He never said Jodi Arias was his stalker?"

"No," Mimi said.

On redirect, Martinez asked Mimi what Travis had told her about his stalker.

"She slashed tires, sent emails, followed us on a date. She'd sneak into his house through the doggie door."

"Do you know whether he was temple worthy or a priesthood holder?" Martinez posed.

"I think he told me he was not worthy to go to the temple. I actually remember him talking about how he used to work in the temple. He said he was no longer worthy to go. I didn't ask why, that's private . . ."

The next witness was Sterling Williams, a patrol officer with the Mesa Police Department. In a familiar strategy, the prosecutor seemed to be alternating personal accounts with forensic and police testimony. Officer Williams had been summoned to Travis's home on June 9, 2008. He described going directly upstairs upon his arrival that day, and leading fire personnel to the body. "They didn't work on him," he recalled. "They visually inspected him and were able to declare that he was deceased."

Officer Williams said the body was "crammed in the bottom of the shower stall" and appeared to have "a neck wound from ear to ear." In a grisly aside, the officer said Travis's "neck wound would bubble, gasses escaping from the body,"

During the officer's brief testimony, Martinez introduced three gruesome crime scene photos of the body that had been taken at the scene. Travis's sister Tanisha immediately began to sob and leaned forward in her front row seat to avoid even a glimpse of the graphic photos displayed on monitors all over the courtroom. Other siblings silently cried and turned their heads away from the screens. The pictures depicted Travis's nude body crumpled in the shower stall, clean of blood despite the gaping neck wound. At the sight of her handiwork, Jodi covered her nose and mouth with her hand. Occasionally, she dabbed at her eyes with a tissue. Many observers remained convinced that Jodi was faking her sobs, and in their coverage of the case, *Dateline NBC* even referred to being unable to spot actual tears. Prosecutor Martinez contended that Jodi had attempted to stage the scene, possibly to delay detection. When the defense had no questions for Officer Williams, the judge declared the proceedings officially over for day one.

The prosecution's case continued for eight more days. Day two was filled with the testimony of two law enforcement witnesses from the Mesa Police Department, Homicide Detective Esteban Flores and Heather Conner, a crime scene technician and latent fingerprint examiner. Flores, the lead investigator, was there to testify to the very lengthy phone call he had with Jodi on June 10, 2008, the very day after Travis's body was found. He said Jodi had called the Mesa police department twice right after the news of Travis's death broke, but he had not actually spoken with her until then. The entire call, just over thirty minutes long, was played for jurors, who could hear Jodi's phony ignorance of Travis's death. "I heard a lot of rumors, and that there was a lot of blood," Jodi could be heard saying to Flores.

During the call, Jodi appeared to pump Flores for information to see what the cops knew, and where their investigation was headed. She asked about what had happened, but the detective couldn't oblige. She denied she had even been with Travis, claiming she hadn't seen him for months and hadn't spoken to him for days. At one point, she sounded emotional when the detective told her that people were pointing the finger at her. "Gosh," she had responded with feigned hurt and surprise.

In addition, Jodi had countered by volunteering a false suspect, suggesting the detective should check out one of

Travis's former roommates, a guy Travis had kicked out, and even giving the cop his name. "He got kicked out because he was considered like borderline sexual predator, not like a rapist, but coming onto girls and it is just really looked down upon in the church." She suggested this ex-roommate was big and dumb and "a little bit thuggish."

She told Flores she and Travis kept their relationship secret from people, and that she had moved to Mesa because of Travis and she had moved away because of him. When the detective had challenged her with a question about jealousy issues, she said both she *and* Travis were jealous and that he would send her "mean emails" when he got upset with her. Still, she expressed regret at not having been with him when he was attacked.

For the detective's cross-examination by the defense, Kirk Nurmi focused on things Jodi had said that bolstered her claim of being victimized by Travis. In particular, there was the French maid's outfit, the "ropish material," found at the scene, and emails that had already been put into evidence by the prosecution.

He began with the French maid's outfit. "Do you remember seeing an email where [Travis] provides [Jodi] a picture of the French maid's outfit that he would like her to don while she cleans his home?" he posed.

"No," Flores replied.

As for the rope, Nurmi wanted to bolster his co-counsel Jennifer Willmott's claim during her opening remarks that Travis liked to tie Jodi up. Flores told Nurmi that police had recovered short "pieces of fabric rope" from the master bedroom and on the stairs leading to the bedroom, but he described them as tassels and pieces of fabric, and added that no ropes had been found at the house.

Shifting gears, Nurmi grilled Flores about email exchanges between Jodi and Travis that had already been entered into evidence by the prosecution and had derogatory sexual terms in them. "Do you recall her saying he [Travis] had said several mean things to her?" Nurmi wanted to know.

"Yes," Flores responded, his voice monotone, his face expressionless.

"Do you remember an email from Mr. Alexander referring to Miss Arias as a three-hole wonder?"

"Yes," he answered.

"As a slut?"

"Yes," said the detective.

"As a whore?" Nurmi asked. There was another affirmative.

There was a shock value to those words as they rippled through the courtroom. Nurmi must have sensed the impact they had, because he would go on to repeat those three terms many, many times during the course of the trial to the point where it became something of a *here we go again* joke to the reporters covering the case.

This first usage, however, showed just how much of this trial would be about the X-rated texts and instant messages between Jodi and Travis; as it turned out, each side had plenty of vulgar quotes to choose from in order to make their points. On re-cross, the prosecutor had Flores read from the very same instant message exchange that Nurmi had used. With each word enunciated equally, in the style of a grade schooler, Flores read Travis's words, "I think I was little more than a dildo with a heartbeat to you." Using this powerful counterpoint, Martinez demonstrated that Travis felt sexually exploited by Jodi and "used" for sexual purposes in the same way that Jodi accused him of using her.

Martinez then tried to convince the jury that Jodi was lying when she said Travis tied her up to his sleigh bed with rope. The prosecutor showed Flores the photos of the purported rope, which Nurmi had hinted was a remnant of their bondage games. Flores said the item looked more like "a small thread." Martinez then showed him Exhibit 63, a photo of Travis's bedroom. The detective identified throw pillows on a loveseat against the wall. The large, square dark brown pillows were bordered with an inch of gold-colored fringe. The prosecutor then returned to the photo Nurmi had used, which was a bunch of these fibers. He offered up that Nurmi's "rope" was nothing but decorative pillow tassels. Flores was excused for the time being. He would be recalled to testify a number of times about many other aspects of his investigation.

Heather Conner's testimony revisited the crime scene by way of crime-scene photos and disturbing evidence found there, including Travis's undergarments, a T-shirt, and a bleach-stained towel found in the washing machine. It began with Juan Martinez putting up pictures of various rooms in Travis's house, and Conner elaborating on anything relevant. The guided tour of the home ended in the master bathroom. The photos that ended the day were of a blood-spattered sink that looked like something out of a slasher movie, a bullet casing that had landed in a pool of blood on the floor near the sink, and another large blood stain on the carpet at the entrance to the bedroom from the hallway leading to the bathroom. The Alexander family was one more time visibly traumatized. Jodi, watching the photos displayed on her own monitor in front of her on the defense table, hid her face in her hand.

Day three of the prosecution's case had Heather Conner back on the stand. Prosecutor Martinez used the crime-scene technician to conduct a blood-soaked tour. Every bloody photo introduced as evidence popped up simultaneously on several large screens scattered around the courtroom, enhancing the horror of the image and provoking a visceral re-

sponse in the gallery. He asked her to elaborate on the blood
on the bathroom walls, the pool of blood on the carpet, and
items of clothing. The Alexander family in the front rows of
the public gallery appeared shaken, but stoic. Also a latent
print expert, Conner discussed her conclusions about the
bloody left palm print Jodi left on the hallway wall, which
contained a mixture of Travis's and Jodi's DNA. The photo
of Jodi's palm and fingers, etched in blood, was also projected on the monitors for the jury to see. The pictures were
hard to look at, but what made them truly difficult was the
story they told—a story of how Travis bled and stumbled to
his final breath.

However, none of the crime scene photos were as horrify-
ing and disturbing as the ones about to be displayed during
the testimony of Dr. Kevin Horn, the Maricopa County
Medical Examiner. He had performed the autopsy eight
days after Travis died, though, at the time, no one knew his
exact date of death. An abhorrent, ghastly autopsy photo of
Travis's face, which, like the rest of his body, was bloated
and beginning to mummify, was projected on the screen
for the jurors, who winced at the image. Travis's teeth were
visible and his now dark lips had receded. Jodi's head immediately went to her hands, where they remained until the
photo went away. It was Dr. Horn's opinion that Travis had
fought for his life, and the cuts on the palms of his hands
looked like classic defensive wounds. The official cause of
death was loss of blood, but Dr. Horn had the opinion that
one of the knife wounds was primarily responsible, in that it
hastened his death. The gunshot would have killed him, too,
had he not already been mortally wounded.

The scenario Dr. Horn painted was brutal and hard to
listen to. He said that the deep, aggressive stab wound to the
chest entered Travis's body between his third and fourth ribs
and penetrated three and a half inches deep near the base

of his heart, cutting a major vein that supplies blood to the heart. He didn't die immediately, though, because he had time to move around and raise his hands.

Then came perhaps the most shocking visual of the trial. Stifled gasps were heard as prosecutor Juan Martinez posted what became known as the "neck" photo. "Oh my god," one reporter texted, "she didn't just stab him, she cut him open." In the photo revealing Travis's neck, he appeared almost decapitated; his head was tilted back making it seem as though a big half moon chunk of his flesh and muscle was missing from right beneath his chin, the gap stretching ear to ear, six inches across and straight back to his spine. It was as if he had been sawed almost in half. This revolting image had suddenly appeared larger than life on multiple screens, as prosecutor Martinez asked the medical examiner to describe the injury. It was around this time that some of Travis's sisters jumped up and ran from the courtroom in tears.

The medical examiner explained that the fatal neck cut would have been enough to render Travis unconscious within seconds, so traumatic an injury was it in terms of blood loss. Still, many in the gallery wondered how long it took Jodi to produce that cut. It severed the carotid artery, his airway, and other major vessels in Travis's throat. If Travis's neck were slashed while he was still alive, as Horn was suggesting, this would be the "act of extreme cruelty" that made Jodi a strong candidate for the death penalty. In Horn's opinion, the third fatal wound was the gunshot to the forehead, although it was certainly unnecessary to make sure he was dead. He was dead. The gunshot wound showed no signs of bleeding, which was why Horn thought it was postmortem, though it was hard to say with certainty as Travis's brain was so decomposed.

On cross, Jennifer Willmott tried to refocus the rattled

courtroom on the state's most intriguing evidence photo, the one that Juan Martinez described as capturing the killing in progress. This murky photo was much less graphic and required some description to give context to the dark, muddled image. The prosecution had tagged the vertical light blue stripe on the left half of the photo as being Jodi's pant leg. Travis lay at her feet. Willmott's goal was to minimize the cruelty of the assault. She suggested that blood coming from Travis's right shoulder was from the gunshot wound. His head appeared to be raised which, she implied, could indicate that he was not yet incapacitated and was able to raise it himself.

On redirect, Horn countered that the blood on Travis's shoulder was more consistent with a slashed throat. Horn insisted the shot to the head was last, and likely a gratuitous shot. Had Travis been shot first, Horn believed he never would have been able to move around the bathroom, and, more important, that there would have been no defensive wounds. This issue of the order of the wounds would become an issue throughout the case, with the defense arguing Jodi shot Travis first in self-defense when he lunged at her, while prosecutors said that Jodi ambushed Travis with a stab to the chest, only shooting him at the very end, after he was already dead.

On day four, Ryan Burns took the stand. Ryan was a Mormon and an associate of Pre-Paid Legal, two things he had in common with Travis and Jodi. He was also a potential love interest of Jodi's. They had met at the PPL convention in Oklahoma City in April 2008, soon after Jodi had moved out of Mesa and back to Yreka. They had spent the next few weeks talking on the phone three to five times a week. Toward the end of May, the two planned that she visit his home in West Jordan, Utah, when she was in Salt Lake City in early June. They wanted to see where the relationship might go, beginning with the PPL event on June 5, 2008. Ryan was handsome, with the chest of a linebacker and well dressed. In a certain way, he looked like Travis, as they both had a clean-cut, all-American style.

Juan Martinez began with questions about the timeline for Jodi's early June road trip. Ryan had expected Jodi in Utah on Wednesday, June 4; however, she did not arrive at his home in West Jordan until midmorning the following day. She told him she had gotten lost and pulled off the road to sleep. He also said she was no longer a blonde, as she had been when he met her in Oklahoma. She was now a brunette. He noticed that she had bandages on a couple of her fingers and asked her about them. She said she had cut herself on a broken glass while bartending at a Margaritaville restaurant in Yreka.

Ryan said after Jodi got there, the two drove to a PPL luncheon meeting. They went in separate cars, and, en route, Jodi was pulled over by the police and given a warning for having a rear license plate affixed upside down. Jodi later told the group at lunch that some kids were playing with her license plates when she had come out of a Maverick restaurant on her trip to Utah. As for her demeanor at lunch, she appeared totally normal. After the luncheon, he and Jodi went back to his house, where they started fooling around. "Every time we started kissing, it got a little more escalated," Ryan recalled. "She seemed to be in the moment. It didn't feel awkward." Not lost on anyone was the fact that Jodi had made out with this man a day after having sex with and then killing Travis. After the kissing session, they went to a PPL business briefing at 7 P.M. for an hour. They then met a group of friends for dinner at a local Chili's.

Martinez wanted to know how Jodi was behaving at the

restaurant. "She was fine, laughing like any other person," Ryan recalled. "Never once did I feel like anything was wrong."

After the meal, the two went back to Ryan's house to nap. "The second we woke up we were kissing. She got on top of me pretty aggressively; she was right on top of me," he said. He said the interaction went no further than kissing and mild fondling. Nothing got too carried away, as Ryan did not want either one of them to have regrets later. Jodi left sometime after midnight that very night. She told Ryan she needed to be in Yreka for work the next day. Of course, Ryan didn't know that Jodi had quit her job during the last week of May and was already going to be a day late in returning the rental car.

On cross-examination, Kirk Nurmi needed to minimize the mountain of evidence of premeditation Martinez was presenting. He asked Ryan about a phone conversation between Jodi and him on the Tuesday before they had planned to meet. Nurmi steered his questioning toward the fact that Jodi had told Ryan she was still in Los Angeles on June 3, and that she would be arriving in Utah the following day. Had she set out on the trip with a plan to kill Travis, she would definitely have fine-tuned her cover story to tell Ryan that she wouldn't arrive in Utah until Thursday the fifth. At least that was the defense argument. It may not have been a strong point, but Nurmi's eye was on the end game: saving Jodi from the death chamber. The defense attorney moved into another area as he began what would be a relentless attack throughout the trial on Travis's character. He asked Ryan if he knew much about Travis being a flirt.

"Mr. Burns, you made a statement with Detective Flores that you heard Jodi shouldn't date Travis because he was a ladies' man," Nurmi asked during a time when the jury had been excused.

"Travis had a reputation for being a 'fun flirt,' " Ryan replied. "He was flirtatious."

In the testimony, Nurmi asked Ryan if he knew about the sexual relationship between Jodi and Travis in spite of Travis's religious belief. "She told me she didn't want me to say anything to anyone about it . . . said they went a lot further than they should have . . . She didn't say they were having sex . . . but at one point, I did ask, and I found out they had had sex together."

"During those conversations, did she ever badmouth Travis?"

Ryan said Jodi did talk about him cheating and being unfaithful. "She felt he wasn't being honest with her. Besides trust issues, she said he inspired her and he was a great guy."

To counter the implication that it was always Jodi who was sexually aggressive, Nurmi produced emails Ryan and Jodi had exchanged. In them, there were no come-ons from Jodi, and it was clear that Ryan was the one pursuing her. Jodi did, however, call Ryan "hottie biscotti" in some of those exchanges. After several hours on the stand and a few questions from jurors, Ryan was dismissed.

The prosecution case over the next several days included testimony from Nathan Mendes, a former detective with the Siskiyou County Sheriff's Office in Yreka, California; Police Officer Kevin Friedman from the Yreka Police Department; and Michael Galieti, a former police officer in West Jordan, Utah. Detective Mendes testified that there was no restaurant named Margaritaville in Yreka, undermining Jodi's assertion that she had cut her fingers bartending there. He also had Jodi under surveillance the evening of July 14, 2008, and noted she appeared to be packing as if to leave her grandparents' home. Officer Friedman said he was the investigator for the theft of the gun taken from Jodi's grandparents' gun cabinet a few days before the murder. "I thought it was odd that the suspects did not take a large amount of loose change lying in plain sight and other firearms that were stored in the gun cabinet," Friedman testified.

Officer Galieti testified that he had stopped Jodi Arias on June 5, 2008, because the license plate of her white Ford Focus was attached upside down. "My friends must be playing a joke on me," Galieti recalled Jodi saying. Her demeanor was "pleasant and a little surprised." He said he gave her a warning, but no ticket. The upside-down license plate would become the closest thing to a running gag in the case as Jodi would offer bizarre explanations for how it ended up that way, suggesting skateboarders armed with screwdrivers were responsible. One theory was that she had intentionally turned it upside down in order to avoid easy detection. The more likely scenario is that she removed both plates once she arrived in Travis's neighborhood so no one could easily trace the car. Then, in her haste to leave after killing him, she mistakenly attached the rear plate upside down. Jodi's later explanation, however, provoked snickers in the courtroom.

Ralphael Colombo, the owner of the Budget rent-a-car franchise in Redding, California, also testified for the prosecution. He said on June 2, 2008, when Jodi rented the car, she refused the red one first offered her, saying she didn't want a loud color, preferring the white one. He also added a key point for the state. Jodi had rented the vehicle as a blonde, but returned it as a brunette. He said during the post-trip inventory, the car was missing its floor mats, and there were what appeared to be Kool-Aid stains on the front and rear seats. Colombo told the jury that Jodi had said she needed the car for some short trips in the area. He was surprised that the odometer had logged 2,834 miles and asked her about it. "I decided to take a longer trip," she explained. She also returned the car a day later than the original agreement, which listed a return date and time of June 6, 2008 at 8:15 A.M.

Jody Citizen, a custodian of records for Verizon, was called to testify about phone calls between Jodi and Travis between May 31 and June 15, 2008. He would not discuss the content of the calls, just what the phone records showed. Some of the corresponding voice mails, however, would soon be played for the jury through the next witness. In total, Jodi had called Travis fourteen times, and he had called her twice. Ten of Jodi's fourteen calls were made before his death, and four were made after. Travis's two calls to Jodi were made in the early morning of June 2, the day she left Yreka.

Jurors got a chance to view the call logs. Jodi had called Travis three times in one minute alone between 1:08 to 1:09 P.M. on June 2. She called him again at 3:21 P.M. for five seconds; at 4:03 P.M. for 298 seconds; and at 5:28 P.M. for 168 seconds. The next day, June 3, she started calling again at a little after noon for seventeen seconds, then again at 1:51 P.M. for 170 seconds, at 8:16 P.M. for 129 seconds and at 8:34 P.M. for 49 seconds.

On June 4, Jodi's first call to Travis's cell phone, forwarded to his voice mail, was made at 11:37 P.M. and lasted thirty-one seconds. Jodi had killed him several hours earlier, so she was clearly working on an alibi track. Eleven minutes later, at 11:48 P.M., she called again for 269 seconds, approximately three minutes. The last call that day came in just before midnight, at 11:53 P.M., and lasted 961 seconds or sixteen minutes. The maximum length of a voice mail message is five minutes, suggesting the sixteen-minute call was actually Jodi listening to Travis's phone messages. Oddly, there was one final call made by Jodi to Travis's phone at 9:20 P.M. on June 14, five days after his body was found, that went straight to voice mail.

On cross-examination, Jody Citizen was asked about the

length of the two calls from Travis to Jodi. He said that one was made on June 2, at 3:04 in the morning and lasted 1,011 seconds, just under eighteen minutes, which indicated that a conversation took place. Seconds after that call ended, Travis called Jodi again, this time for 2,450 seconds, slightly under forty-one minutes. The contents of those phone calls may never be known. One message police were able to retrieve was the 11:48 P.M. voice message to Travis on June 4, just hours after the slaying. Juan Martinez called Detective Lawrence Gladysh, a homicide detective with the Mesa police department, to testify about the message. It was played for the jury: "My phone died," Jodi said in a very upbeat, sweet voice. "I drove one hundred miles in the wrong direction . . . fun, fun, tell you all about that later. Talking about the calendar, Heather and I are going to see *Othello* on July 1. We'd love for you to accompany us. Let me know; talk to you soon." When she left this voice mail on Travis's phone, Jodi was actually forty-five minutes north of Kingman, Arizona, twenty-five miles south of the Nevada border and 250 miles from Mesa.

Michael Melendez, also a Mesa police officer, analyzed the camera recovered from the washing machine. He was responsible for the smoking gun evidence in the case. In fact, without the incriminating photos that Jodi deleted and he recovered, Jodi may not have faced a first-degree murder charge. Melendez took the jury through the five steps one must take to delete a photo. There were approximately ninety pictures still on the camera. Only the ones from the crime scene and of the nude photos of Travis and Jodi earlier on the same day had been deleted. The deleted photos had been taken over about four hours, beginning with the sexy poses earlier in the afternoon. They ended with the shower photos and the pictures clearly taken accidentally during the course of the killing. Melendez also analyzed Travis's laptop collected from the office inside his home. He had found no pornography—adult or child—on the computer. There were also no pornographic websites on Travis's browser history.

On cross-examination, Jennifer Willmott noted that the last activity on the computer took place at 4:54 P.M. on June 4, 2008. (The last *email* activity, however, was at 4:19 P.M. This later usage at 4:54 P.M., Melendez said, could have been from Internet surfing or playing a CD.) This was corroboration that the laptop was used just half an hour before Travis's murder. The defense would argue that it also supported Jodi's story that the two had rough sex in his office around that time by at least placing them in the office.

Throughout the prosecution's nine days of testimony, Detective Esteban Flores was repeatedly called back to the witness stand to testify about various pieces of evidence. During one cross-examination by Kirk Nurmi, Flores had to acknowledge that he had given incorrect testimony about the sequence of Travis's fatal injuries at a critical hearing on August 6, 2009. At that time, he had testified that Travis was shot before he was stabbed. This was a hearing to establish if there was probable cause to go forward with the case as a capital case.

"So, your testimony that the gunshot occurred first was inaccurate . . . Your testimony was a mistake," Nurmi suggested.

"No, my testimony wasn't a mistake," Flores countered, saying that at the time, he had misunderstood what Dr. Horn's determination had been.

The defense attorneys moved for a mistrial, arguing that another judge's 2009 ruling that probable cause was established for the aggravating factor of "especially cruel" was based on false testimony. Nurmi argued that Flores had flip-flopped. Therefore, Jodi's due process had been violated, the defense argued. "We have an aggravating factor founded on testimony that was inaccurate. There can be no dispute about that because Flores testified about it this afternoon. It stands in complete violation of the fifth, eighth, fourteenth amendments," Nurmi spouted. "We ask that it be dismissed or a new trial be submitted." The court ruled that regardless of which wound came first, there was enough evidence to find the crime especially cruel either way and denied the defense's motion for a mistrial. There would be other points along the way where the two defense lawyers, dedicated to the cause of their client, would again and again move for a mistrial, always to no avail.

Jodi's PPL friend, Leslie Udy, was the last witness on the prosecution's list. She took the stand on day nine of the trial, January 17, 2013. She was one of the people at the Chili's restaurant with Jodi, Ryan Burns, and others the day Jodi had arrived in Salt Lake City. When Martinez questioned her about Jodi's demeanor, she said she hadn't noticed anything unusual. "She was acting like Jodi," was her reply. The two had spent several hours together, and had talked about photography and Jodi's ex-boyfriend, Travis. Jodi told her the two had broken up amicably. She told Leslie that Travis and she planned to remain friends, and had even joked that one day their children would probably play together. Such a drift into this kind of hopeful fantasy after she had just butchered him could only be considered extremely odd and cold-blooded.

Leslie said Jodi called her on June 10, crying and upset. Jodi claimed that she had just learned that Travis had been murdered, and she couldn't fathom anyone wanting to hurt him, saying he was such a wonderful person. In the wee hours of the morning, Jodi called Leslie a second time. Again, she was really upset. She said this was the hour that she and Travis usually talked and with him gone, she didn't know who else to call or what to do.

Nurmi was in charge of the cross-examination. In a nutshell, he wanted to know if Leslie could imagine Jodi committing such a horrible crime. "The person I know was a very quiet, soft-spoken, gentle person," she said. "I couldn't imagine her doing something like that." When prompted, she also recalled a night spent at Travis's house, when she had overheard him talking on the phone around 1 A.M. She had even jokingly said to him, "Say hi to Jodi." Nurmi's final question had to do with Leslie's knowledge of the relationship. She admitted that she thought it was sexual.

For redirect, Martinez, with his usual enthusiasm, jumped up and approached the witness. He showed her a photo of Jodi nude, the ones taken just hours before the murder. "Do you know her?" he asked.

"Yes," she answered, looking very worn out.

"Who is it?" Martinez continued.

"Looks like Jodi," Leslie said shaking her head, tired that she had to answer such an obvious question.

Martinez showed her another nude picture with the same question, and again she responded it looked like Jodi. "I don't mean to be indelicate with you, but you say you know her? Do you know anything about that aspect of her life?"

"No."

"You said that you knew her really well . . . is it your belief that she would have confided in you in certain things?" Martinez posed.

"Yes."

"Objection, calls for speculation," Nurmi interrupted.

"Overruled," said Judge Stephens. "You may answer yes or no."

"Yes," Leslie answered quietly.

"She confided in you about the relationship, right?" continued Martinez.

"Yes."

"She never confided in you that she killed him, did she?"

"No," Leslie said, shaking her head.

"I don't have anything else," Martinez said. With that, the prosecution rested. Everyone in the courtroom rose to their feet, as the jury was excused and court was recessed until January 29, when the defense would begin its case.

CHAPTER 17

THE DEFENSE

Making Jodi into a sympathetic person was going to be a tall order, especially after the gruesome details that had been presented in the state's case. Jodi and Travis moved in the same social circles in Arizona, so it was no surprise that the defense witnesses included mutual friends and even a PPL colleague. On Tuesday, January 29, the first defense witnesses took the stand in an effort to show another side to Jodi and Travis's relationship.

Jodi sat in her usual seat nearest the far wall of the courtroom, with Jennifer Willmott in the middle of the defense table, and Kirk Nurmi closest to the prosecution. Wearing a shirt so pale it was either the faintest shade of blue or straight-up white, along with her big glasses and long bangs, Jodi almost looked too conservative and naïve to have murdered someone so brutally—almost. The first witness was Gus Searcy, a balding, middle-aged gentleman with far more hair on the sides than on the top. He was impeccably dressed in a dark suit and golden tie. A friend of Jodi's at PPL, he seemed to be something of an informal mentor. He had worked with the firm long enough to have a special ring awarded to the company's top earners of $100,000 and above, and he held the position of executive director.

Gus knew both Jodi and Travis. He, too, had been at the convention in Las Vegas in September 2006, which was where he believed he'd first met Jodi, although he wasn't one hundred percent certain. In his approximately one hour on the stand, he described Jodi as responsible, well mannered, and conservative when it came to her appearance. He had met her several times during the course of their platonic relationship, and he never saw her being slutty. "She was always dressed feminine, but very conservative dresser— long sleeves, high neck, long dresses, or slacks—nothing provocative in any way. She was very professional." She did not act sexually inappropriate or out of control, either, in those times, which included company parties. As a PPL trainer, he took professional image mistakes very seriously, knowing that a woman who projects a sexy appearance may not be taken seriously in the business.

Also important to the defense, Gus Searcy had knowledge of a phone call between Jodi and Travis, one that left Jodi shaking and crying. He wasn't able to elaborate, as hearsay objections by the prosecution were almost always sustained, but the point was made that Travis had said something negative that upset Jodi.

During his cross of this first witness, Martinez blew his cool; however, the reason for his hot-and-bothered posturing wasn't clear. Gus Searcy wasn't that much of a threat to the prosecution, yet Martinez started to pace and raise his voice. "You don't get to ask the questions, I do," Martinez scolded the witness during one heated exchange. Searcy, too, turned up the sarcasm and antagonistic behavior, saying he knew how to speak English when Martinez made the same point in slightly different words. At a hearing out of the presence of the jury, the two really went at it, when Martinez suggested Searcy was far more interested in making this trial about him, rather than Jodi, because he had an agenda of self-promotion. Eventually, the defense and the prosecution both finished with the witness, and Judge Stephens read the jury's questions for Mr. Searcy as the dust settled. She then called for a well-deserved lunch break before the next witness, Jodi's former boyfriend Darryl Brewer, took the stand.

Darryl specifically asked the court not to show his face during the broadcast of the trial, so television audiences never got to see the tall, very handsome man in a dark gray suit who took the stand. The wrinkle lines on his face and his slightly graying hair confirmed the fact that he was substantially older than Jodi, but his chiseled good looks were enhanced by a broad, charismatic smile. Jodi stared forlornly at the man she had dated exclusively for almost four years and who had clearly loved her. Occasionally, she could be seen wiping away tears.

Darryl had a gentle, gracious manner of speaking, markedly less confrontational than the previous witness. He began his testimony recalling when and where he had met Jodi nearly a decade earlier. As for her personality, he said she was never jealous or possessive, but was a wonderful, hardworking woman, who often held two jobs. "She was a responsible, caring, loving person," he revealed, clearly holding no anger toward her. He said she was great with his son who was only four or five years old when they met. Darryl, however, said they had no plans to marry.

Darryl described a marked change in the relationship, especially in their sex life, after she began working for PPL in the spring of 2006. By the fall, she became more and more interested in the teachings of the Mormon faith and she no longer wanted to be intimate. According to Darryl, she was now saving herself for a future husband, so they began to live apart within their home. Jodi said she didn't want any more cursing in the home, either. Not long after, Mormon missionaries began coming to the house, where they sometimes had prayer sessions. When Darryl was asked if he remembered Jodi's September 2006 trip to Las Vegas, he said he did. Pre-Paid Legal is not affiliated with the Mormon Church, but it has a large group of employees who are members.

There was never a formal break-up conversation between the two. Darryl said his ex-wife relocated from southern California to Monterey in the fall of 2006 and took their son with her. The nine-to-ten-hour drive north was onerous, so he focused on developing a strategy to get back to Monterey and closer to his son. Meanwhile, Jodi was changing and becoming less financially responsible. She stopped paying household expenses and, after the fall, she didn't even pay her share of the mortgage. Darryl moved north to Monterey in December and couldn't carry the mortgage past February 2007. The house went into foreclosure.

The couple left it open that they might get together again in the future, but at that moment, their lives were taking different paths. In fact, Darryl told the jurors that he hoped Jodi would be back with him after they resolved the house issue. They remained friends on good terms, who talked to each other once in a while on the phone.

Unfortunately for the defense, Darryl's rosy portrait of Jodi did not last.

On cross-examination, Mr. Martinez dropped a bombshell. Picking up where Mr. Nurmi had left off, that Jodi and Darryl were friends who talked to each other by phone, he asked Mr. Brewer if there had been a conversation with Jodi not long before the murder. "Isn't it true that in May of 2008, you received a telephone call from the defendant, Jodi Arias?"

"I could have, yes."

"Isn't it true that during that telephone call, she was asking you for a favor . . . for gas cans, so she could make a trip to Mesa, Arizona, you remember that?"

This time, Darryl took a little longer to think. Finally, in a subdued, almost embarrassed manner, he faintly answered, "Yes." It was eventually established that Jodi had picked up two five-gallon gas cans from his house near Monterey on June 3, 2008, and she had never returned them. But, more important, she had told Darryl that she was going to Mesa—key evidence of her planning.

Mr. Martinez proceeded to show Darryl some sales receipts for gas purchases made at two gas stations close to each other, and then put the pieces together. The state's theory was that Jodi had borrowed the cans, bought the gas, and traveled to Mesa so that she could make the trip without stopping for gas and leaving a trail. With the gas cans in her car, there would be no record of any transaction at a gas station. Perhaps more important, there would be no attendant to testify that he saw her in the middle of the night on the road to Mesa and there would be no footage of her on any gas station cameras. As long as she had those cans, she probably figured there would be no way to prove that she went to Arizona that night. This, according to the state, was evidence of planning, forethought, and premeditation in the calculated murder of Travis Alexander.

When Martinez exhausted his questions about the gas cans, he moved into the sex life of Jodi and Darryl. He wanted to know when it began, how often they did it, in what fashion, was it photographed, who was more aggressive, and a slew of other personal details. Darryl said he and Jodi were both equally enthusiastic, and that Jodi may have taken pictures of him when he was in the shower.

It was a chilling parallel, and taken with the rest of Martinez's well-constructed cross-examination, it was not a good ending for the defense's first day. Jodi, the self-described photographer, had taken naked pictures of at least one man prior to Travis—in the shower no less—and she had also borrowed two gas cans for a trip that would have taken her past countless gas stations no matter in what direction she was traveling.

The following day, January 30, the defense called Lisa Andrews, now using her married name, Lisa Daidone. Perhaps the state had opted not to call her as its own witness, in part because her testimony was expected to be so inflammatory against Jodi that Martinez may have feared it might be grounds for a successful appeal. This way, he got to cross-examine her and lead her to the answers he wanted. Mostly, it was her knowledge of Jodi's stalking, in particular, the tire-slashing incidents, that was so damaging. If she were to testify about them, the jury might conclude that Jodi had been the perpetrator of those uncharged crimes, even though there was no police report or hard evidence tying her to the incidents. Lisa became a defense witness instead, based primarily on an angry email she had once sent to Travis.

Lisa was a beautiful young lady, very composed, with casually combed blond hair and nice eyes. In the four years since Travis's murder, she had married and given birth to her first child. Lisa inhaled deeply as Jennifer Willmott began her questioning. Lisa was called as a defense witness because, during her eight-month on-again, off-again relationship with Travis, she had witnessed a side of him the defense wanted to feature. In hindsight, Lisa said he had not been abusive or that sexually aggressive with her and, in fact, it was she who had initiated their first kiss. She also thought they were going too far, too fast when Travis got an erection during a make-out session. However, when she discovered that he was cheating on her with his old girlfriend, Jodi Arias, she broke up with him. The very next day, she sent him an angry three-page email about her feelings on a proper Mormon relationship, which Willmott was introducing now. She went through the entire email with painstaking care, it being one of their most important pieces of evidence in their quest to prove that Travis wasn't a saint, but was a sex-obsessed cheater.

"Do you remember this email, where you were talking to Travis about breaking up and that it was the right thing to do?" Willmott asked.

"Yes."

"Did you hope he came to the same conclusion?"

"Yes."

"Did you talk to him about starting off the relationship . . . wrong?"

"Yes," said Lisa quietly.

"Did you feel that way because you thought *you* might have tempted him to kiss *you*?"

Lisa agreed, saying she thought it was too soon to be behaving like that.

"Did you talk to him about the fact that you were making out too long?"

"Yes."

"By making out, what do you mean?"

"Kissing," Lisa said with a small smile.

"Did you talk about how each time you made out, it progressively got worse?"

"Yes."

"Did you talk to him about when you used to make out with him in the beginning, you didn't think about sex?"

"Yes."

"But, eventually, it would creep into your mind?"

"Yes."

"Was that something you were not comfortable with?"

"Yes," Lisa acknowledged.

Willmott asked if she thought sex was on Travis's mind, too. Lisa replied affirmatively.

"Did you tell him that sometimes you thought he wanted you just for your body?"

"I did say that in the email," Lisa said.

"And that your kisses didn't mean anything to him?"

"I did say that in that email."

"That you felt it was a way for him to let out sexual tension . . ."

"I did say that in the email," she said with a deep swallow.

". . . that he had so much of?"

Lisa was becoming a little embarrassed. "Again, I said that," she said, subduing a crooked smile.

"Did that make you feel used and dirty?"

Lisa acknowledged that she had mentioned that in the email, and that if Travis truly cared for her, it wouldn't have been about passion and lust.

"Do you remember that you told him that you had previously told him not to grab your butt?"

"Yes."

"And especially not in public?"

"Yes."

"But that he persisted in doing it?"

"Yes." Lisa admitted that at the time, she felt Travis was not listening to her, acknowledging that she had asked Travis not to talk about sex so much, but he did anyway. She thought it made a man vulgar and unattractive to talk about sex as much as he did. She believed Travis was a virgin, and she told him that he'd get sex some day, but he just had to be patient.

Willmott pointed out in the email that Lisa had used the

words "immature," "insensitive," and "selfish" when she was discussing Travis's behavior. The same email still in evidence recalled a day trip the two took together to Sedona, where Lisa had complained that Travis was on the phone too much. He implied that she should be grateful. She also mentioned that he was being selfish when he wanted to have conversations with her late at night, and she was too tired to talk. Late night calls were the norm between Travis and Jodi but clearly Lisa, young and unaware of those calls, was unwilling to engage in a similar practice.

Nonetheless, Lisa said they got back together, mostly due to Travis's persuasiveness and persistence. However, she called it off again, this time because she thought Travis was getting too serious about marriage. The third time they got back together was even more short-lived. "Strange things" had been happening and, by mid-February 2008, she didn't want to continue the relationship, at least until Jodi was out of Travis's life. Though the jury wasn't allowed to hear the details, these bizarre occurrences included the tire slashings on two consecutive nights the previous December. Lisa suspected Jodi was behind the criminal mischief and was fed up. She also found out Travis was in touch with another past girlfriend, Deanna Reid.

To end her questioning, Willmott wanted to know how Lisa had felt after Travis's death, when she learned he was not a virgin. She said she had been "shocked."

At this point, Willmott turned the witness over to the prosecutor, and all hell broke loose. It began well enough. Martinez walked Lisa through her complaints about Travis that the defense had made into character issues, and Lisa agreed that many of them had been reversed after she had made Travis aware of her feelings. In her words, Travis had become more respectful, more attentive, and more gentlemanly after that. She even agreed with Martinez that many of those early complaints of hers about Travis being too sexual had been the product of complete naïveté on her part, as she knew very little about the biological process of arousal. In hindsight now, she seemed to feel silly that she had thought Travis's erection had been from sick thinking, not human biology.

Martinez also pointed out that Travis sincerely wanted to marry Lisa, and at that point he was doing everything he could to be the man she would want to be with. It was Travis who was trying to conform to what Lisa wanted, not the other way around. After they got back together, Travis was the one who stopped anything even remotely sexual, from hugging to kissing, from going too far so that Lisa wouldn't feel adversely affected. Even the third time they got back together, Lisa admitted that Travis never "foisted" himself on her.

"If he was kissing you, that was something that was welcome by you, right?" Mr. Martinez inquired.

"Correct," Lisa agreed.

"If you were kissing him, that was something you wanted, right?"

"Correct," Lisa said again.

"When you were in public, was it a situation where you would be glomming onto him, grabbing onto him, and hugging him?" Martinez asked, alluding to testimony where Jodi had been described as being overly sexual and inappropriate when out with Travis.

"No," said Lisa, more comfortable now that she wasn't undermining Travis. Martinez described the relationship with the analogy that they were like a couple of high schoolers, and Lisa embarrassedly agreed, also concurring that the email she had sent was along the lines of a "high-school maturity."

"In retrospect, do you think some of the comments you made were a little unfair to him?"

"Yes," Lisa nodded enthusiastically.

Martinez strode over to the prosecution table while rambling about what a proper relationship *shouldn't* look like, selected a particular photo from underneath another upturned one, and started to carry it up to the projector. "Do you think, in regards to everything he did to you, and how you feel, and in the circumstances, do you think in your mind, it is appropriate to take a knife and slash somebody's throat?" Martinez bellowed, slapping the photo down onto the machine. There were audible gasps and yelps in the courtroom at the unexpected grisly display.

"Objection!" barked Willmott, jumping to her feet as an autopsy photo of Travis's face tilted slightly back, bloated, gray, exposing a gaping wound across the neck, came onto a humongous screen and multiple smaller ones visible throughout the courtroom, but meant for the jury. "Completely irrelevant!" she exclaimed. Nurmi joined Willmott in a standing objection as they stormed to the bench.

The damage had been done. As Judge Stephens called for an immediate sidebar, the courtroom went into meltdown. Lisa sat stunned, her hand across her mouth. Tanisha ran from the gallery, sobbing, followed at the heels by a male relative. Her sister, Samantha, threw her head down and folded her hands on top of her head in a desperate attempt to hide from the image. The man beside her leaned over her to shield and protect her. Jodi hid behind her hair, which she pulled entirely over her face as she, too, appeared to sob openly, pinching her nose on occasion. Her mother and aunt, while not crying, looked stunned. Other people in the gallery also fled for the hallway.

When order was restored, Judge Stephens admonished everybody in the courtroom that it was imperative to keep their emotions under control. Martinez continued with Lisa along a different line of question, acting as if no disturbance had been created by his ambush. Nurmi would later use Martinez's stunt as the basis for one of myriad unsuccessful motions for a mistrial throughout the trial. He asked that the judge remove Travis's family from the courtroom to the witness room, where they could watch the trial on a monitor, if there were further emotional outbursts.

The next two witnesses were Desiree and Dan Freeman, the sister and brother friends who had taken two trips with Jodi and Travis, one day trip to Sedona and the Grand Canyon, the other a three-day trip to Havasupai Falls in the Grand Canyon region. Desiree testified first. She said Travis became quite enraged at Jodi on one occasion when they were all together, and seemed "over the top." She even used the word "shocked" when Jennifer Willmott asked her how she felt witnessing the confrontation.

Desiree's brother was next. In 2010, Dan Freeman had actually been considered as a witness for the prosecution as well as the defense, and he had even stopped watching the news about this case in the event he was called. At the time, he was caught in the middle, as he regarded both Travis and Jodi as friends. On the stand, he tried to stay completely objective. He testified that he had seen Jodi and Travis fight on more than one occasion, but nothing extraordinary. He and his sister accompanied Travis and Jodi on the September 13–15, 2007, trip to Havasupai Falls that started out with a fight between Jodi and Travis at Travis's house. Sometimes, he got the distinct feeling that Travis didn't want to be alone with Jodi, lest he lose his willpower and do something sexual he'd regret later. Dan reinforced that Travis was cozier with Jodi when fewer people were around.

The prosecutor objected to some of the evidence from the defense's next witness. Lonnie Dworkin, a computer forensics examiner who had examined various devices, including Travis's and Jodi's laptops, Jodi's cell phone, and Jodi's

Canon camera. He recovered video and images from all the devices. Most important to Jennifer Willmott was a photo of an erect penis that Dworkin claimed he had recovered from Jodi's hard drive. Because Dworkin had no idea whose genitalia it was, Martinez objected. Dworkin was allowed to testify about the photo but it wouldn't be displayed in open court until later in the trial.

Dworkin also found thousands of photos from Jodi's own personal Canon camera, including four that the defense deemed significant to the case. Three photos showed Jodi as a brunette with reddish blond streaks, date-stamped about a month before Travis was killed. The state was arguing that Jodi dyed her hair from blond to brunette between June 2, 2008, when she rented a car at Budget car rental in Redding, California, and June 4 when she killed Travis. This, said the state, was part of her planning and premeditation. But the defense was arguing, through these photos, that Jodi became a brunette at least a month before the killing. The fourth picture, curiously taken on July 12, 2008, just three days before her arrest, was of the gray "Travis Alexander's" T-shirt and the pink "Travis" panties, a reminder of what the defense claimed was Travis's possessive, controlling nature. The prosecution would counter that there was no evidence outside Jodi's questionable word that the items in the photo were given to Jodi by Travis.

Defense expert Bryan Neumeister, a thirty-two-year veteran specialist in video and audio enhancement, was called to present a much-anticipated piece of evidence—a recording of a telephone call between two people. One voice, the clearer of the two, was identified as Jodi's, and the second, a male voice, was Travis's. With the requisite foundation requirements met allowing the recording to be played, this particular phone call would soon become the sex tape heard around the world.

CHAPTER 18

EIGHTEEN DAYS

Would she or wouldn't she?

As the defense case progressed that became *the* question that hummed through the courthouse in speculative chatter. As each defense witness stepped down, the pulse of the reporters would rise. Would Jodi be next to take the stand?

The wild card in any criminal trial is whether a defendant will take the stand in his or her defense. A person charged with a crime has a right to remain silent from arrest through trial, and that silence cannot be used against her by the jury. But when self-defense is asserted, it almost always calls for a defendant to get on the stand and explain why the conduct in question was justified and, hence, not criminal. Jodi Arias was no exception.

From the outset of the trial, few people believed an outright acquittal was even remotely possible; however, Jodi could help her case if she could offer some explanation as to why the brutal slaying of Travis was not premeditated first-degree murder, and, perhaps more important, why she lied for two years before admitting she killed him. Beyond the sheer barbarity of it, the fact that she told three stories made her seem even more of a depraved monster than had she not waited two years to admit she killed him. By then, when her final claim, that she had acted in self-defense, bubbled up through the lies of the masked ninja story, it seemed not only desperate, but ludicrous.

Still, if, in spite of the past lies, Jodi could come across as sympathetic and believable on the stand, it could turn the tide in the case. Calling Jodi as a witness was risky, but it held the potential to reshape the trial and possibly avoid a conviction of first-degree murder, or at least the death penalty. Given the circumstances, either of those outcomes would have been a victory for the defense.

But of all the people to take the stand in any criminal case, the defendant has the most to lose and, thus, the greatest motive to lie—and Jodi was already an admitted liar. She had a lot to explain, and she needed to do it in a credible way. Everything about her would be scrutinized, from the content of her testimony to her demeanor and delivery. Jodi needed to make the jury believe it was she who was the victim. She would need to make a convincing argument that she had never planned to kill the love of her life, but rather had been the victim of her oversexed, two-timing boyfriend's abuse. If only she could connect with a few jurors, or even one, who would actually believe her, then maybe her life would be spared. There was no question that it was a stretch of epic proportions and a gamble, but Nurmi and Willmott rolled the dice.

On Tuesday, February 4, right after the lunch hour, the defense wrapped up testimony from two computer forensic and audio/video witnesses. At about 2:00 P.M., the attorneys approached the bench to have a private discussion with the judge. Judge Stephens gave jurors a break and sent them out of the courtroom for just a few minutes. Sidebar conferences and juror breaks were quite common at the trial, so the spectators in the public gallery had no reason, on that basis alone, to suspect that something extraordinary was about to happen. Once the jurors were gone, Jodi, dressed in a black short-sleeved top and white slacks, briefly left the courtroom through the side door closest to her seat, accompanied by the uniformed bailiff, probably to use the restroom. She came back in through the same door a couple of minutes later and headed straight for the witness box, appearing to be in a state of anxious, yet controlled, composure.

In an instant, the hum in the courtroom ceased, as all eyes were trained on Jodi. The atmosphere was electric. Her decision to testify certainly made her the exception to the mega trial rule. When it came to the biggest trials of the era, from O. J. Simpson's murder trial to Michael Jackson's child molestation trial, and the murder trials of Scott Peterson and Casey Anthony, all had chosen not to take the stand in their own defense. Jodi's moment had finally arrived.

Jodi's hair was off her face, her frameless glasses not shielding the apprehension in her eyes. Her life was on the line and, by anyone's admission, things were not looking good. Judge Stephens asked that the jury be returned to the courtroom, and Jodi Arias stood in the witness box to be sworn in.

It took no time for the testimony to stall. No sooner had Judge Stephens told Mr. Nurmi "You may proceed," and he had delivered his first question, "Hey, Jodi, is this a position you ever expected to find yourself in?" than the word "Objection! Relevance!" stopped the answer cold. It was clear that Jodi was going to be the witness of the day for a long time to come.

Nurmi began again after a brief sidebar conference. He looked directly at Jodi.

"Did you kill Travis Alexander on June 4, 2008?"

"Yes, I did," Jodi answered.

"Why?"

"The simple answer is that he attacked me and I defended myself."

That it was "the simple answer" was an understatement. The formidable task in front of Nurmi was to make it a *believable* answer. With that in mind, the defense attorney's line of questioning went straight to Jodi's childhood, the good and the bad parts of it. Jodi answered each question by rotating slightly toward the jury, looking from person to person on the panel as directly as she could. She recalled everything at home being close to ideal until about the age of seven, when her mother started spanking her with a wooden spoon. Jodi appeared to tear up at this memory, although no actual tears started to flow.

With that, and perhaps taking a page from Casey Anthony's highly publicized bombshell acquittal, Jodi threw both of her parents completely under the bus. She talked about escalating violence in the home, and beatings that would leave welts on her. She said her father was as much a party to the behavior as her mother, often using a belt to inflict punishment. Once, after he shoved her during an argument, she fell into a doorpost and was briefly knocked unconscious. When she came to, her mother, also involved in the argument, told her father to be more careful. Jodi said she became so tired of the excessive discipline and physical abuse that she finally dropped out of high school after her junior year and moved out. Also similar to Casey Anthony's case, the defendant's mother, seated supportively but helplessly in the gallery, had to endure every moment of her daughter's accusations. However, whereas Casey had let her lawyers do the character assassination for her, in this trial, Jodi was accusing her parents of abuse with her own words from her own lips, all while sitting mere feet from the mother she was lambasting. On occasion, Sandy Arias's twin sister would help Jodi's mother maintain her stoicism by holding her hand.

For eighteen consecutive court days, from February 4 to March 13, Jodi would return to the witness stand. After her first day on the stand, the judge ordered that the cameras in the courtroom could not shoot her walking to the stand. She wore a security device on one leg that was obscured by the loose-fitting slacks she always wore. Locked onto a knee, it would prevent her from running should she decide to make a fast move, and it caused a slight limp, which could no longer be captured on camera.

Jodi spent the first few days of her testimony recounting her relationships with three previous boyfriends. She began with Bobby, her first boyfriend and the person she moved in with after she left home. For the most part, she talked about him fondly, remembering how he liked dressing in eighteenth-century Goth. And even as she went on to claim that he was occasionally abusive toward her, her demeanor remained flat. They ended the relationship "mostly because of housekeeping issues," adding there was no lingering anger or obsessive feelings once they were no longer an item. While Bobby had managed to stay out of the trial vortex, never taking the witness stand, sources who had investigated Jodi's time with Bobby described the end of their relationship very differently, hinting that, as she would later do with Travis, Jodi had remained obsessed with Bobby for a long time after their breakup and stalked him.

Matt was another ex Jodi had once lived with. She was as cheerful walking through that relationship with Nurmi as she had been with Bobby. In fact, she was so soft-spoken that, at one point, Judge Stephens asked the jurors if they were all able to hear her. Concerning Matt, Jodi said he was kind, spiritual, and treated her well. Their relationship did include sex, but she loved him, so sex was only part of it.

After about a year and eight months, when Jodi learned he was being unfaithful, she confronted him in person, and the relationship was over. The ending was not heated or violent. Rather, it was tearful and emotional, but it was over. Again, the other side was never told.

Nurmi proceeded to ask Jodi about what happened next. She said she moved to Big Sur, where she met Darryl Brewer. The four years of their relationship had no evidence of violence or disrespect. Darryl, when he was on the stand just a few days earlier, had already corroborated everything Jodi revealed. On the stand now, Jodi confirmed that their main sticking point had come when she had found a new spiritual calling in the Mormon faith and had decided to be celibate until she found a marriage partner, a decision that by her own account did not last long. She also agreed that their breakup was remarkably simple and mature, despite their long history together. If one were looking for anger or resentment in Jodi's body language about any of these men, it just wasn't there. She openly and confidently answered Nurmi's every question, no matter how titillating or embarrassing it might have been.

Then came Travis. Because he was unable to speak for himself, Jodi was the only one in the relationship left to talk about what had gone on between them. Lots of prior witnesses had attested to certain things they had seen, or overheard, or discussed with one party or the other. However, they weren't in the bedroom with them. Even if Travis were alive, he and Jodi may have defined the relationship completely differently, as in every classic he said, she said scenario. Here, however, there was only she said. Jodi's version had little to no chance of being taken seriously because the prosecution had already established her as a profligate liar.

On the other hand, the portrait of Travis seemed hard to believe as well. Until this point, he'd morphed from man into saint, which wasn't realistic either, and the defense had the added obstacle of taking on Mormonism, morality, and hypocrisy as it tried to find a saleable story line in the torrid sexual landscape of Travis and Jodi. While the defense attorneys themselves may not have relished attacking the victim of such a brutal, angry murder, they had an obligation to defend their client. They knew Travis had been admonished by his church for losing his virginity outside marriage long before he had ever met Jodi. If there was to be any kind of meaningful defense, it had to build on the reasonable assumption that Travis was *not* absolutely chaste and pure of mind, while Jodi mercilessly cajoled him into the bedroom to fulfill her one-sided, insatiable sex drive. That scenario just wasn't realistic, and the defense would emphasize this point in its attempt to represent Jodi as best it could.

Of course, to those around Travis, the experience felt very different. To them, Jodi was slaughtering Travis twice, first by physically killing him, then by attacking his character in an equally vicious fashion, knowing full well that he was no longer there to defend himself.

Nurmi took no time in getting Jodi to talk about when she met Travis for the first time at the Las Vegas convention, moving her swiftly along to when they first had oral sex, which she testified was exactly one date and about ten days later. Nurmi paused so Jodi could delve into every minor detail, not wanting her to broad brush it for the sake of the jurors, who had sworn they had no opinion on the case during its exposure in the press. Yes, Travis had come into a guest bedroom where she was sleeping; yes, they started to French kiss when she had been expecting conversation or at most, minor kissing; yes, he started taking off her clothes; yes, he was in his temple clothes, but they undressed him together; yes, the oral sex went both ways. Nurmi wanted Jodi to let the jury know why she had been so willing to jump into sex this quickly. As one of Travis's friends pointed out, any born and bred Mormon girl who was asked for oral sex on a first date would have slapped the man in the face.

Perhaps trying to sound like a reasonable person, Jodi took some responsibility, albeit in a rather backhanded way. She didn't mind at all that he liked her sexually, and the way she described it, it would have been way more awkward to get out of it after a certain point of no return rather than just go with the moment, so to speak. They were two consenting adults, and even though it moved faster than she would have liked, she didn't have the will or inclination to hold back. Even assuming it happened the way she said it did, questions still remained about what aspect of Jodi's behavior had made Travis correctly conclude that she was the kind of girl who wouldn't slap him.

And so the testimony went, Jodi recalling incident after incident of sex between the two with a straight face, while the audience blushed and the jurors squirmed. The explicit nature of the sexual discourse went far beyond what even the most seasoned court veterans had expected. Jodi was very comfortable with Nurmi, so Jodi actually seemed more like an intern on a clinical assignment or an observer of sexual behavior rather than someone who had done the things she was talking about. Sometimes, she'd laugh, sometimes, she'd act more coyly, but she seemed to be dead serious. Her ability to recall detail was astonishing, unless, of course, she was making it up. After all, these episodes had happened years earlier, and she could even remember the kind of drink each of them ordered at a Starbucks on their second date, which, coincidentally, also ended in a one-way oral sex act on Travis. Jodi again said the feeling of attraction was mutual, but she was beginning to feel degraded.

Prosecutor Juan Martinez sat stewing on the side, but without any seriously dramatic outbursts. He knew he would get his chance. He would occasionally feverishly write down a note on his legal pad or lean over to exchange a whisper with Detective Flores, who was sitting beside him at the prosecution table.

Meanwhile, Jodi continued to follow Nurmi's prompts, discussing the spiritual toll the sex was having on Travis and her. She talked about Travis giving her *The Book of Mormon* and her baptism into the faith a month later. She explained to the jurors what her interpretation of chastity was, especially when she relied on Travis to be her guide. Her recollection of a night of sex right after the baptism, including the first anal sex of the relationship, outraged the audiences in and out of the courtroom. Based on frequent media surveys done throughout the trial, the majority of people following the case considered this story and many of Jodi's other sexual anecdotes to be a lie. Their opinion was that there was no way in hell Travis would do that on the very night he baptized her into his religion, no way in hell.

Jodi had spent a week on the stand when, on Monday, February 11, the attack on Travis's character was ratcheted up. If trial watchers thought the details of their sex life to date had been uncomfortable pornographic fabrications, the story she was about to relate was despicable. More awkward, Jodi's father Bill Arias was in the gallery with her mother Sandy. He looked tired and beaten down and always had on his now-oversized outdoor jacket, appearing as though he was just arriving or just about to leave. He tended to lean away from Sandy, rather than lean close in, more of a posture of solidarity. Jodi's younger brother Joseph was also present. The two were expected to be at the trial for the remainder of the week.

The testimony began with Travis's supposed Valentine's

Day gifts to Jodi soon after they became a couple in February 2007. One of the gifts, according to Jodi, was a package of boys' Spiderman underwear, which were ill-fitting and tight. She said Travis told her she was "hot" in them and wanted her to wear them in the future for "sexual interaction," the term Nurmi used. Next, Nurmi directed Jodi to a May 2007 between-the-sheets incident that Jodi claimed was their first vaginal intercourse.

Jodi explained, "I wanted to stay with the Law of Chastity, felt our relationship would be blessed if we followed that." Nurmi, followed up with a question, "When you went to sleep, were you dressed?"

"Wore cotton shorts, pretty high," Jodi answered.

Nurmi had another follow-up. "When you woke up, what was happening?"

"He was in the act," Jodi replied. "My first thought was uh-oh. Worried about spiritual consequences."

While there's no doubt they ultimately did have sexual intercourse repeatedly, a lot of people suspected this particular incident never took place, at least not the way she described. Not only was Jodi slathering it on thick when it came to her own spirituality, but many questioned how Jodi could remain asleep during the process of having Travis remove her shorts and penetrating her vaginally. According to her testimony, when she became aware of what was happening, she got out from under him and performed oral sex on him. "He began to quicken his pace. I don't know if I scooted out . . . He pushed my head under the covers." And why did she go along with something that she was now painting as degrading? "I just wanted to follow through," was her non-answer answer. She said no words were ever spoken about it, as she lacked the "moral courage" to bring it up, adding that they still spent the rest of the weekend together.

Jodi moved through their timeline together, their trips

to Disneyland, Huntington Beach, the Sacred Grove, and Niagara Falls. The problem with Jodi was no one really knew where any of her lies began and where they ended. She added more sexual details than travelogue tidbits but, of course, that was the purpose of the testimony, to show Travis's insatiable sexual appetite. She talked about them breaking up over the phone, because she had discovered that he was cheating on her, but they were still going on trips together.

"Why, after you get back to California, are you still willing to put up with this?" Nurmi asked his client. Jodi said she was in denial, and that the sexual interactions made her feel loved. Nonetheless, according to Jodi, they broke up on June 29, 2007.

After the breakup, Jodi moved to Mesa. She said Travis encouraged the move and had listed the positive attributes of living there. That, of course, was contrary to what Travis's friends said outside court—that he "freaked out" when he learned she was moving to Mesa—but, for now, jurors were left with the impression that Travis actually wanted her to be nearby. Jodi explained that they continued a sexual relationship, but that it was essentially a secret life, with no signs of affection for each other in public. She needed money, and he hired her to clean his house. An indignant Nurmi displayed a drawing of a woman in a French maid's outfit that Travis purportedly suggested via an email that Jodi wear while cleaning. Though she never wore such clothes, the defense strategy was to pile on as much questionable conduct by Travis as they could to prove that Jodi was his dirty little secret, and that he emotionally abused her.

"When you were cleaning the house, working as his maid if you will, did he ever express desire to have sex with you while you were working for him?" Nurmi asked.

"Occasionally."

"How did you feel about that? You're at his house, and he wants to have sex with you."

"It wasn't unpleasant . . . it made me feel good."

With Nurmi's prompting, Jodi began a lengthy list of "wheres," now that the two were finally able to have access to each other regularly, something that had not happened during the preofficial and official portions of the relationship. In addition to Travis's house, the clandestine trysts took place in Jodi's car or behind the bushes on the front porch of her house. Jodi testified that the porch scenario occurred more than once and was a sexual fantasy of Travis's.

"He wanted to drive up to the house," she began, "it was a more private porch, stucco column, a big bush that created a shadow—it would occur at night—drive up to the home, have me come out of the house, me give him oral, he ejaculate on my face, and he would drive away." She said they did this three times, and once, he dropped Toblerone candy on the grass beside her for a reward.

No wonder her father never took off his coat, in case there was a chance to escape and avoid hearing more of his daughter's kinky sexual history. Jodi even said on the stand how embarrassing these stories were to relate with her parents sitting in the front row. Nonetheless, that purported self-consciousness didn't stop the sex narrative from continuing—sex on the freeway in Texas, sex here, sex there, anal sex, oral sex, vaginal sex, and finally, after a day with so much sex that even the most prudish were desensitized, Nurmi brought it all back home to the boys' Spidey underwear and sex. This was where the story sank to a new low.

On January 21, 2008, Jodi said, she'd gone into Travis's room to retrieve a porcelain angel he had given her, and she'd caught him masturbating.

"I got kind of embarrassed. Kind of awkward. I was headed toward the dresser. Trying to think of something funny or witty. He started grabbing at something, papers. One of them went sailing off his bed and landed faceup near my feet. A photograph."

"What was in the photograph?"

"A picture of a little boy."

"How old?"

"Five-ish, six."

"Was the boy dressed?"

"In underwear, like briefs."

Jodi described being horrified, of running from the room feeling nauseous. Travis was calling her name, but she ran for her car. She got home and threw up in the bathroom. She discovered that Travis had left her three voice mails but she was so repulsed, she drove right to the temple center to try to collect her thoughts. Finally, she thought maybe she was actually saving little boys from Travis's advances because of her willingness to wear boys' underwear, that she was mitigating his sick obsession. Also, she thought Travis himself had been violated as a child, and this was his acting out. She might be the vessel that would swing his obsession away from children. With her as a pliant, flexible sex partner, he would be the normal, heterosexual man he wanted to be. When she was done with her story, much of it through weak attempts at tears, she admitted that she still didn't want to end it with Travis because of the idea that she was saving him.

With this testimony, Jodi certainly wasn't saving herself. The backlash was immediate and ferocious from the public watching the trial on television. Jodi's accusation that Travis had the tendencies of a pedophile made people furious with her, and they vented their rage by calling television and radio shows, and writing scathing posts online. It appeared that Jodi Arias had just surpassed Casey Anthony as America's most hated female.

What had begun as a critique of Travis's character and

proof of his involvement in their sexual relationship had metastasized into something far more grotesque. Like the suggestion that she had suffered abuse at the hands of her parents, this accusation had come out of nowhere. Never had she spoken about it in any of her previous interviews, and no evidence of child pornography had ever been found on any searches of Travis's property, physical or digital. One news producer noted the theatricality of her story, how a photo flew through the air and just happened to land faceup at her feet—just one of many convenient occurrences in Jodi's lies. There was little believable about her tale; yet the fact that she had the audacity to tell it spoke volumes. To hear such an extreme story from a source with so little credibility displayed an arrogance and a boldness that was disturbing. This was a woman who would apparently say anything about Travis, go to any lengths, in her quest for freedom. It was hard not to hear these extreme allegations about Travis without replaying Jodi's famous words to the media: "No jury will convict me." The same brand of assuredness that had led her to proclaim her future freedom meant she would stop at nothing in her search for vindication.

The courtroom gallery was aghast and incredulous, although the jurors, true to their oath, showed no particular reaction. Nobody but Jodi was crying. Travis's sisters, in their front row seats, shook their heads in disbelief, their expressions revealing their disgust over what the defense was doing to their dead brother's reputation. By the time the day ended, with Jodi testifying that Travis physically abused her by kicking her in the ribs and breaking her left ring finger, the sentiment against Jodi had coalesced. From that moment forward she would be universally despised.

CHAPTER 19

THE SEX TAPE

In the aftermath of Jodi's outrageous allegations of pedophilia, few thought that the defense would be able to top itself. As it turned out, Nurmi and Willmott were just getting warmed up.

The following day included a highly anticipated piece of evidence, salacious fodder for the trial junkies. There had been a lot of buzz about the recording that Jodi had made of Travis and her engaging in phone sex, and this was the day that the tape was finally going to be played. Judge Stephens spent quite a bit of time telling the gallery audience that the testimony they were going to hear was going to be more sensitive and sexually explicit than usual, and that any spectator in the gallery could raise his hand and excuse himself now, before proceedings got under way, if he thought this was something he would not be able to handle. Not a single hand went up.

At that, the jury was brought in and seated, and exhibit 428, the audio recording, was placed into evidence. The tape had been recorded by Jodi on May 10, after she had moved away from Arizona back to Yreka, less than a month before she killed Travis. She claimed that he had asked her to record it for him, but the prosecution believed that Jodi had recorded it surreptitiously. If Travis had wanted to record it, he would have recorded it himself on his cell phone. Travis was in Mesa, although from the conversation, it appeared that he was planning a trip to northern California to see Jodi sometime that early summer. The two were talking very amicably. Only if one knew what was coming would there be any clue to Travis's setting the mood. "Why don't we just talk for a little bit? About happy things and getting normalized for a minute, and then we'll see where it takes us."

"We'll see where it takes us. I like that. I like the get happy and get normalized part," Jodi responded, most chipper.

There was light talk about travel dates and upcoming PPL events. Jodi wasn't sure she could afford to travel to Washington, D.C., although she wanted to try. They both thought the upcoming event in Palm Desert wouldn't be worth it—too hot, too much drinking, too many soulless people. Lots of laughs and jokes were exchanged. Finally, Jodi managed to introduce something sexual, talking about something that had happened at Team Freedom.

"I think you grabbed my ass in front of [someone] in Vegas," Jodi said. "I love it when you grab my butt, but you only do it when you're trying to prove a point."

"You can't say I don't know how to work that booty," replied Travis.

"It kind of screams for attention, it sticks out," said Jodi. "You're an A plus."

"I'm not the tossed salad type, but I would do that to you," Travis blurted out, using a slang reference that denotes anal sex delivered orally, although it's possible he may have gotten his terms mixed up.

The mood was well on its way, as they complimented each other's past performances and—it would seem—his abilities and enthusiasm when it came to performing oral sex on her.

"You've chomped. Gone to town. All-you-can-eat salad bar," squealed Jodi.

"I went to town on it for forty-five minutes!" Travis said in agreement.

Jodi loved the memory. "Most incredible stamina I've ever dreamed."

"We've had two to three hours sessions any time—it's because I pace myself," Travis recalled.

"I don't mind receiving while you're doing the giving," was Jodi's response.

"I like you to play any role. If you handle me, I'll handle you," quipped Travis.

"I like being handled," said Jodi. "I will totally handle you."

Jodi sat in the witness box with her head in her hand appearing, at times, to cry. It was always possible that she was acting, but she may also have been crumbling from the humiliation of it all, actually feeling sexually sentimental, or some combination thereof. She, as well as everyone else, was hearing the voice of Travis as if he were in the room with them. Many people in the gallery were openly weeping. As for the reporters who were, by trade, trained to keep their emotions in check, some were still distinctly uncomfortable. They were being forced to eavesdrop and become voyeurs to intimacies that are almost never to be shared, especially not with a whole nation. The fact that this conversation was being broadcast on television, with a delay to accommodate any need to bleep profanities, was kind of mind-blowing. This courtroom was truly opening bedroom doors. So much for that old saying that nobody ever knows what goes on behind them. Then again, it's the nature of trials to reveal secrets.

On the audiotape, Travis and Jodi had gotten off the sex

track a little, but they were soon back in the moment. They tried to recall the time they had both been "injected with aphrodisiacs."

Jodi began by "trying to think of an example. I just pull you on the bed and start. I fell asleep and you woke me up by pulling down my shorts and licking my pussy. That was hot. I would have been content just sleeping with you, but you had another agenda."

"There are not many guys who would just do that," he told her.

"I don't know the ratio, but I get the feeling there aren't a lot of Mormon guys like that," said Jodi. "I would like to marry someone who'd like to be freaky . . . I have plenty of blossom time left."

Travis seemed to like where this was going as much as Jodi. "I'm going to tie you to a tree and put it in your ass."

"That is so debasing, I like it," Jodi replied.

". . . tie your arms around a tree, blindfold you."

"Oh, my gosh, you're full of ideas. We've gotten way creative in the past," Jodi urged. "I'm game with everything you come up with. You're quite the source."

"I didn't like the Pop Rocks as much as the Tootsie Pops," Travis recalled. Jodi said she had liked the bathtub, candles, and braids, and Travis agreed wholeheartedly about the braids.

"I want you to ride my face like a horse," he continued, ". . . in that bath, hot."

"When we are in that bath together, you are amazing. You make me feel like a goddess, so sexy, so hot. Oh gosh."

Things were heating up. "You *are* hot," Travis complimented her. "Seriously, baby. Start touching yourself."

"I am already."

"I just started."

"Imagine my hands giving you a hand job," Jodi said.

"Before I met you, I never jacked off. Once a month, every few weeks. Since you left, every day."

"Are you serious?" Jodi gushed.

"Fucking you . . ." Travis grunted.

"I wish you were here. We'd shut and lock the door, have a big fuck fest. You need to cum, I mean come here," she teased.

"I can't wait to jizz on your face," was the response.

"Yeah, definitely," said Jodi in reply to that idea, adding how much she loves having intercourse with Travis.

"You make me so horny, I think about sex with you every day. How it feels to have your cock deep inside me."

"Is it wrong that we started fucking?" Travis whispered.

"If it's wrong, I don't want to be right!"

"Jodi, oh, JODI!"

There was talk of "jizz" and "cream pies," and "jerking off"; lots of compliments directed at Jodi about being the "prototype of hotness," the "super woman." Finally, there were the climax moans, which for others might have been enough. But, true to the stamina each had already complimented the other about, they kept the sex going.

He said, "That was hot, like a twelve-year-old girl having her first orgasm."

"You make me feel so dirty," she responded, her voice dripping with pleasure. And, in an apparent reference to how Travis kissed her nipples, "I like how you suck on them like lollipops."

Travis requested an update, "Still touching yourself?"

"I am," she responded. "I like the way your dick feels. It's nice how you're smooth. I like putting my lips all over it. I really, really, really wanna suck your dick right now." Jodi's attitude on the audio tape was a really, really, really far cry from her testimony, where she repeatedly insinuated that she was a reluctant sex partner being pressured into oral sex.

Travis moved on to talking about "outfits." She thought clever role-playing would be that he busts her for being nude in public, and he gets to redeem himself. At one point, Jodi had to break away from the call, thinking she heard somebody outside her room, but she was back in stride in no time. More "dick," more "face sitting," some "horny toad," and a little "titty fucking" was sprinkled into the next few thoughts. By now, things were coming to their second climax, and sounded as such. Jodi would claim on the stand that she faked the orgasms heard on the tape that would live in legal infamy as one of the more pornographic bits of evidence ever admitted in a high-profile trial. Her explanation was that she needed two hands to reach climax and couldn't because she was holding the cell phone. Was she faking or wasn't she became a hot topic on social media. If she was faking it, there was a sense that she missed her calling; she should have gone to Hollywood and become an actress.

"Oh, yeah, huge! I just jizzed like fifteen pumps!" Travis exclaimed. Jodi had earlier received her superwoman compliment and she wanted to make kind remarks in return. "You are like superhuman, I hope you know."

Sprinkled throughout all of this was chatter about pictures and "a porn star thing" and camera angles; how his "dick" would be in focus but everything else blurry; how Jodi would sit on Travis's face and be the point of view of that scene. They both participated in this discussion and it seemed pretty clear that this was a story line for the purposes of achieving orgasm as opposed to an actual preproduction meeting.

A little minor sex talk ensued, when Jodi told Travis to go get cleaned up. Less than a minute later, they were back to ordinary small talk. They talked about movies, especially superhero movies. Travis wasn't a *Spiderman* fan, but *X-Men* was good, and *Batman* was okay. They talked about Vermont, Johnny Cash, and the Grateful Dead, considered by Travis to be one of the most amazing bands of all time. They talked again about the Washington, D.C., trip. Joking around together, they even hummed what sounded like a couple of bars of the national anthem, messing around with the lyrics. Finally, they sent each other off to bed with a cheerful good night.

When the audiotape was over, Judge Stephens announced to the court that there would be a very well-deserved break. There was an air of exhaustion and sensory overload; nobody could say anything that would top what had just been heard. It was as if a hand grenade had been tossed into the trial, and the spectators were left somewhat dazed and disoriented. Reporters struggled to put it into context, and it was unclear how all the dirty talk would impact the trial. Where some saw a home run for the defense that painted Travis as sexually obsessed; others felt it might actually benefit the prosecution because it revealed Jodi as an active, willing, and eager participant herself.

Perhaps most significant, there was the issue of why this had even happened in the first place. Why would Jodi record the most private of sexual intimacies? Speculation immediately coalesced around the theory that Jodi was creating a blackmail tape, a tape that she could threaten to play for those who thought Travis was chaste, a tape that she could dangle in front of Travis as a threat to use if Travis didn't change his mind and take her, Jodi, to Cancún, instead of Mimi Hall. Taking this speculation a step further, it was easy to see how the tape could have been the real cause of the argument she and Travis had sixteen days later, on May 26, when Travis angrily wrote to Jodi that she had betrayed him and was evil. It certainly made sense to those who'd been following the case, especially since Travis never revealed exactly why he was so upset with Jodi. When he had talked to his friend Taylor Searle the day after the fight, he had made it seem that Jodi's Facebook hacking was beyond acceptable, and that was the reason for the fight. However, Jodi had done that before. But if she had held the phone sex tape over his head in some threatening fashion, *that* would have made him livid. After all, if you're being blackmailed you are not going to mention the thing that someone is using to blackmail you.

In a desperate attempt to help police solve the case, Sky Hughes studied the contents of the May 26 text/IM fight and was struck by something Jodi said in response to Travis's fury at having been mysteriously betrayed. "There's something there where she says, 'I'll call my attorney.' Something in there like that." Could it have been that Travis told her she was breaking the law by taping him without his knowledge given that Jodi was calling from California, which is a two-party consent state, meaning both parties on either end of the call must consent to be recorded? Is that why Jodi responded that she would call a lawyer? It's interesting that Jodi also fails to mention—despite the considerable length of the argument—exactly what they are fighting about, which would also make sense if she was blackmailing him with the sex tape.

Beyond the headlines of the graphic sex tape, there was something deeper that troubled people, the haunting echo of Travis's voice. As the tape had played, Travis seemed to come to life in that courtroom. Unsettling as the tape was, it wasn't just about him revealing his darker impulses. It also showed him as a real person—not just a ghost—who loved to joke and laugh and even sing. When the recording ended so did the mirage. Travis would not be coming back.

The afternoon was taken with Nurmi reviewing and dissecting the contents of the tape. Pretty much any line that had been uttered was pulled out and gone over for context, for timing, and for interpretation. There could be no denying this was a critical piece of evidence for his client. The prosecution had painted Jodi as a lying, conniving sex vixen and femme fatale. Here was proof that there had been sex, lots of it, and very consensual. If nothing else, she wasn't lying about every single thing.

It took two more days for Jodi to describe the days leading up to her killing Travis. However, the climax of her testimony was when she described the minutes she and Travis were in the master bathroom on June 4, 2008—the minutes it took her to kill him. This is how she described it:

She arrived in Mesa in the wee hours of June 4, 2008. Travis was awake, waiting for her, as he supposedly knew she was coming. She entered the house through the side door, her usual entry point, bringing her small piece of luggage, backpack, purse, and laptop with her. Jodi described how she leaned against the door frame at the office entrance and watched him watching music videos, his dog, Napoleon, by his side, who failed to bark at Jodi's arrival. Travis, apparently, didn't know she was standing there for thirty seconds or so.

Jodi was exhausted from the drive. The two went upstairs to sleep. This was the first they had seen of each other in two months, since Jodi's move to Yreka. By the early afternoon on June 4, they were having sex. Jodi told the jury that they decided to try a little bondage, and Travis tied Jodi up with some decorative rope. Travis, she testified, unrolled the long rope from the bedroom to the bathroom. He cut an appropriate length and left a kitchen knife either on the night stand or in the bathroom.

Jodi had provided conflicting details when recounting this story to expert witnesses who interviewed her at the jail in preparation for trial. These details would wreak havoc on her credibility. At trial, she explained that Travis draped the rope around the sleigh bed's headboard and wrapped loose nooses around her wrists, but she had previously told an expert that her ankles were also bound.

She was naked; he was wearing his temple garments, which he discarded right before giving her oral sex. She wanted him to shave his pubic area before she reciprocated, so the bondage role-playing stopped, and they had more traditional sex. In breaks from sex, the photos were taken. Because Travis liked Jodi in braids, she wore her hair that way for the naked photo shoot. The sex went on for hours.

As Jodi told it on the stand, they were in his downstairs office at around 4:00 P.M. Jodi had brought a CD of photos from trips they took together and wanted to show them to Travis, but the CD didn't operate. It was scratched or had a virus. Whatever the cause, it frustrated and annoyed Travis. She was hanging with Napoleon on the floor, but Travis was getting angry. Everything about his body language changed. Jodi testified that he threw the CD against the wall.

Napoleon left, which was typical Napoleon behavior; he didn't like it when Travis got mad. Jodi tried to calm Travis down by rubbing his back. The next thing she knew, he rotated her around, leaned her over his desk, and applied his whole body weight to her. Trapped underneath him, she went along with him, hoping to calm him down. They were both wearing clothes, but Jodi claimed Travis pulled down her pants and, after a few thrusts, ejaculated on her back. Jodi said that she wasn't angry about it, as it had seemed to do the trick.

The two hung out for a while more, then Travis went upstairs to shower. Travis had just lost forty pounds, so even though he wasn't one who loved having his picture taken, he was up for some photographs of himself that day. For a few months, Jodi had been aware of his pending trip to Cancún. She knew that she wasn't his guest and, according to her, she was fine with that. She thought taking a few pictures of his new body would make him happy.

The day's evidence ended on that cliffhanger, but it had been another extremely long day. It was six thirty in the evening, and Judge Stephens dismissed the jurors until ten thirty the next morning. The next morning did not find anyone looking particularly refreshed. By now, even Jodi's outfits were being recycled through the jury box. She was still mixing up hairstyles, whether or not she was wearing glasses, but everything else seemed the same, same likely staged remorse, same head hanging in the same manner as the day before, and arguably the same fake tears.

Nurmi picked up his questioning where the previous day ended, reminding Jodi that she and Travis were about to engage in a photo shoot. Jodi said they selected the shower because of the water effect. They were also going to use Travis's new camera, as hers was already packed. He was the model, but she picked the poses. What she testified to from this point forward is the following story that prosecutors would later argue was a complete fabrication. She told jurors she was squatting on the floor a few feet from Travis. He was seated in the shower. She leaned toward him and reached into the shower to show him some photos, but the camera slipped out of her hands and hit the tile floor of the shower.

Travis flipped out, screaming that a five-year-old could handle a camera better than she. He then stepped out of the shower and body slammed her on the tile. Her story was already suspicious. Back in April, Jodi had blown the engine on Travis's BMW, and it didn't upset him nearly as much as the camera dropping apparently did. It seemed incongruous that a dropped camera would make him as maniacal as Jodi described. In her telling, though, this explosive reaction was just the beginning.

When he started spitting at her, she ran down the bathroom hall into the master bedroom, and pivoted right, straight into his closet. She slammed the door, knowing she could run out the other end of the closet. Jodi could never really explain why she didn't pivot left and out the door of his bedroom. Going that way, she could have fled down the stairs and diffused the situation or run out of the house. Instead, she stayed within the confines of the closet and master bathroom. She knew that he had a gun in there, and she stepped on a shelf to grab it from the top shelf. Nurmi got her to the most anticipated testimony of the trial. "What happened next?"

"I grabbed the gun, and I ran out of the closet. He was chasing me to the middle of the bathroom; he kept running like a linebacker until he grabbed my waist. The gun went off; I didn't mean to shoot him. It was just pointed at him, and went off. He lunged at me and we fell, really hard towards the wall. If he had been shot, nothing was different. I didn't want him to get on top of me. I can't get out of those holds. He's grabbing at my clothes, screaming angry. He said, 'I'll fucking kill you, bitch.' " He was calling her names like "fucking idiot" and she was crying, but he was still trying to lunge at her even after he was shot in the head.

How did he end up with multiple stab wounds and a slashed throat? The explanation everyone—jurors, the courtroom gallery, the television audience—had been hanging on for turned out to be no explanation at all. After she broke away again, she remembered "almost nothing." As Jodi calmly explained to the jury, after shooting Travis there was a "huge gap" in her memory that lasted at least five hours.

"Most of my next memory is driving in the desert," she asserted to Nurmi. Between the gunshot and driving in the desert, she claimed her memory was essentially blank. She had no recollection of stabbing Travis over two dozen times or slashing his throat. She didn't remember dragging him back to the shower. She had a vague recollection of putting a knife in the dishwasher but she couldn't be sure it was a memory from that day. She couldn't recall deleting incriminating images from the camera and putting it, along with Travis's clothing, in the washing machine. She didn't recall collecting the gun and the rope, and maybe the knife, to dispose of far from the house. Somehow, Jodi did all that without leaving a trace of the vicious killing anywhere in the house but the master bathroom suite and the washing machine, which she hoped had destroyed any incriminating evidence.

Elaborating on this elusive answer, she explained that she was able to remember the "feeling," but not the details. She said the feeling was "mortal terror." She recalled recognizing that she wouldn't be able to rewind the clock as she drove west in the desert, the sun in her eyes, the many stoplights, the sky getting darker. Somewhere, she threw the gun, but she didn't remember precisely where.

The anticlimax of her words was striking. After years of lies and alternating versions of events—not to mention weeks of testimony during which she had repeatedly vilified Travis's character—this answer about the "huge gap" in her memory was impossible for many to swallow. It had the same air of convenience as her story of walking in on Travis masturbating and the photo of the small boy just happening to float to her feet. For a woman whose credibility had been stretched thin for years, this excuse that she simply didn't remember what had happened felt more suspect than almost anything else she'd said. In many ways, this gap in her memory—what prosecutor Martinez would eventually call Jodi's "fog"—became a metaphor for her entire persona and a lens through which all of her testimony could be scrutinized. The same woman who could remember the kind of latte she purchased at Starbucks years earlier somehow couldn't recall sticking a knife into her lover's chest or nearly decapitating him.

Jodi said at some point before the Hoover Dam she realized that she had blood on her hands and clothes. She stopped driving and tried to clean herself up with some bottled water she had in the trunk. She knew that Travis was probably dead, but she had no clear memory of him being dead when she left. On fleeting occasions, she thought maybe it was all a nightmare. Driving in a daze, she finally got her bearings when she saw a sign: "Las Vegas, 100 miles."

Jodi said she knew her life was pretty much over. She couldn't call 911 because she couldn't imagine telling them what she had just done. She was scared of what would happen to her and her family. She was angry with herself and just wanted to die. Determined to carry on, she continued on to Utah, and her fifteen-hour visit with Ryan Burns and other friends before heading back to Yreka.

When asked why she attended Travis's memorial service in Mesa on June 16, Jodi explained: "I thought if I didn't show up it would look suspicious. People knew we were close." Through tears, Jodi explained that she had made a promise to Travis and it was important to her to keep it.

"Why?" asked Nurmi.

"He would have come to mine even if it was in Antarctica."

The night after the memorial service, Jodi said she lay in bed alone: "I felt like he was there. It helped me to know he was okay; that he was in a better place, that maybe he wasn't mad at me anymore."

Kirk Nurmi brought his direct testimony home by asking

Jodi to explain why she had created the alternate stories to Travis's murder.

First, Jodi was asked to explain why she told *Inside Edition* that no jury would ever convict her.

"Those were the bitterest words I ever had to eat," Jodi replied.

"Why?"

"You can't convict a dead person. I planned to be dead long before a trial."

"Since his death was discovered, you told one version of events in which you weren't there. In another version, intruders came into the home, killed Travis, and you escaped. Why did you then decide to *tell us what really happened*?"

"Objection!" rumbled Juan Martinez, offended by Nurmi's reference to what "really happened" as though Jodi was being truthful on the stand.

"Rephrase," said Judge Stephens.

Nurmi tried again. "Why did you then come forward with all these things you were hiding, Alexander's sexual interest, the violence?"

"It felt fraudulent from day one, especially when there were people who believed me. It wasn't an overnight decision by any means," Jodi answered. "I would rather have gone to the grave with it . . . By the time spring of 2010 rolled around, I confessed."

With that, Nurmi finished his direct questioning of this witness, and Judge Stephens summoned the attorneys yet again into her chambers.

CHAPTER 20

—— ❦ ——

JUAN'S TURN

It was on February 21, 2013, the twenty-first day of the trial, that Juan Martinez had his chance to go after Jodi. Everybody knew that his cross-examination was going to be confrontational and dramatic, offering none of the softball questions from defense attorney Kirk Nurmi's direct. The bulldog was ready, and he had a lot to work with.

Still, it wouldn't be a slam dunk for Martinez. One area in which the defense had been successful was in humanizing Jodi. She had come off as intelligent and well-spoken. Then there was the issue of the sex tape, which seemed to be something of a split decision: It had certainly gotten headlines and supported Jodi's claim that sex happened. However, it also proved that kinky sex had been mutually embraced. If Jodi was being debased by Travis, she seemed to be enjoying every second of it, which is not unusual. Entire industries are built around the concept of erotic humiliation, also known as dominance and submission or D&S, with the so-called subs enjoying the sexual roller coaster as much or more than their doms. Even if she was faking her enjoyment, that certainly didn't justify Travis Alexander's brutal death. In her testimony, Jodi tried to turn their sexual play into emotional and physical abuse. The sub wanted to be recast as a battered woman so she could claim self-defense.

As a result, in the previous eight days, Jodi had also introduced four stories of physical abuse at the hands of Travis, along with the stories of their salacious sexual escapades. It was prosecutor Martinez's job to tear those down and expose them as lies. Like many parts of her testimony, there was no corroboration for her allegations. At least two friends testified they had seen Travis losing his temper, and he had snapped at Jodi on occasion, but that was a far cry from physical abuse. There were no witnesses to substantiate any physical abuse, no medical records to support the claims, no photographs, no calls to the police, and no disclosures to friends.

As part of her campaign to cast Travis as the abuser during her direct testimony, Jodi had held up a crooked left ring finger for the jury to see, telling them that the day after she found Travis masturbating to the photo of the small boy in underwear, Travis broke her finger in a violent outburst. Jodi claimed that Travis, threatened by her discovery of his shameful secret, became increasingly hostile and violent toward her, to the point at which she had to kill him to defend herself. However, her story line was all over the map, with her tangle of lies repeatedly contradicting each other. While her defense attorney left those contradictions unaddressed, prosecutor Martinez couldn't wait to get at them and rip apart the cocky self-assurance she exhibited while lying. The question was whether Jodi would be able to stay human in the eyes of the jury, and keep all her stories straight under Juan Martinez's onslaught of tough questions.

Taking the stand, Jodi looked extremely apprehensive, with her hair straight down and the glasses she wore on occasion perched on her nose. That day her clothes were particularly conservative: a black tailored jacket piped with white, worn over a white lace-trimmed shirt. Before everyone stood for the jury, she sat with her head down and her eyes closed, possibly praying, until finally sucking in an enormous amount of air and letting it out with a sigh. With the reminder Jodi was still under oath, Mr. Martinez went right for the jugular, straight out of the box, on a very personal level.

He showed her a photo of her sister and her, dated May 2008.

"[It's] a picture of your dumb sister, Angela, isn't it?"

"She's my sister, but she's not dumb."

"*You* tape-recorded a conversation on May 10, 2008, where you said, 'I honestly think she's a little bit dumb.'"

"I called her dumb and stupid."

"Did I ask you that, ma'am? I'm not asking you if you love her. I'm asking if you indicated it."

The conversation Martinez was referring to came straight from the casual, nonsexual part of the sex tape recording. Martinez was throwing her off her game. Surely, Jodi didn't anticipate this question. If she denied saying it, she'd be lying since it was on the recording. But, with her family sitting right there in the courtroom, it was tough to have to admit she'd called her sister dumb. Perhaps Martinez was establishing that Jodi said things that she didn't mean. He was setting the stage to prove that this witness either lied about absolutely everything or betrayed everyone who loved her—or both.

Martinez operated at high speed almost all the time. He was hot tempered, which was quite a contrast to Jodi's cool and calm delivery. Sometimes, his aggression seemed unnecessary, so well-established were the points he was trying to make, but his tactics were actually brilliant. He started big, *Jodi was not truthful*. He would take no time to get to *Jodi was a person with a very selective memory*. She couldn't remember at what point she thought Travis must be dead, she couldn't even remember the murder; yet, minutiae about other arguably irrelevant events were exaggeratedly accurate. Martinez also skillfully managed to bring up Jodi's licentiousness by emphasizing that she was lying on top of Ryan Burns kissing him within hours of slaughtering Travis.

Jodi didn't seem to mind fighting back. The two went at it over her convenient memory lapses.

"Problems with your memory, is it a recent vintage?" Martinez asked.

Jodi sidestepped. "Define recent."

Martinez replied with sarcasm, "I don't know, since you started testifying . . . If it benefits you, you have a memory issue?" Then he added a question, his voice rising. "What factors influence your having a memory problem?"

"Usually when men like you are screaming at me or grilling me or someone like Travis doing the same," Jodi shot back.

Getting sassy with the prosecutor was most likely not a great idea. One TV producer in the gallery expressed what many felt when she said, "Speaking as a human being, not a journalist, I wanted to slap her. Why was she talking to him like that?" But Jodi's mission was to make at least one person on the jury take her side, and exploiting the prosecution's consistently aggressive style and barking tone was one way to achieve that. Their sparring became absurd. If Martinez asked: "Did you like it?" Jodi responded, "What do you mean by 'like it'?" Spending time challenging the prosecutor on word nuances came off as arrogant, but most likely, she was hoping that it would make him look like a bully.

Just as the defense had the sex tape in its arsenal, the

prosecution had a weapon of its own: Jodi Arias's journals. Jodi had been faithfully journaling for years. Her private feelings for Travis were written in her own hand, so there was no reason to believe these entries were anything but truthful. After all, they were supposedly written from the heart, for no one else's eyes . . . until now. Martinez took only a few minutes into his cross-examination to raise one of those journal entries. He used it not only to demonstrate Jodi's boundless affection for Travis, but also to undermine her various accusations against her lover, among them that he was a pedophile and had assaulted her, injuring her finger.

She had written in her journal on January 20, 2008, but the next entry wasn't until January 24. In between those dates, on January 21, she had supposedly caught Travis masturbating to the photo of the boy, and then the next day, January 22, she said Travis had broken her finger. Yet her January 24 entry began with "I haven't written because there has been nothing noteworthy to report."

"Did you write about significant things?" Martinez asked Jodi, coming from a point of reference as to when she had hurt her finger.

"Some things . . ."

"You knew you could write anything because it would stay private?"

"No."

"Take a look at the first five or six lines," Martinez growled, opening up the journal, which had been entered into evidence as Exhibit 242. "You wrote that?"

After a sidebar, he continued. "'I guess it's a good thing nobody reads this because I love Travis Alexander more than can be.' You confronted him because you loved him and you didn't want to let him go?"

By pointing out the date, Martinez managed to completely undermine Jodi's story of the angry, raging, finger-breaking Travis that very day. Jodi would go on to testify that she never wrote anything negative in her journals about Travis because of her belief in the Law of Attraction, which urged that one think positive thoughts.

With the deftness of a furtive welterweight, Martinez rapidly fired questions, taking aim at Jodi's sex life with Travis and using the sex tape to show Jodi was more than a willing participant. For days on end, Jodi had been insisting she was degraded and humiliated by the amount and types of sex acts, and made to feel "like a used piece of toilet paper." The inordinate amount of time Martinez used to get to Jodi's diary entry about "the Pop Rocks and the Tootsie Pops" was painful, but eventually the point was made that Jodi had written that she enjoyed the experience.

The interchange between Martinez and Jodi was fascinating to watch. It was hard to know exactly how well the prosecutor was scoring with every juror. Sometimes his point was so belabored that it was easy to forget the original focus. Jodi didn't mind toying with Martinez, either. She sometimes seemed to enjoy trying to help him with an excruciatingly precise question by being even more exact, such as deciding if journal entries in the same color ink meant it was the same entry carried forward to the next page. She'd flip back and forth, back and forth, deciding if she agreed. Several times, a few one-line zingers added levity to a moment, allowing Martinez a moment to pause from his ceaseless pacing.

When the day had begun, Jodi had been ready for the fight, feeling empowered; after all, she had been observing Martinez in action since January 2 and knew how he operated. However, as the afternoon wore on, she sometimes lost the flat affect that had been her façade throughout her eight days with Nurmi. She was definitely showing signs of losing control, as instances of smirking, contempt, and smug, feigned delight filtered through her composure.

Both sides had time to regroup over the weekend. Court resumed right after noon on Monday, February 25. Jodi continued to wear black, this time a completely black, scoopneck, long-sleeved top. The day began by dissecting Jodi's statements to Detective Flores on the day of her arrest on July 15, 2008. Prosecutor Martinez's questions bounced around from past to present to past again, rarely going in a linear fashion. It's a technique used by law enforcement to trip up habitual liars. Within a few questions, the now familiar sparring between the two resumed. Martinez began rolling the interrogation footage, and everyone present could see and hear the detective say: "A lot of details in this case have not been released to the public. Details known only by us and people who did it. One of the reasons I'm here, I think you can help us." Jodi's response to that was, "I'd like to help you in any way I can." Martinez pushed the pause button before addressing Jodi.

"Not true, is it?" he snapped.

"Depends on what 'help' means," Jodi replied, indicating she was no more willing to surrender a single answer this day than she had on Friday. It was certainly going to be another long afternoon in court. With truth, lies, and consequences on the line, Martinez asked Jodi which lies were true.

"You told us, the reason you lied was you were thinking about your family."

"Yes."

"If there's a good reason for it, it's okay to lie?"

"I didn't say that."

"You were concerned about your family?"

"Yes."

"Your reputation?"

"Yes."

"Thinking more of yourself when you were making this statement to the detective, right?"

"I can't say that."

Even the smallest points became the focus of semantic debate. Martinez was focused at all times. He tried one more time to get Jodi to admit that her use of the word "help" with detective Flores was totally self-serving and misleading. If she had really wanted to help him she would have admitted to knowing the things that only the killer would know for sure.

"Other than you, who would be sure?" he asked her in subdued frustration.

"God," Jodi answered after a quick pause to think it through.

"Well, we can't subpoena God, can we?" Martinez shot back.

Jodi even answered the rhetorical. "I don't think so," she said, turning to address the jury, as was her habit. Martinez's response to that was quickly objected to, and sustained, by Judge Stephens. Even spectators would know it was argumentative, and irrelevant.

The rest of the afternoon was spent highlighting Jodi's lies to Detective Flores about the crime itself. "The whole interview was a lie," was the way Martinez summarized it best.

The prosecutor was clearly getting annoyed at Jodi's evasiveness and attitude. Jodi slipped into one of her self-serving answers that she had contemplated suicide, and Mr. Martinez started to smoke through the ears. He told Jodi she really needed to stop talking about her suicide attempts, saying she had played that card many times. That, of course, brought up the definition of the word *many*. Juan Martinez then made an insightful point he would resurrect months later in his summation. Jodi conceded that her weak attempt to slit her wrists shortly after her arrest was too painful to carry out. The tiny razor cut to her wrist had "stung" too much. Martinez dove in: "Can you *imagine* how much you must have hurt Mr. Alexander when you stuck that knife in his chest? That must have really hurt, right?" Martinez was seething. Again, Nurmi's "Objection!" was sustained.

For the people watching the case from the outside, many loved that Martinez was scolding Jodi the way they wanted to, leading the prosecutor's star to rise fast in social media. Systematically, he was dismantling each and every claim of physical abuse Jodi made against Travis, claims that many felt made a mockery of battered women's syndrome and made it that much harder for real victims of domestic violence to be believed. Outside the courthouse "Juan Martinez for Governor" buttons and signs had begun to pop up.

Another area Martinez probed was Jodi's diabolical and cruel behavior toward Travis's loved ones after she killed him. Jodi had gone out of her way to offer condolences to Travis's family. She had the gall to send a bouquet of irises to his grieving grandmother coupled with a note reading "you are in my prayers." Not surprising, his grandmother threw the flowers away as soon as they arrived. Jodi sent an eighteen-page letter to the same grandmother on what would have been Travis's thirty-first birthday, July 28, in which Jodi explained in detail how two masked intruders butchered and shot Travis and how she had escaped. It was hard to fully comprehend the mentality of somebody who would butcher a man, then cozy up to his devastated family and feed them intricate lies on the premise that she wanted to console them.

The evidence against Jodi was overwhelming but, even by the third day of cross she refused to be rattled; if anything, she seemed to rattle the prosecutor, or at least annoy him. He would ask a long question, pause for her answer, only to have her respond with an "I guess," and get him ranting again. After one showdown, Jodi said she couldn't even remember the question. "I think I'm more focused on your posture, your tone, and your anger," she told her infuriated opponent.

It was yet to be seen if the seasoned prosecutor's theatrics were playing well with the jury. Some court observers complained that much of the testimony was going adrift from the brutal, cold-blooded killing of Travis Alexander and had a lot to do with showboating. Others said Jodi's disrespect of the prosecutor played right into his hands, showing jurors she was far from the pliant wallflower she claimed to be with Travis. She was revealing herself as a passive aggressive manipulator who not only liked playing mind games, but was good at them.

One area of cross that landed squarely was Martinez's examination of Jodi's infamous gap in her memory that began right after she shot Travis. Martinez pounced on the idea that her blackout when it came to murdering Travis was way too convenient, too unbelievable. Prosecutor Martinez showed just how absurd it was by explaining how Jodi deleted numerous photos from Travis's camera after killing him and how each deletion involved a complicated process, not the kind of intricate maneuver one accomplishes in a blackout.

The fourth day of cross began with sex, sexual aggression, sexual fantasies, and more lies. Martinez was not afraid to elicit details, so those attracted to the case for prurient reasons were certainly satisfied. Jodi was delightfully happy through much of the sex testimony. She seemed to take amusement in watching someone as clever, sophisticated, and old as Martinez use terms generally spoken in the bedroom. Not as amusing were the questions about the murder. Parts of the CBS *48 Hours* hour-long program featuring Jodi's early interview were aired. There she was on the courtroom screens, larger than life, spewing what everyone now knew were outright lies and doing it believably in the same calm tone she was using during her testimony. Someone might as well have been screaming, *Liar, liar, pants on fire*.

The last day of cross-examination was Thursday, February 28, and the twenty-fifth day of the trial. Martinez wrapped up his grilling of the defendant by focusing on the critical minutes in Travis's bathroom when she slaughtered him, and her bizarre conduct afterward as she tried to cover her tracks.

Jodi was in tears, or pretended to be, for most of the testimony. She was squeezing a tissue and sipping water for composure, but Martinez was relentless.

By this time Jodi rarely swiveled in her chair to address the jury seated to her right. She tried to address Martinez, but even then she often preferred to look down. Martinez relentlessly punched holes in Jodi's story about what happened in the final seconds in Travis's bathroom. The state said she ambushed him in the wet shower with a knife to the chest, then stabbed him repeatedly in the back, then slit his throat and finally shot him with the gun she stole from her grandfather. The prosecutor stressed what many of Travis's friends kept saying on television, that Travis didn't own a gun for Jodi to grab from the top of the closet. No holster or ammo box were even found, to which Jodi postulated that she thought Travis kept the gun unloaded. However, Jodi was still insisting that Travis body slammed her after she dropped his camera so she ran into his closet, grabbed his gun, and shot him as he came at her again like a linebacker before going into a fog. The prosecutor shattered her version of events with a simple question.

"How is it if you are shooting him [first] the shell casing . . . landed in blood?"

"It didn't land in blood," Jodi replied contradicting a crime scene photo that clearly showed the shiny metal shell stuck in a coagulated pool of red blood.

Prosecutor Martinez ignored her. "If the gunshot is the first blow there should be no blood?"

"I don't agree," Jodi said, ignoring the obvious reality.

There wasn't a detail Jodi had previously given that wasn't challenged. If Jodi said the camera bounced this far when it hit the tile, Martinez would point out how that was impossible. If Jodi said her head was facing south after the body slam, Martinez would point out that that made no sense, to know which way your head was facing when you were knocked out. He also said that Travis would never have been able to body slam her with one leg in the shower and one leg out, as she had testified previously. The holes just kept coming. How could she roll out from under him to get away? How could a man in good shape, as Jodi had described him, not be able to catch her?

"He doesn't catch up to you?"

"That's correct."

"There's a door there?" he asked about the closet.

"Yes." Jodi was crying uncontrollably or at least pretending to.

"Able to close it?"

"I slammed it," she managed.

"It have a lock?"

"Not that I know." The tears had no bottom.

"Ma'am, were you crying when you stabbed him?"

"I don't know," she sobbed.

"Take a look, you're the one that did this?" he asked in a tone gentler than before, showing her the all too familiar autopsy photo of Travis's back with the cluster of stabbings.

"If he is being stabbed in the back, he's no threat to you," he stated more than asked.

"I could only guess. I don't know what you're asking me," Jodi mumbled back, hanging her head and covering her face. But Jodi's oh-so-clever sidestepping had stopped working.

"Would you agree that you are the person who slit his throat from ear to ear?" Martinez demanded.

"Yes."

Martinez then confronted her with voice mails, a text, and an email she sent Travis in the hours and days after she murdered him. "There's no reason to leave a message for a dead man?" Martinez asked.

On June 6, 2008, at 9:58 A.M., she sent Travis the following text: "Hey, I need to know when you're going to deposit that check." This was a reference to the two-hundred-dollar check she had mailed him a few weeks earlier as payment toward the BMW Travis had sold her. The police found the uncashed check during a search of the house.

Martinez asked if she had sent that text as part of a cover-up. Jodi, crying again, said she didn't want to face the consequences of what she had done.

Martinez then produced an email Jodi sent to Travis on June 7 at 10:21 A.M. He asked Jodi to read it aloud. Through her tears, she started to read it, but broke down. Martinez took over. "Hey you, I haven't heard back from you. I hope that you're not still upset that I didn't come to see you. I just didn't have enough time off. It's okay, sweetie, you are going to be here in less than two weeks. We're going to see the sights, check things off 'The List,' and all kind of fun things. Oregon is beautiful this time of year. Yay!! Be happy!!"

As he neared the end of a five-day cross-examination, Martinez replayed part of Jodi's 2008 interview to *Inside Edition,* in which she said no jury would ever convict her, because she was innocent.

Martinez followed up. "You believe you're going to be acquitted because you came in here and told those stories." Jodi reiterated that she intended to commit suicide before the trial. Martinez shot back, "But you said 'I'm innocent.' Even that's a lie, isn't it?"

Soon after, Juan Martinez turned and walked back to his table.

The trial had begun the day after New Year's Day. The state presented twenty witnesses in nine days. The defense case began in late January. Jodi was the defense's eighth witness but, when Kirk Nurmi went to begin his redirect examination of Jodi, spring was around the corner. It was March 4, almost eight weeks since the start of the trial. As expected, Martinez had eviscerated much of her story, and Nurmi was going to try to rehabilitate her reputation by once again trying to elicit the human side, not the cold sociopath that Martinez had jack-hammered to the surface. Damage control was tantamount, and this was probably his last opportunity. Even though the expert mental health witnesses were waiting in the wings, Jodi did not seem like someone suffering from mental illness, who was so delusional she could not distinguish between right and wrong.

By this point, Jodi had been on the stand for thirteen days, eight on direct and five on cross-examination. Spectators were experiencing so-called Jodi fatigue. Perhaps the jury was too, weary of the same flat affect punctuated by the rare sob. If Jodi's testimony was anything, it was too long. The questions weren't particularly difficult, but often, the minutiae were tedious and circuitous, with the back and forth trumping the issues. Nurmi was no dynamo, but he hoped Martinez had perhaps made it possible for him to make Jodi a bit sympathetic. Four of Travis's siblings, sitting behind the rail in the front row and directly in Jodi's line of sight, would scoff at any attempt to elicit pity for their brother's killer. Their solidarity was as daunting as it was admirable.

Nurmi began by asking Jodi if she killed Travis, just as he had when she first took the stand a month ago. Jodi again took personal responsibility, admitting she killed him, adding only that she killed him after he tried to kill her. She had no intention of killing him when she arrived, she told her attorney, ignoring the now overwhelming evidence of her premeditation.

Nurmi tried to rehabilitate Jodi on a number of points. One was whether her bent left ring finger was injured during the killing or months earlier in a violent outburst by Travis. He displayed for the jury a photo of Jodi and her younger sister Angela from May 2008, that he said showed the injury to the finger. Nurmi also attempted to diffuse what seemed to be strong evidence of Jodi's jealousy. Then, of course, there was the sex, which was rehashed, realigned into lists of who initiated what and how many times this or that happened. With Nurmi's guidance, Jodi repeated the many things she did sexually, emphasizing what she claimed she did not enjoy but had done anyway just to please Travis.

A key focus of the redirect was on Jodi's journals. Several pages had been torn out, and Jodi explained she had removed them because her writings might have upset Travis. There was also her purported adherence to the Law of Attraction, an ask and ye shall receive philosophy of positive thinking. Jodi said she was determined to keep her journal positive, especially knowing Travis might read it. Explaining to the jury that she wanted to protect Travis, she said she deliberately kept her journal free of negative entries, like Travis's supposed incidents of violence or the alleged sexual act with the photo of the young boy, instead accentuating only the positive. To the overwhelming majority of the public who thought Jodi had made up the beatings and the pedophilia, this excuse about her journals felt like just another lie of convenience.

Still Nurmi soldiered on, asking Jodi to read aloud from a journal entry she wrote on August 26, 2007. "I love Travis Victor Alexander so completely I don't know any other way to be. . . . He makes me sick and he makes me happy. He makes me sad to miserable, and he makes me uplifted and beautiful. All in all, I shouldn't be wording this as if he *makes* me feel these things. It all originates from within. All of my darkness is the result of my own creation. It is the fruit of my thoughts, planted continually and without too much repetition."

When the redirect finally ended, there was only one more thing keeping Jodi on the stand: questions from the jurors. Throughout Jodi's fifteen days of testimony, jurors had submitted so many questions for her that the attorneys needed hours to review them. The judge told the jurors not to return the following day until midday. Meanwhile, the attorneys used the morning of March 6 to review more than two hundred questions and prepare their arguments for which ones, if any, should *not* be asked. The jurors' written questions had been collected by the bailiff at every court break during Jodi's testimony. The clerk maintained them in the order in which they were received. When asked by the judge, they would stay in that order. For the remainder of that day and half of the next, Jodi answered questions such as:

Why did you put the camera in the washer?

You told Darryl you wanted to abstain from sex before marriage. If so, why did you have sex with Travis?

What is your understanding of the word skank?

Why would you take the time to delete the photos off the camera after you killed Travis?

How is it that you were so calm on the television interviews?

Did you see a doctor for your memory issues?

Would you decide to tell the truth if you never got arrested?

After all the lies you told, why should we believe you now?

Questions the judge did *not* allow included: What was your reason for switching defense attorneys? Considering all of the lies you've told and admitted to, would you consider yourself to be a pathological liar?

After the jurors' questions were asked, Nurmi and Martinez got another round of follow-up questioning of Jodi based solely on the jurors' questions. However, those questions were broad, covering most areas of the evidence. For his part, Martinez took time to grill Jodi on her pedophilia accusation and whom she had told, possibly hinting that a particular friend was willing to lie on her behalf about Travis's attraction to boys. Martinez also had a Perry Mason moment, when he whipped out the proof that Jodi had three gas cans with her, not two, on her trip from California to Arizona and on to Utah. In addition to the two she borrowed from Darryl Brewer, a third one was purchased in Salinas, California, on June 3, 2008. Martinez also produced gas receipts from Jodi's gas purchases in Salt Lake City to prove that she had bought enough gas to refill her car and the three five-gallon cans.

The final grilling was about how Travis was first attacked—was it with a gun, as Jodi insisted, or a knife, as the state argued? Martinez wanted to know why she pointed the gun at his head if she didn't think it was loaded. He also wanted to know where the knife came from.

"Did you have the knife in your hand when you shot him?" Martinez wanted to know.

"No, I did not," Jodi replied.

"That means you needed to get it from somewhere if you didn't have it in your hand."

"I don't know. I don't know where it was," Jodi said. Many felt Jodi's entire rope bondage story was told solely so she could claim a knife happened to be within easy reach.

Which fatal wound came first, the stab wound to the heart or the gunshot to the head could be important to the question of cruelty, the factor that qualified the case for the death penalty. According to the state, the injuries sustained by the knife wounds followed by the shot were crueler. A juror's question following Martinez's conclusion asked why Jodi hadn't just shot Travis twice, rather than switch weapons if she was that scared. She explained that the gun had fallen in the scuffle and was impossible to find, and the knife was at hand. At the end of the day, it probably didn't make that much difference which fatal blow came first. Twenty-nine knife wounds and a shot to the head? That was beyond hellishly cruel in any order.

CHAPTER 21

WADING THROUGH
THE FOG

After the prosecutor's devastating cross-examination of their client, the defense had an even taller mountain to climb if they were to convince the jurors that Jodi Arias was not a cold-blooded murderer, that she had acted in self-defense when she had taken Travis's life.

In a bid to reach that summit, the defense paraded out two mental health experts, Dr. Richard Samuels, a clinical and forensic psychologist, and Alyce LaViolette, a psychotherapist and domestic violence expert. Dr. Samuels was called to explain Jodi's alleged memory loss at the time of the killing. He would argue Jodi did go into a fog, which he labeled "dissociative amnesia," and "post-traumatic stress disorder"; Ms. LaViolette was going to support the defense claim that Jodi had been abused, and, thus, was justified in killing Travis, or at least in defending herself. If believed, Jodi could be convicted of something less than first-degree murder or, at a minimum, save herself from the death chamber. The defense lawyers and the witnesses may have felt emboldened by the specter of the death penalty, telling themselves since Jodi's life was on the line any theory was fair game, no matter how farfetched or offensive to the family of the victim. What few saw coming was the monumental backlash that awaited them, a public outrage so intense it even sent Alyce LaViolette, the domestic violence expert, to the hospital reportedly with anxiety attacks after a public campaign was launched against her.

Dr. Samuels took the stand first. His arrival in court on March 14, Day 31 of the trial, was met with a smile from Jodi. Dressed in a dark suit, blue button-down shirt, and red tie, the balding, bespectacled witness appeared relaxed and composed as he settled into the witness box, pages of hand-written notes in his lap. The jurors also seemed alert and interested. They were finally going to hear from an expert witness for the defense, who would hopefully have a credible explanation for Jodi's bizarre and violent behavior.

Jennifer Willmott handled the questioning, giving her co-counsel Kirk Nurmi a break. Willmott began with the routine foundation questions—name, education, and credentials. Dr. Samuels had a Ph.D. in biopsychology and thirty-five years of experience working with people who suffered from post-traumatic stress disorder (PTSD), police officers among them.

According to Dr. Samuels, Jodi had been traumatized by the violence of Travis's death, which had caused her to develop dissociative amnesia (DA), a memory loss associated with severe trauma, thus rendering her unable to recall the killing. He said in cases of DA, the sufferer typically complains of foggy memory just after the start of the traumatic event and just before the ability to remember is restored. But there are times when memories are not even created so there's nothing to restore. That occurs when the part of the brain responsible for creating and storing memory is impaired, which he suggested may have happened with Jodi.

Samuels based his opinions on twelve interviews he conducted with Jodi at the jail during the three-year period from September 2009 through 2012, as well as psychological tests he had administered between November 2009 and January 2010, nearly two thousand pages of case material. He also used Jodi's media interviews. He rendered two main opinions: She suffered from PTSD brought on by acute stress disorder as a result of killing Travis and from dissociative amnesia brought on by severe trauma, which explained her "fog."

"How did you conduct the interviews with Ms. Arias?" Willmott asked.

"I always began by asking her what was on her mind that day," the psychologist replied. "I usually have my agenda, some areas I want to explore, and I will get to the those [*sic*] areas . . . You can easily tell what's most difficult for the individual, because they skirt around that particular issue, and that allows me to develop an approach later on down the line to finally get the information."

Dr. Samuels recalled that the first time he met Jodi in September 2009, she was still telling the "two intruder" story. "It wasn't until I confronted her about the truthfulness of that story that she admitted to killing him in self-defense," he recalled.

"Is this unusual?" Willmott posed.

"I've had patients that I've worked with who haven't told me the whole story, so yes, this is not at all unusual," Dr. Samuels said, noting that it is common for defendants not to tell the truth at first.

Willmott next asked him to speak about biopsychology, the study of how the brain functions. Martinez vehemently objected to the use of the prepared PowerPoint presentation that Dr. Samuels was about to deliver, as Martinez was entitled to review it in advance and was given no notice of it. After some discussion, Judge Stephens agreed to allow jurors to consider it, but ruled that she would not allow them to take a copy into deliberations with them. Throughout the trial the judge gave considerable leeway to the defense to pursue their strategy, and most legal pundits presumed it was to make absolutely sure she didn't give the defense a solid basis for appeal. The fact that the death penalty was a possible outcome seemed to make the judge doubly careful that she not give Jodi an excuse to later claim she had received an unfair trial.

A colorful diagram of the human brain was flashed up on the screens, while Dr. Samuels pointed out the area where memories and emotions were created and described what effect stress could have on the brain's ability to store memories.

"Do humans have any control over how their brains record memories?" Willmott asked.

"No," was Dr. Samuels's answer. To address Jodi's contention that she had been in a "fog" after the murder, Samuels contended that a person fleeing a scene was operating on "automatic." He maintained that while stress could render a person unable to control their emotions, it did not prevent him from fleeing a traumatic situation, hence Jodi's ability to flee the house and drive herself into the desert. "In this 'fog' people can even drive cars. It's entirely possible and actually highly likely that someone would not be able to recall anything about a situation. Or, if they do, it would be foggy or bits and pieces. But this is common, this is well known, and it's not really arguable." Martinez seemed to be itching to ask, *Could they also clean up crime scenes, dispose of evidence, and execute cover-ups?* But the prosecutor's turn would come.

Dr. Samuels emphasized that a person suffering from "dissociative amnesia," the term he used to describe Jodi's state immediately after the killing, may only remember bits and pieces, and even experience a sense of detachment, similar to that of an out-of-body experience. "Perpetrators of horrible crimes can also develop post-traumatic stress disorder for having acted as the source of the crime," he said, an observation that certainly didn't help his cause.

Throughout his six days of testimony, Dr. Samuels likened Jodi's alleged PTSD to that of police officers and soldiers, a comparison that enraged the public and did not sit well with at least one of the jurors, who would later ask if it wasn't true that both police and soldiers kill as part of their job and duty.

When asked why Jodi had not told anyone what had happened, Dr. Samuels explained it was "a classic symptom of acute stress disorder." He maintained that Jodi was in a state of "acute stress," a precursor to PTSD, on the night she killed Travis, as evidenced by the excessive strength she exhibited in dragging his body to the shower and her inability to recall the most violent details of the killing.

"What does that tell you when someone the size of Miss Arias is lifting up someone the size of Mr. Alexander?" Willmott asked.

"It would tell me that she is in a flight or fight mode," the expert replied. Dr. Samuels speculated that Jodi had lied to investigators as a way to cope with the trauma of killing Travis and that much of her behavior following the attack was associated with PTSD. In a description that made the Alexander family—listening feet away—livid, Dr. Samuels described Jodi as a "pacifist," and theorized that she likely could not reconcile her behavior with her personal beliefs, which may have been why she created a story in which someone else killed Travis.

In response to questions about Jodi's journals, and the absence of any mention of abusive behavior on the part of

Travis Alexander, Dr. Samuels said he was not surprised. "Some people go through life with a defense mechanism impeding their lives," he said.

Dr. Samuels explained that Jodi's heavy make-out sessions with Ryan Burns just hours after brutally killing Travis was "another way for her to cope with the horror." Sending flowers to Travis's grandmother may have been an expression of "genuine sorrow," according to Dr. Samuels but it was also consistent with behavior of an "alternative reality." He explained that amnesia can help protect a person who may also create an alternative reality to put distance between them and the horrific event in which they participated.

By the time it was his turn, Juan Martinez was more than ready to attack Dr. Samuels's opinions, which Martinez believed were all based on his blind acceptance of Jodi's lies. But before Martinez dismantled this acceptance, he first suggested that Dr. Samuels's PTSD diagnosis was severely flawed, obscured by his affection for Jodi. Martinez noted that the psychologist had "gifted" Jodi the self-help book, *Your Erroneous Zones,* by Wayne W. Dyer. It was Martinez's position that Dr. Samuels had compromised his objectivity as an expert by crossing the line into therapy. "There is a code of ethics that prohibits you from providing gifts to the defendant," Martinez barked. "Isn't it true you provided the book to her because she was depressed?"

"For her low self-esteem," replied Dr. Samuels, denying that the nine-dollar book he purchased for Jodi on Amazon. com was a gift. He said he had sent it to her because she was contemplating suicide, and he knew she could not get the book on her own. He vehemently denied giving Jodi "therapy," explaining that he had informed her lawyers of her suicidal ideations. He also denied being in Jodi's thrall, despite Jodi's now established reputation for turning on the charm with men, as she clearly tried to do with Detective Flores in her interrogation tapes, where she tossed her hair and stretched seductively.

Going after Samuels's methodology, Martinez also suggested that anything gleaned from the tests for PTSD was completely unreliable. He administered them to Jodi in January 2010 when she was still adhering to the two-intruder story. In other words, he was building his diagnosis on the framework of her outright lies. Dr. Samuels had concluded at the time that she *witnessed* the trauma—the murder of Travis—and suffered from PTSD as a result. In a stunning admission, Samuels was forced to acknowledge that, even though he later learned she had lied to him and that she committed the killing herself, he did not re-administer the tests. It was a jaw-dropping lapse that had people in the gallery looking at each other with raised eyebrows.

"All the answers here are based on a non-sexual assault by a stranger," Martinez steamed. After a prolonged, heated back-and-forth, Dr. Samuels finally agreed that he had erred and should have repeated the test after Jodi changed her story.

Martinez ripped into Dr. Samuels about other lies from Jodi that he ignored or failed to include in his written report, mostly in the sexual arena. Jodi had told him that Travis was the only man she had ever had anal sex with, which was a lie; it had been established earlier in the trial that she'd had anal sex with Darryl Brewer. Martinez also pointed out that Jodi's description to Dr. Samuels of being bound at both the wrists and the ankles in the hours before she killed Travis was not consistent with her testimony, where she had said only her wrists were loosely bound. It was also inconsistent with the nude photos taken the day of the murder, in which there was no evidence of rope on the bed.

Another inconsistency that Martinez raised was a detail

that Jodi gave Dr. Samuels about the killing. She had told Dr. Samuels that Travis "was pulling at her sweater while chasing her into the closet." On the stand, Jodi told the jury that once she ran into the closest, she slammed the door shut. Surely, she could not have done that *and* retrieve a gun from the top shelf if Travis was so close that he was pulling on her sweater. Finally, Jodi had told Dr. Samuels that there were many pictures of women's breasts on Travis's computer, which was yet another lie. Police found no such photos in their thorough search.

"So it's not important to you that the defendant lied to you?" Martinez wanted to know.

"These inconsistencies did not affect my opinion," Dr. Samuels responded.

"Generally speaking, if an individual lies to you about something that you consider insignificant, no harm no foul?"

"The presence or absence of breasts . . . I did not see the need to pursue it any further. I didn't see it as relevant . . . it was my judgment call not to include it."

Martinez railed into Dr. Samuels for failing to corroborate Jodi's stories with the facts, after she had consistently demonstrated a pattern of lying. His home run was the doctor's failure to retest Jodi after she changed the story to self-defense. Martinez also accused the doctor of upping Jodi's score on her post-traumatic stress diagnostic test. After misplacing some test papers, the doctor rescored the test and gave Jodi a higher score.

"I scored it twice," Samuels admitted.

"That's a change, right?" Martinez drove home.

"That's a change," Samuels concurred, adding that with either score Jodi still met the criteria for PTSD. But the damage had been done—the witness had effectively been disarmed.

Even though many court observers thought Samuels had

gotten cut to shreds, jurors could be seen stuffing their questions into the basket throughout his testimony, and it would take an entire court day to answer them. When he was finally done, Dr. Samuels had been on the stand longer than anyone except Jodi. He had made his first appearance on March 14, trial day thirty-one, and now it was March 25, the thirty-sixth day of the trial. It had been an exhausting stretch, and his relief at being dismissed was palpable.

Through it all, Jodi sat fiddling at the defense table. Jodi seemed to relish the experts; they were here for her, supporting her side of the story with technical terms and educated assumptions, while their presence validated her and stroked her ego. They were even willing to fall on the sword of Juan Martinez to do so. For a very limited amount of time, Jodi could fantasize that she was understood and was even winning. Dressed in a brown shirt beneath an ivory V-neck sweater, she appeared pleased to see the next defense witness, a domestic violence expert with a national reputation.

Alyce LaViolette was a psychotherapist who was in court to support Jodi's claims of abuse. Until this trial, LaViolette had a great reputation as an advocate for abused women. Her lengthy and impressive résumé spanned twenty pages and included lists of her projects—both paid and volunteer—on behalf of victims of spousal abuse. One of her initiatives, *Alternatives to Violence,* was one of the first programs in the United States for men who were abusing their domestic partners. LaViolette had developed domestic violence training programs for the Departments of Children and Family Services in both Los Angeles and Orange County, California, had published numerous articles on the topic, and had received awards for her work on behalf of women. What's unclear is whether she initially knew she was risking her reputation by taking the stand in support of the defendant in a case that had become increasingly emotionally charged as the testimony progressed.

Testifying at the *State of Arizona v. Jodi Ann Arias* trial would not be her first time in the witness box. She had occasionally served as an expert witness in both criminal and civil court. She had first been contacted by Jodi's attorneys in September 2011, after Jodi had claimed she had killed Travis in self-defense, in a "justifiable murder." Jodi's attorneys had wanted LaViolette to establish that, at the hands of Travis, Jodi was an abused woman, and thus she believed her life was in imminent danger. The plan was to make it seem reasonable for Jodi to believe the words Travis allegedly spoke in the bathroom—"I'm gonna fucking kill you"—while supposedly lunging at her. However, it was unclear whether LaViolette truly understood the stakes at play in the trial. By putting herself in the position of defending a habitual liar, she ran a risk—to herself professionally and to the cause she'd spent a lifetime supporting—and in the process she would soon be accused of betraying the millions of genuine victims of domestic violence.

LaViolette was not a psychologist, so she was not licensed to administer psychological tests. She reached her conclusion that Jodi was abused by analyzing the defendant's journals, as well as a few of Travis's. She had also examined some of their texts, emails, and IM exchanges and the statements Jodi had made to authorities. Finally, she and Jodi had spent more than forty-four hours in private conversation, and she would use those conversations as well.

LaViolette was going to run into a lot of the same problems that tripped up the witness before her, Richard Samuels. Critics say like Samuels, she, too, had bought hook, line, and sinker into the sex, lies, and audiotapes propagated as the truth by Jodi. Juan Martinez, aware of where she was going, was already chomping at the bit to grill her. Alyce took the stand on the afternoon of Day 36, March 25, looking confident in a bright blue blazer, her gray hair trimmed short. She may have later rued the day.

After being sworn in, the middle-aged professional took her place in the witness box. Soon she was giving the jury a tutorial in domestic violence using a chart called the "Continuum of Aggression and Abuse," a tool she had developed that she used in her assessment of domestic violence. She broke down her continuum into five columns, each labeled with a type of domestic abuse, increasing in severity from left to right. They are: "Common Couple Argument," "High Conflict," "Abuse," "Battering," and "Terrorism."

LaViolette spent nearly two days defining a range of abusive behavior exhibited at each level. She also laid out the basics of "what is a battered woman?" and "why someone battered would stay."

"When someone who loves us is tearing us apart, nothing hurts worse than that," she said. It wasn't until her third day of testimony that LaViolette started to apply her continuum to Jodi and Travis, and according to her, the most severe that seemed to apply to them was the third column, "Abuse," considered low-level domestic violence, although she would testify to some characteristics at the next level, "Battering." There was some corroborative evidence of severe name calling in late May 2008, which LaViolette said was character assassination, but there were extenuating circumstances that LaViolette apparently didn't consider. Beyond that, it was all Jodi's word and her word just didn't count for much. On television, there was a lot of debate over whether in treating Jodi like a truth teller this witness threatened her own credibility in a big way.

Willmott first asked the witness what she knew about Jodi's childhood.

"I learned that in Jodi's family there was a certain amount of physical discipline, some, which I would consider went over the line and some that didn't . . . when you leave welts on a child, and that was information that I was given, that they were hit with spoons . . . between Jodi's mother and father. Jodi's father was controlling and manipulative and made derogatory statements if her mother gained weight . . . he was jealous and didn't want [Jodi's mother] to spend time with family members, particularly her sisters," LaViolette reported, saying she had found support for this description of Jodi's father in statements from some family members. Given the lack of other corroboration of Jodi's claims, one has to wonder if some members of Jodi's family were inclined to try to lend support to her claim of abuse because her life was on the line.

LaViolette also said that she read interviews with Jodi's family members, and according to her, Jodi's father had supposedly made sexually inappropriate comments to Jodi about her breasts and butt. "He would talk about Jodi's body, about her boobs being too small, her friend had a smaller booty than she did," LaViolette recounted.

According to LaViolette, Jodi also explained that her mother had taught her to stay in a relationship, even if it wasn't what she wanted. "Through thick and thin," LaViolette said. She added that Jodi's grandparents believed that Jodi had issues with her mother, because Sandy Arias had not protected her daughter from her father.

The defense expert next described Jodi and Travis's first meeting at the PPL conference in Las Vegas. "He pursued her and it was pretty exciting, and I believe that was when he told her that he was Mormon and she was very impressed with the family values of the Mormon faith . . . she was very disappointed that she wasn't married and didn't have children," she said, remarking on the "power difference" between the two. "When someone has power, when someone is a high roller, when someone is prestigious in their faith, when someone courts you and woos you and pulls you into a situation, there's a power difference." LaViolette had already told the jurors that when she does couples counseling she looks for power differences. That dynamic can foster abuse, and she had found such an imbalance between Jodi and Travis.

Jodi was in the market for a husband when she met Travis, LaViolette recounted. At first the relationship had not been abusive, but Jodi was particularly vulnerable around the time she met him, having just gotten out of a long-term relationship and wanting to please Travis. LaViolette opined that may have been why she didn't say no to the oral sex that first weekend at the Hugheses' house, accepting the story as Jodi had painted it.

"I think that one of the things that happens is, for many young women it is very difficult to say no, especially if they're attracted to someone . . . when they feel pressured, they're not sure how to stand up for themselves. This certainly isn't every woman. I'm not trying to say that at all. But when you're a more vulnerable woman, when you're not an assertive woman and maybe when your boundaries aren't good, you're much more likely," the defense expert suggested. Given that the court and the country had just watched Jodi go toe to toe with one of the toughest prosecutors in anyone's memory, this statement struck some as absurd. It didn't fit that Jodi could be so dismissive and insolent with the prosecutor and still be considered non-assertive.

LaViolette weighed in on Jodi's spirituality. "Ms. Arias's baptism was very important to her," LaViolette said. Jodi told her it was extraordinarily special to her that Travis baptized her personally. They were sharing a spiritual experience, and it demonstrated a connection between the two, she said. Some journalists taking notes began to squirm, as they had been studying Jodi for months, a couple of them for years. Perhaps this expert would have fared better had she given Jodi a lie detector test first. Her wide-eyed acceptance of Jodi's stories rankled not just the Alexander family but even some reporters and TV producers who found her analysis wildly naïve or perhaps even willfully naïve.

LaViolette explained how Jodi told her that she and Travis engaged in anal sex after the baptism, something Travis's friends doubt occurred on such a sacred day. "The conflict is, there is sex and she's now part of that. She's in a sexual relationship, she's not supposed to be sexual in the same way, but she's got a spiritual mentor who's telling her that the sex isn't so bad and they can do this and so she's now implicated, she's now part of it," she said.

The next piece of testimony was a potential bombshell for the defense, perhaps the biggest yet. The prosecution had tried to keep the email exchange between Travis and his best friends, Chris and Sky Hughes, in January 2007 out of evidence. LaViolette said the exchange pointed to a pattern of Travis's emotional abuse of women. Although the jury would not see and read the actual email, the judge did allow LaViolette to paraphrase it.

Sky had written that Travis had issues with women, and if her sister wanted to date Travis she would forbid it. "There was reference to a particular woman and his manipulation of that woman," LaViolette recalled. "There was information about Mr. Alexander calling Ms. Arias a skank and then acting like it was a joke. There was information about the way he ignored her in public places and would not allow her to put pictures of them up in places where other people could see them. Just basic ways he treated her, or they felt he mistreated her . . . that they indicated were abusive, that he called rough around the edges and they called abusive."

When testimony resumed the following day, LaViolette picked up where she had left off the day before. There was no doubt in her opinion that Jodi's relationship with Travis fit the pattern of an abuse victim and abuser. First, the Hugheses suggested in January 2007 that she "move out of the relationship" with Travis based on his history with women. Then, six months later, Jodi discovered he was cheating on her. Still, she held out hope that they'd be together forever one day. LaViolette described Travis as "jealous, controlling, deceptive, and manipulative" and theorized the abuse escalated over the course of their relationship.

From Jodi's testimony, the jury was already familiar with Jodi's four claims of physical abuse at the hands of Travis, but LaViolette walked through them all once more—from the first occasion in October 2007, when, after a terrific argument, she said he shoved her, pushing her to her knees, to the last encounter in April of 2008, when he purportedly choked her until she nearly lost consciousness after she claimed she handed him a mental health services pamphlet to address his supposed affinity for boys. After itemizing these examples of supposed abuse LaViolette put forth an explanation for Jodi's overkill of Travis. "When somebody is defending their life, I think sometimes people do more than they need to do," she explained at one point during her testimony.

What many found flawed about her assessment was her uncritical assumption that Jodi had been truthful when she had detailed a handful of violent encounters with Travis. Critics complained that she simply accepted Jodi's words as the truth; even when Travis's own words offered stunning clues that there was another side of the story, LaViolette refused to wade into territory that might shatter her pat theories.

Case in point, LaViolette concluded that Travis had committed character assassination against Jodi, particularly on

May 26, 2008, during Travis and Jodi's now infamous text and instant message argument nine days before she killed him. On that day Travis berated Jodi relentlessly, calling her a "freaking whore, cheap whore, corrupted carcass, and a three-hole wonder," said LaViolette, referring to his sixteen-page instant message diatribe. He had called her names before, but never as angrily as on May 26. The defense got LaViolette to read some of the text and instant messages out loud. Travis had called Jodi a "sociopath" and "evil" and said to her "you are sick and you have scammed me."

What went unsaid in LaViolette's testimony, and indeed the whole trial, was speculation about what had caused Travis to get so upset. Travis's friends had studied his comments during this fight and had come up with their plausible theory about why he would tell Jodi "You have betrayed me worse than any example I could conjur [*sic*]," without mentioning exactly how she had betrayed him. To them, the fact that Travis never clearly says what he was so upset about is telling. Since Jodi had broken into his social media accounts before, it was unlikely that another hacking would have provoked such intense indignation. Only something new, it seems, would have sparked the kind of anger he displayed during this exchange.

One wonders if the defense experts had stopped to ponder the very real possibility that Jodi had informed Travis that she had a tape with his voice, clear as day, indulging in sexual fantasies that would have given his Bishop a coronary. The speculation made sense. After all, it was never made clear why Jodi recorded that sex tape in the first place or whom she intended to play it for. Given that Jodi was clearly capable of slitting someone's throat ear to ear, it seemed equally possible that she was capable of saying, *Hey, Travis, are you sure you don't want to take me to Cancún as your date, instead of Mimi Hall? I have something that just might convince you to change your mind. Mimi or Lisa or Deanna or the Bishop would certainly be shocked to hear this. Listen.* A threat like that certainly would have justified Travis's response when—hurt, angry, and betrayed—he told Jodi, "You are the worst thing that has ever happened to me," adding that he wanted nothing ever to do with her again. With everything that the American public knew about Jodi's life, none of this seemed like a stretch. Neither did the fact that two days after this fight erupted over texts and instant messages, the burglary at Jodi's grandfather's home occurred, a burglary that resulted in a "stolen" gun of the exact same caliber as the bullet that was found in the head of Travis Alexander.

While Martinez would say that this argument between Jodi and Travis was the spark that triggered Jodi's murder plot, the speculation about blackmail would not come up at trial. Martinez and his trusty detective had likely toyed with the blackmail scenario as a possibility, among others, but Juan Martinez would never be able to argue it in any kind of formal setting. Nevertheless, the prosecutor had other tricks up his sleeve.

On cross-examination, Martinez dove into battle. He took direct aim at a keynote address LaViolette had given a couple of years earlier titled "Was Snow White a Battered Woman?" It sure sounded like LaViolette was making the claim that the fairy tale character was a victim of domestic violence. LaViolette defended her keynote by repeatedly telling Martinez that it was just a catchy title. Martinez basically accused LaViolette of being able to take any woman's relationship and call her a battered woman, insisting she twisted the facts to fit the ends and had a totally one-sided view of the case. At one time during a heated exchange,

LaViolette didn't answer the question, but instead responded with a question for Martinez:

"Mr. Martinez, are you angry with me?"

The question drew laughter from the gallery but, at that moment, it was as though LaViolette was no longer a witness but rather a therapist assessing the angry man before her. Another time, when she felt particularly badgered, she told him that if he were a member of her group therapy, she would give him a "time-out." The judge admonished her for her disrespect of the court.

One of the battles between Martinez and LaViolette was over her unwillingness to concede that Travis was a stalking victim. She disagreed with Martinez's claim that Travis was afraid of Jodi, maintaining that his actions were not those of a person in fear for his life. In fact, she noted that he had continued to communicate with Jodi right up until the time of his murder. "People usually try to stay away from their stalkers," she said.

Martinez, however, pointed to an email Travis had sent to a female friend on May 19, 2008, in which he expressed "extreme fear" of Jodi, although she was living one thousand miles away in northern California. LaViolette pointed out that Travis had not sought a restraining order or filed a police report or tried to relocate to distance himself from Jodi. In fact, he was still communicating with Jodi after the May 19 email was sent. Martinez believed that LaViolette was not objective, that she came to her conclusion and then made the facts fit them, rather than vice versa.

Indeed, there was national debate as to whether her testimony was so one-sided that it strained credulity, yet she didn't waver even when the public outcry against her became threatening. LaViolette was being attacked in the court of public opinion. Victims of physical and domestic abuse were outraged at her advocacy for Jodi, someone with a weak case at best, and probably a completely fabricated one. LaViolette had accepted the word of what many had concluded was a pathological liar with a motive to deceive and had made glaring mistakes in her sifting of facts. An all-out cyber war erupted against LaViolette, with people posting angry comments on blogs, and encouraging each other to trash a book she had co-authored, *It Could Happen to Anyone: Why Battered Women Stay,* which was flooded with poorly rated online book reviews. The outrage and threats were overwhelming. An afternoon court session was cancelled suddenly when the witness was unable to appear. It was later confirmed that she had been taken to the hospital, with her condition rumored to be heart palpitations and anxiety attacks. In part, the well-organized campaign against her may have played a role. Her telephone number had been posted publicly and people were encouraged to go to her website to "Show your disgust with LaViolette." Petitions circulated to have her removed from a director position and guest speaking engagements. As LaViolette testified about Travis's character assassination of Jodi, her own character was under assault outside the courtroom. The angry mob mentality was over the top and became a story in itself with an editorial in the Huffington Post titled "The Mobbing of Alyce LaViolette," which decried the "wholesale demonization of Ms. LaViolette."

Of course, jurors knew nothing about the angry mob. Their questions for her came directly from the testimony in front of them. They had one hundred and fifty-nine of them, many of them asking the same kinds of things Martinez was asking. Why was LaViolette so willing to believe everything Jodi said? And why hadn't she fielded any opinions from the other side?

To rebut the defense's mental health experts, the state introduced testimony from psychologist Janeen DeMarte.

Considerably younger and less experienced than Dr. Samuels and LaViolette, she nonetheless came across as confident and knowledgeable. DeMarte concluded that Jodi suffered from borderline personality disorder, equating her behavior to that of an immature teenager disposed to angry outburts and blaming others for her anger and hostility. DeMarte testified that during the twelve hours she spent interviewing Jodi, she had exhibited seven out of the nine symptoms of borderline personality disorder—suicidal thoughts, a sense of emptiness, a fear of abandonment, a lack of identity, a tendency toward unstable relationships, rapidly changing emotions and inappropriate and intense anger. She pointed to some of Jodi's behaviors as evidence of a borderline personality disorder: moving to Mesa *after* she and Travis had broken up, spying on Travis and reading emails, idealizing men she dated, and changing herself to fit in with the people around her, in this case joining the Mormon Church. To highlight Jodi's anger outbursts, DeMarte pointed to an email Jodi sent to Travis on February 14, 2007, in which she wrote that she had kicked doors and smashed things.

"People with this personality experience hostility, agressiveness, but they're not displaying it necessarily," DeMarte testified. "When they feel wronged, they have these violent outbursts. These individuals externalize blame." She also described flaws in defense expert Richard Samuels's psychological testing. One glaring error, which Martinez himself had raised, was that Samuels had concluded Jodi had PTSD in 2010 when she was still maintaining the two-intruder theory. DeMarte did not believe Jodi suffered from dissociative amnesia.

The final expert to testify was called by the defense to refute DeMarte's testimony. Robert Geffner, a neuropsychologist, said Jodi's psychological test results did not suggest a personality disorder as DeMarte had opined, but instead all of the test results supported anxiety problems or issues caused by trauma. He said he could not diagnose Jodi because he didn't have the full picture. However, he was willing to hypothesize.

In rebuttal to the defense case, Travis's ex-girlfriend Deanna Reid was among the witnesses called by the prosecution. It was the twenty-third of April when she took the stand, more than four months into the case. She described her relationship with Travis as always loving and respectful, never abusive. On cross-examination, defense attorney Nurmi asked Deanna whether she had a sexual relationship with Travis.

Deanna clearly looked uncomfortable as she truthfully answered. "Yes, well into our relationship, after we moved to Arizona."

Their sexual relationship lasted about a year. They ceased when they visited their respective bishops to confess and seek guidance. Nurmi asked Deanna a litany of embarrassing questions about Travis that he surely knew the answers to. But it was strategic—to emphasize once again what Travis had said about or to Jodi: "Did he ever use phrases with you like 'you're the ultimate slut in bed'?"

"No," Reid answered.

"Did he ever talk to you about blowing enormous loads every time?" Nurmi had a text message from Travis to Jodi: "U put me on another planet. You are the ultimate slut in bed. No wonder I blow enormous loads every time."

Deanna was becoming noticeably uncomfortable. "No," she said.

Nurmi wasn't done. "Did he ever ejaculate in your face?"

"No," said Deanna.

"Did he ever call you a whore, a slut, a three-holed wonder?"

"No."

"Did he ever tell you how he wanted to tie you to a tree, and quote, put it in your ass?"

"No."

"Did he ever tell you the way you moan is like a twelve-year-old girl having her first orgasm?"

"No."

"Did he ever tell you about wanting to cork the pot of a little girl?"

Deanna answered all in the negative.

Martinez jumped to the floor. His questions were not about sex, but abuse. "Did he ever call you names?" he asked Deanna with animated hands.

"No, he did not," Deanna answered.

"Did he ever strike you or physically advance on you? Or inflict any physical violence on you?" Martinez concluded.

"No, never," said Deanna. With that, Judge Stephens recessed court for the day.

CHAPTER 22

CLOSING ARGUMENTS

As hard as it was to believe, the closing arguments were finally at hand. Thousands of questions had been asked in fifty-four days of testimony. There had been twenty prosecution witnesses, eleven defense witnesses, nine rebuttal witnesses (although three had previously testified in the state's case in chief), one surrebuttal witness, and two sur-surrebuttal witnesses (one was a recalled witness). The grand total: thirty-eight witnesses. More than six hundred exhibits had been presented. The jurors themselves had asked hundreds of questions, many exhibiting skepticism about the testimony of certain witnesses, primarily Jodi and her experts. However, no matter how seasoned the trial attorney or court watcher, it was impossible to predict what a jury would do. The verdict in the Casey Anthony trial had left the legal community befuddled and the public outraged. It appeared this panel sitting in judgment of Jodi Arias had adhered to the judge's instruction to pay attention to the testimony and avoid all news about it outside the courtroom.

The jurors and the worldwide audience were saturated with testimony about sex and lies; abuse and lies; the Law of Chastity and lies; *The Book of Mormon* and lies; and the story of the murder itself. The spectacle had been five years in the making and had so far lasted four months, a little short of the five months Travis and Jodi had officially dated. As the trial was coming to a close, Maricopa County officials confirmed that the cost to the taxpayers of Jodi's defense was approximately $1.6 million, a figure that was expected to rise.

It was widely known that Jodi could be executed for killing Travis. The prosecution made the decision to seek the death penalty within two months of Jodi's extradition to Arizona in early September 2008. Jodi's hope for acquittal was remote; her second-best shot, second-degree murder, had slim-to-none odds, while manslaughter also seemed a long shot. A conviction for premeditated first-degree murder was the prediction. If so, the trial would then move forward to the next phase, the aggravation phase. If the jury also unanimously concluded that an aggravating circumstance was proven, namely that the killing was especially cruel, then there would be a final phase to the trial where the jury would decide if Jodi lives or dies by lethal injection.

Given that the evidence of Jodi's premeditation was overwhelming and that the defense had failed to drive holes in the state's case, the focus shifted to speculation about whether there would be jurors who connected with Jodi and would at least spare her life. After all, they'd spent a lot of time with her face to face and, while their questions showed they didn't buy her act, their familiarity with the defendant could make it harder to vote to kill her.

It was Juan Martinez's job as prosecutor to make sure that, as the jury went into the deliberation room, they felt no such sympathy for a killer. That was the goal of his closing argument, and as always, he began with passion and graphic precision.

"This individual, the defendant, Jodi Ann Arias, killed Travis Alexander. And even after stabbing him over and over again, and even after slashing his throat from ear to ear, and then even after taking a gun and shooting him in the face, she will not let him rest in peace. But now instead of a gun, instead of a knife, she uses lies."

The lies of Jodi Arias would be a theme of the closing argument, lest there was a juror left who might have been suckered by a Jodi "story" of abuse. "She uses these lies in court when she testified to stage the scene for you, just like she staged the scene for the police after she killed Mr. Alexander."

Next, Martinez brought in Jodi's crafty, almost cruel use of the media after the killing. "This woman, who would stage the scene, has even attempted to stage the scene through the use of the media. She has courted the media. She has gone on national television . . . has also attempted, or gone out in search of, the limelight. She has signed a manifesto, just in case she becomes famous. And to top it all off, she has indicated that she is innocent and that no jury will convict her, that none of you will convict her . . . Well, she is an individual, as you have seen, who has craved the limelight. So it seems that it is only fitting that . . . she now bask in a different kind of light, the light of truth."

Martinez moved to the manipulative side of Jodi. "This is an individual who will stop at nothing, and will continue to be manipulative and will lie at every turn and at every occasion that she has." Martinez used the examples of the gas cans and the gas receipts from Salt Lake City to illustrate his point. He reminded the jurors that Jodi's story changed from having never been in Salt Lake City, to having never purchased gas in Salt Lake City, to admitting it was true only after being handed the three receipts with her name, "Jodi Arias," on the printout from the Salt Lake City

Tesoro two days after the murder. She was adept at adapting her lies.

Martinez noted that Jodi always cast herself in the role of victim. Whatever predicament she was in, it was always somebody else's fault. She may have killed Travis, but it wasn't her fault. "This individual that attempted to manipulate you believes based on what we've heard, that even though she may have engaged in actions, that she may have done certain things—none of it, absolutely none of it is her fault. Why could it possibly be her fault? If you look back in her history, which is the important part of it, involving her relationship with men, what do you see?" He summarized every significant relationship Jodi had been in, portraying her as a vine swinger, a stalker, and a self-pitying participant in them all. With Darryl Brewer, her longest lasting relationship, he sarcastically highlighted her as a victim of pathetically bad luck: "It's not her fault because, well, Mr. Brewer doesn't want to marry her. What's a girl to do? It's not her fault. She's got to look for another guy, and it appears that he doesn't want to have any kids, and she does. And so again, it's not her fault. How could it possibly be her fault that somebody has free will? Absolutely not her fault, that's what she tried to tell you." But, he went on that, ever resourceful, Jodi started her hunt for a new man to manipulate. "To Travis Alexander's misfortune, he was that *boy*." (Well, Travis was almost thirty, but that was the word Martinez used.)

Martinez's next focus was to put the sex and Mormonism in the proper context. "Can't point the finger enough at Mr. Alexander, can't point the finger enough at the fact that he's a bad Mormon because he's having sex with her? If he's such a bad Mormon, then why stay with him? You're the one that chose him. If he's such a bad guy, why are you hanging out with him? And to compound things, well, she's also

Mormon, too. Why does she keep pointing the finger at him, when she is just as Mormon as he is? She converted in November of 2006." After pointing out the absurdity of Jodi's claim not to know the meaning of "chaste" he continued. "It is almost unconscionable for her to point the finger at Mr. Alexander when she's in the same situation as he is. She has the same knowledge that he does. But again, she wants you to feel sympathy because, again, it's not her fault."

Stressing the misfortune of Travis meeting Jodi, Martinez said that at least in the beginning, when they resided in different states, Travis had had a chance to enjoy life before the "stalking" started. "Luckily for Mr. Alexander, I guess, in the beginning, this relationship was from a distance, and I say luckily because at least when she was in Palm Desert and he was in Mesa, Arizona . . . at least during that time, she couldn't reach out and stab him, she couldn't reach out and shoot him in the face. She couldn't stalk him, couldn't come over unannounced, she wasn't living the ten minutes away. At least fortunately during that time, Mr. Alexander had some extra time to live."

The stalking was as much a feature of the closing argument as the lying. "So what else does Jodi do? She does what every person who has caught their boyfriend, according to her, being unfaithful. What does she do? She moves close to him, moves from California to Arizona, specifically to Mesa, very close to him after they have broken up in the end of June of 2007. That's what she does. Well, now this is when this stalking begins."

Martinez elaborated by noting what she *didn't* do in Mesa. "And what does she do when she comes out here? Well, rather than dating, rather than becoming involved in some sort of social scene in the Mormon Church or finding friends and that sort of thing, no. And something else, she begins to be *more* attentive, that's the word." He mentioned the August 2007 incident when Jodi peeped in Travis's living room window one night and saw him kissing another woman on the couch. "And after she starts stalking him, or after this event of stalking, she doesn't leave him alone. No, she comes over the next day, because she's in the right. They've broken up and it's okay if you're broken up to come over and peep at your ex-boyfriend's house and then in peeping, find him doing something and then wanting to get an explanation. What possible explanation could he ever have owed her at that point?"

As for the alleged violence against Jodi, Martinez emphasized, again, the complete lack of corroboration. "The reason there are no 911 calls is because it never happened. Everything in this case points to the fact that it did not happen. There are no medical reports; there are no friends. There is no one that can come in and say anything about this . . . There is absolutely nothing." He ripped into Jodi's assertion that the Law of Attraction prevented her from journaling negative events, reminding the jury that these "abuse" days were filled with entries of fond memories of kissing and snuggling. Even the abuse events she can't keep straight, Martinez insisted with disdain, saying she was manipulating the evidence to fit the goal. He peppered his argument with examples of the numerous times Jodi was out of control: going to his house unannounced and totally unwelcomed at Christmas; hacking into his email account and reading his email; peeping through his window to watch him in his living room with another woman.

The prosecutor also took the opportunity to lay to rest Jodi's most hideous lie, that Travis was a pedophile. "It is a hateful allegation with nothing to support it," Martinez said about Arias's claim that she'd caught Travis masturbating to a picture of a little boy. "This is really the pinnacle, doesn't get higher or worse than that."

Moving on to the May 26, 2008, text/IM messages exchange filled with derogatory names about Jodi and used by the defense as corroboration of emotional abuse, Martinez explained, "And much is made by the defense that . . . he's mean to her. Well, why wouldn't he be mean to her? Yes, there are names that people are being called; that's correct. There are not any nice names. But he is extremely afraid of her stalking behavior on May 26th when those names are called, and there is anger that is being exchanged back and forth and he sort of, capsulizes it by . . . using a term that's not quite so sexual, but really capsulizes what it is going on here, and how the defendant attempts to manipulate the truth, when he says, 'I am nothing more than a dildo with a heartbeat to you.' That's what he tells her, because that's how he feels."

Martinez continued arguing about this text exchange. "At that point when he's writing that, he is extremely afraid of her because of her stalking behavior. And he does think she's evil. And how prophetic, looking at the next words, how absolutely prophetic, no one can dispute that that is the truest . . . those are the truest words that are spoken in this case and they are spoken by Mr. Alexander, even though he is not here, through his writings. 'You, Jodi Arias, are the worst thing that ever happened to me.' Any doubt that that's the truth? Do we need to look at the picture of his gashed throat? Do we need to look at the sort of frog-like state that she left him in, all crumpled up in that shower? Or do we need to look at his face, where she put that bullet in his right temple to know that what he says there is true? 'You are the worst thing that ever happened to me.' "

Martinez could have stopped there, so powerful was the message, but he had yet to bring up the premeditation behind the murder. At this point, the prosecutor, totally on his A game, reminded the jury that the gun—allegedly stolen from Jodi's grandparents' home only two days after the big May 26 name-calling argument and days before the murder—had been the same caliber as the one used to shoot a bullet into Travis's head. He elaborated on the phone call to Darryl around the time the gun was stolen, where Jodi told her former lover she was going to Mesa and needed to borrow his gas cans.

As part of her plan, Jodi even knew what color car she wanted or, rather, what color she didn't want for her well-planned journey. It couldn't be the red one she was initially offered. That would be too noticeable. The rental car was just for some local trips, according to what she told the car rental agent, even though when she returned it, the odometer showed she had driven 2,834 miles, the same distance as a cross-country trip from Los Angeles to New York. The rental agent also talked about her changed appearance, from blond when she rented the car on June 2 to brunette when she returned it on June 7, a day later than the agreement stated. Her hair color was another detail in the plan to mask her identity, as folks in Arizona only knew her as a platinum blonde. Martinez reminded the jury about Jodi's cell phone being off during the very hours when pings would have otherwise placed her in Mesa at the crime scene and the removal and fiddling with the license plates on her rental car in an attempt to prevent identification.

Each one of these details pointed to planning and forethought, but taken as a whole, it formed a powerful, cohesive narrative of premeditation. "You know she's premeditating the murder. She's thinking about killing him. That's all that's required. The state doesn't even need to prove a whole plan such as this. All the state needs to prove is that the defendant thought about the killing before she actually carried it out." He added more to his point, just to eliminate doubt. "This is an extensive amount of planning, days, six days in advance, six to seven days in advance of her killing him, a week or so." In other words, she began plotting a couple of days after Travis had told her to get out of his life for good in the May 26 text/IM breakup. The implication was that Jodi stewed for a day or so about his extremely negative reaction to whatever she had done and then got busy planning her revenge, which she executed on June 4.

The prosecutor continued to elaborate on Jodi's long litany of lies, manipulations, and inconsistencies, occasionally broken by a defense "Objection! Not in evidence!" until court was recessed for lunch at around 12:00 noon.

After lunch, Martinez picked up with Jodi's lies, scoffing at a defense witness's characterization of those lies as merely an "exaggeration."

"Those statements to the police are important because they show how she can attempt to manipulate things and is able to say whatever fits the story at the time. So initially, when the police came to her, when Detective Flores came to her and asked her, well this is what we have, let's talk about it, she denied everything. She kept saying, 'Let me see the photographs. I want to see the photographs.' The reason she wanted to see the photographs is because she wanted to conform her story to what the police knew, or what she thought the police knew."

Addressing Jodi's memory lapses, he trashed her performance on the witness stand. "She has an incredible memory, alright, when it comes to lying. And the witness's manner while testifying, how it was that she testified . . . Well, you saw her at times attempt to cry, you saw her at times get angry, you saw her at other times just sullenly stand there, and you saw her at times, when the questions were getting difficult snap out, and try to, somehow, make the person that was asking the questions the villain, saying, 'Well, you're scrambling my brain. It's not my fault.' Again, *it's not my fault* . . . That's exactly what's going on here. So, that it's 'not my fault that I keep lying here on the witness stand; it's *yours,* because of the way you're asking me the questions; the fact that you're raising your voice, that's whose fault it is.'"

Martinez emphasized that his role as prosecutor was to get to the truth, but Jodi wanted him to be the bad guy. "And that's why I can snap at you from the witness stand; I can smirk at you from the witness stand, and look knowingly towards the jury, because it's not her fault. It's the person who's asking the questions." As Martinez emphatically pointed out, the only person with motive to lie was Jodi Arias herself.

The gruesome crime photos and autopsy shots of Travis, the beloved friend and brother, a man of optimism and hope, a spiritual man who could fill a room with his smile, were displayed one more time, accentuating the horror all over again. Martinez talked about the gas cans being the ultimate symbol of the defendant and her stories; the gas cans were the vessels, the gas was the lies. "What the state is asking you, the jury, to do is to not leave this courtroom filled with the stench of gasoline on your hands," he declared in his powerfully poetic close. "The state is asking you that you return a verdict of guilty and that you return a verdict of guilty as to first-degree murder, not only as premeditated murder, but also as to felony murder; for no other reason than it's your duty and the facts and the law support it."

On the morning of May 3, 2013, Judge Sherry Stephens called on Kirk Nurmi to begin the closing argument for the defense. After rising for the jury, Jodi looked ready. As she had been on so many occasions before, she was dressed in black, a black cardigan-style sweater set. She looked relaxed, happy, and resigned, brushing off a random wrinkle on her sleeve and organizing her notebooks on the table in front of her. The media circus outside the courthouse, having grown exponentially since the beginning of closing arguments, could be forgotten in the relative quiet of Judge Stephens's well-controlled, well-behaved courtroom.

"Fear. Love. Sex. Lies. Dirty little secrets," Mr. Nurmi began, pacing slowly and using his hands to stress each uttered word, deliberately putting a pregnant pause between each subject.

"These aspects of the human condition may not be universal," he continued, trying to be dramatic, "but each one of these aspects of the human condition played a prominent role in the relationship that Jodi Arias shared with Travis Alexander. And because these aspects of the human condition played such a prominent role in this relationship, it makes sense that the evidence you've heard, starting on January 2, is a tale of fear, love, sex, lies, and dirty little secrets."

Nurmi really had his work cut out for him. No matter where he took his argument from here, the best he could do was somehow mitigate some of the state's evidence that had room for interpretation.

"Now ladies and gentlemen, one of the other things you were told at the beginning of this trial was that ultimately your job would be to determine one thing . . . what happened. You are the finder of fact." He brought out the time-stamped photos from the fatal bathroom photo shoot as a memory aide, though it's doubtful anyone on the jury needed to be reminded. "What happened in the minutes of time between what we see here, June 4, 2008, 5:29 and 20 seconds and . . . what we see in exhibit 162—Mr. Alexander's body being drug [*sic*] across the bathroom floor at 5:32 and 16 seconds. What happened in those three minutes is ultimately what you are to decide."

Nurmi needed to attack the state's position that Jodi had

planned Travis's murder long before she left Yreka for Mesa. The prosecution had woven together a compelling argument that the steps Jodi took between May 26, the date of the derogatory text message/IM exchange, and June 4, the day of his death, had been in anticipation of murdering Travis. Nurmi had a different explanation. He zeroed in on those critical two to three minutes in the bathroom by repeating Jodi's mantra. Travis overreacted when she dropped his camera, he body slammed her, chased her, lunged and threatened to kill her, leaving her fearing for her own life.

Nurmi took the time to elaborate on fear, not just Jodi's fear of Travis at various points in their relationship, but the fear the jury might have in delivering an unpopular verdict. As the trial dragged on, the rhetoric in the court of public opinion had turned increasingly rageful, with certain hardcore trial watchers directing their fury at those few individuals who'd come out in support of the defendant. Alyce LaViolette had allegedly been threatened for being on Jodi's side. Nurmi wanted to assure jurors that it was their duty to do the right thing, even if the right verdict is perceived to be unpopular.

"It occurred to me . . . that you might have some fear," he told the panel in solidarity. "You've been listening to evidence for more than twelve weeks now, since January second. . . . You may fear how your verdict will be received by those who love Travis Alexander, by those who love Jodi Arias or by the world at large . . ." After pausing dramatically, he continued. "You are not to be guided by sympathy, or prejudice or fear, but instead, by your personal belief. And rest assured, each and every one of you are here because all the parties involved believe that you are the type of people that would have the courage of your convictions to stand by your personal belief, against whatever pressures you may feel. You are asked to put that fear aside and look at the evidence." He tried to dismiss parts of the testimony that had become overtly laughable or were attacks directly aimed at his star expert witness, Alyce LaViolette. "Before we talk about the evidence and what this case is about, I think it's important to talk about what this case is *not* about. It's *not* about Snow White, it's not even about any of the seven dwarfs; it's not about bad haircuts and it's not about the sexual orientation of any of the witnesses."

Nurmi had more important arguments to make. Jodi was despised by so many that he needed to deal with her unlikeability, especially in case jurors felt the same way. Even Jodi couldn't suppress her laughter at Nurmi's next statement. "It's not even about whether or not you like Jodi Arias," he said of his client with a straight face. "Nine days out of ten, *I* don't like Jodi Arias!"

"Objection!" bellowed Martinez.

Agreeing with the prosecutor, Judge Stephens asked the jury to disregard the last statement. The fact that Jodi beamed when her own attorney said he mostly didn't like her showed just how much she thrived on attention, good or bad. It was a telling reaction that spoke to why she stayed with Travis despite her complaints against him. She craved attention in any form.

Mr. Nurmi was struggling to explain why Jodi would drive so many hours and a thousand miles to an abusive ex-boyfriend's house to kill him in self-defense. He emphasized that Jodi had moved *away* from Mesa, that she didn't want to be around him anymore, and in her journals, she had talked about how a cloud had lifted. "Point of fact is, she moved away. This girl who's supposedly obsessed, moved away." He talked about the sex tape recorded on May 10, which completely undermined the assertion that Travis had been fearful of Jodi. Nurmi pointed to the May 26 text message exchange, where Travis called Jodi a "whore, slut and three-hole wonder," concluding Travis was the one who needed to be feared, not vice versa.

Nurmi tried to offer innocent explanations for many of the details the state gave as evidence of premeditation. If she had planned on covertly killing Travis, why would she have been so dumb as to stage a burglary of her grandfather's gun, when she could have taken it at any time? If she wanted to be so covert about her plot, why would she leave a trail of evidence, from the car rental to the gas charges that *were* put on her debit card? If she was on a covert mission, why would she stop and see two former boyfriends on her way to slaughter a third? "You don't stop anywhere; you don't visit any people; there's no witnesses, you go in there clean and you do your business, right? Does she do that? Oh no, she didn't. It doesn't make any sense. What does she do? She stops in Monterey, California. And what does she do in Monterey, California? She visits two former boyfriends. This crazy woman that can't let it go has friendships with two of her former boyfriends," Nurmi argued vehemently.

Still, Nurmi was willing to concede the prosecutor's first point in his closing argument—that Jodi was a liar. "If Jodi Arias were accused of the crime of lying, I could not stand before you and say she's not guilty of that crime. But nowhere in your jury instructions are you asked to convict Jodi Arias of lying. There is no verdict form that you will have that says . . . is Jodi Arias guilty of the crime of lying? Well, of course not, that's not the crime she's being charged with," Nurmi declared.

To Nurmi, Jodi's behavior was inconsistent with a premeditated killing. Who would spend an entire day in bed with someone they had every intention of killing, he wanted to know. In his opinion, that was the most absurd thinking of it all. "The question arises under this theory that the state has perpetrated to you: They're in bed together sleeping.

She's got the gun. She's got the knife. He's asleep! What better opportunity would somebody need? He's asleep. You put the gun to his head and you do it. You put the knife to his throat and you do it. No better time than when he's asleep."

In what was perhaps his strongest argument, he went after the state's evidence that Travis was afraid of Jodi. "We're supposed to believe that he's so scared of her, right? He's afraid of her. So my goodness, how could she just walk right in the house and then sleep with him, sleep in the bed, and then take pictures—he's so scared of her he's taking naked pictures of her in his bed! That is a new level of being scared." Of course, Travis's friends would counter that Travis had become sexually addicted to Jodi and when offered his drug of choice could not resist, powerlessness being the definition of addiction.

Nurmi displayed a photo of Travis that shows him standing in the shower, his back to the camera, as he's being photographed by Jodi, minutes before his death. Emphatically, Nurmi pointed out how easy it would have been for Jodi to take out Travis then and there, had that been her intention. "She's waiting for a moment in time to strike. She's waiting to kill Mr. Alexander. If there's a moment in time, this is it. This right here is it! There he is. He's worn out, he's naked, and his back's to her. His eyes are right against the wall. He wouldn't have seen it coming . . . She could have shot him right there if that was her plan."

Nurmi concluded that it just didn't comport with the facts that Jodi premeditated the killing. He highlighted some of the testimony from his deflated expert witnesses, who had opined that Jodi had been abused by Travis, physically and emotionally. He revisited evidence that Jodi was moving on with her life, having signed up with an LDS dating service in the Yreka area, and having become interested in Ryan Burns. He concluded that whatever happened in those final three minutes of Travis's life, when everything went from peaceful and calm to an unfathomable blood bath, had to have been because someone snapped. "What this evidence shows is that either what happened is that Jodi Arias defended herself and didn't know when to stop, or she gave in to a sudden heat of passion . . . Ultimately, if Miss Arias is guilty of any crime at all, it is the crime of manslaughter and nothing more." Many legal pundits wondered why he hadn't made that far more saleable *snapping in the heat of passion* argument from the get-go instead of throwing it into the wash at the last possible moment.

Mr. Martinez had the last word. "When the law is on your side, you argue the law; when the facts are on your side, you argue the facts; but when nothing is on your side, you just argue. And that's what you had," he said of his opponent's two-and-a-half-hour summation. Martinez painstakingly rebutted every specific point Nurmi had made, in the end bringing it back to Travis's home. Martinez even questioned whether Travis really knew she was arriving in the early morning hours of June 4, 2008, raising the possibility that Jodi had arrived, uninvited, with a plan.

"She wanted him. She couldn't let him go. Even from Yreka, she couldn't let him go. There's never an indication that he said that, or he requested her to come there. Those were her words, and she kept saying them over and over like a mantra. And so on that date, when she finally got there she came ready to go. And by ready to go, I mean she brought over the weapons and she spent some time with him, and then when he was in the shower, he was no match for her. And she took care of business and you know how she took care of business . . .

"I am asking you to return a verdict of first-degree murder, not only of premeditated murder but also of felony murder. Not because it's an emotional decision that I want you to reach . . . or an argument just for its own sake, but because in this case, Travis Victor Alexander was slaughtered by this woman."

"Objection, improper argument," sighed Nurmi.

When the objection was overruled, Martinez brought it home. "She slashed his throat, she stabbed him in the heart, and then she shot him in the face, and all of that thinking about it in advance," he said with a voice hoarse, raspy, and quieter than usual. Martinez lifted his white Styrofoam cup of water and a few papers, and returned to his seat.

Mr. Martinez had ended the guilt phase of his prosecution of Jodi Arias.

CHAPTER 23

MOMENT OF TRUTH

On the afternoon of Friday, May 3, 2013, at the end of all closing arguments, Judge Sherry Stephens gave the jury her final instructions before deliberations. She had already given them detailed instructions at the start of the closings about the crimes and key definitions of legal terms, admonishing them not to be "swayed by sympathy" and to "consider all the evidence in light of reason, common sense, and experience."

Remarkably, the jury was still fairly intact. In the four months of *The State of Arizona v. Jodi Ann Arias,* the panel had lost only three of its members. The first to go had been Juror #5, who had left in tears in April. She had been described as observant and a copious note taker, but she had been excused after Jodi's lawyers accused her of misconduct and requested a mistrial. Even though the mistrial request was denied, the juror was gone. To the surprise of many, Juror #5 returned to the courtroom as a spectator a few days later. She had given a few innocuous statements to reporters who knocked on her door in the days following her dismissal, but within a few days and on the advice of an attorney, she declined to speak to reporters about the case, proving just how mesmerizing the case had become.

Juror #11, the twentysomething Hispanic man in the back row who never seemed to take notes, had been the next to go. He had been sick with a hacking cough for a few days, and in an abundance of caution, the judge had excused him. She didn't want the rest of the panel getting sick and delaying the trial further.

Only a week before the deliberations were about to get under way, the jury lost a third panelist when Juror #8 was excused on April 25 due to a DUI arrest the prior weekend. That left nine men and six women to hear the judge's charge.

Judge Stephens had instructed the panel on the elements of first-degree murder and the lesser-included crimes they could consider. Jodi was charged with one count of first-degree murder under two theories: "premeditated" and "felony murder," which is causing the death of someone during the course of another felony. The crime of first-degree murder/premeditated required proof of four scenarios, though the most relevant was that Jodi intentionally caused the death of Travis Alexander.

The difference between first-degree and second-degree murder was premeditation. Second-degree murder was an intentional killing that did not require premeditation by the defendant. The presumptive sentence for second-degree murder was sixteen years, but the judge could go up or down by six years, so the range in Jodi's case was ten to twenty-two years. Given that she'd already been behind bars for almost five years awaiting this moment, if she got *murder two* she could—hypothetically—be out in five years with credit for time already served, a prospect that horrified Travis's family and friends.

The defense had requested that jurors also be allowed to

consider an even lower form of homicide—"manslaughter," by sudden quarrel or heat of passion, which carried a presumptive sentence of ten and a half years. As with second-degree murder, the judge would have discretion in sentencing. She could go down to seven years or up to twenty-one. Again, Jodi would get credit for the nearly five years she had already served.

Once jurors had heard their final instructions, two women and one man from the panel were randomly selected as alternates. That left eight men and four women in the final panel to deliberate Jodi's fate.

Deliberations began around 3:40 P.M. that Friday and lasted for fifty minutes before jurors were dismissed for the weekend. They returned on Monday, May 6, to begin their first full day in the jury deliberation room. A crowd had begun to form outside the Maricopa County courthouse. Camera crews, producers, and reporters were converging on the courthouse steps mingling with the supporters of Travis Alexander, who were also huge fans of prosecutor Martinez, everyone anxious to be there when the verdict was finally read.

Inside, Jodi was confined to a holding cell in the bowels of the courthouse, where she waited for word on her fate. There was no TV or phone, and she was not given anything to write with, which meant no doodling or journaling during her confinement there. Her meals were served to her in the "tank," and only her attorneys were allowed to see her.

Attorneys from both sides had returned to their respective offices, and would be summoned to the courthouse if the jury had a question or a verdict. Nurmi did not have an office downtown, but Willmott's office was only five minutes from the courthouse. Martinez's office was in a building across the street, about a block away. Many of the other critical parties, including family members on either side, were scattered in residences or hotels ready to come in for a juror question or when word hit that a verdict had been reached.

Monday, May 6, saw no verdict, nor did Tuesday, May 7. The tension was palpable in the fifth-floor hallway of the courthouse, where reporters and others involved in the case would hang out, hovering near the doors to the courtroom where the verdict would ultimately be announced. With every passing hour, it became exponentially more nerve-racking. Outside under the beating Arizona sun, the gathering crowd was getting antsy, journalists interviewing one another as deadlines came and went. The reporters had really gotten to know the most colorful trial watchers, including the woman known as "Cane Lady." Earlier in the trial she had asked prosecutor Juan Martinez to autograph her cane and he graciously agreed, only to have the defense accuse him of misconduct. As the jury deliberated five floors up, Cane Lady sat in the hot sun, the center of a cluster of fervent pro-prosecution citizens who were nervous but confident the jury would see it their way.

At a little before 2:30 P.M. on Wednesday, May 8, the jury notified the judge's bailiff that—after deliberating fifteen hours and five minutes—they had reached a decision.

Word quickly spread that the verdict would be read at 4:30 that afternoon, giving the media two hours to reinforce their armies. Soon several hundred spectators from the community and beyond had formed a crush at the base of the courthouse steps. Chants erupted. "Justice for Travis!" one woman called out and dozens of others joined her, repeating the phrase over and over. The cameras rolled.

Inside the courtroom, Travis's siblings filled the gallery's first row behind the prosecutor. Many of his friends were also present, including his ex-girlfriend, Deanna Reid, and best friends Chris and Sky Hughes. Jodi's mother and aunt were seated several rows back from their usual spot behind the defense table, and neither woman betrayed much emotion. Jodi's maternal grandmother was there looking stoic but frail. Several people fanned themselves with sheets of paper, adding some movement to a packed gallery that was otherwise eerily quiet.

Once Judge Stephens took her seat at the bench, the anticipation in the courtroom was overwhelming. For two very long minutes, not a word was spoken.

Jodi, dressed in a tasteful black pantsuit, sat quietly next to her attorneys. From her expression, it seemed apparent that she did not believe the jury would find her guilty of the most serious charge of premeditated murder. She swallowed hard when the judge finally addressed the court. "Ladies and gentlemen, I understand you have reached a verdict," Judge Stephens began, noting that the verdict form had been handed to the bailiff. After silently reviewing the form, the judge handed it to the clerk.

"We the jury, duly empaneled and sworn, upon our oaths do find the defendant as to Count One, first-degree murder, guilty," the clerk declared to gasps and cries of elation from some in the gallery. Travis's siblings and close friends hugged one another, some smiling, some sobbing, most doing a little bit of both. It was an emotional catharsis after almost five hellish years of living in limbo waiting for justice. Jodi fought back tears, but it was clear to all that she was shocked, saddened, and taken aback. "Five guilty of premeditated, zero felony, and seven premeditated and felony," the clerk continued. In other words, all twelve jurors believed it was a premeditated murder and seven of them believed it was *also* felony murder.

"Is this your true verdict?" Judge Stephens, always the epitome of reserve and professionalism, asked. She then instructed the clerk to poll each juror individually.

Jodi looked forlornly from juror to juror, as if wishing

that one of them would change his or her mind if he or she would just look back at her. But her magical-thinking powers had proved to be as phony as her stories. There was no whooping or hollering inside the courtroom, although outside, the crowd erupted in jubilant cheers.

Because of the advance notice, the courthouse area was a mob scene of massive proportions, with most everyone excitedly cheering and chanting "Justice for Travis!" It was absolutely festive, everyone having waited so long, months and years, for justice. There were no statements on the courthouse steps by the trial attorneys. When the guilty verdict was reached, there were still two phases left to the case, so no one talked.

As usual, Jodi showed her perverse brilliance for pulling focus and bringing the attention back to her. Within a half hour of the verdict, Jodi gave an exclusive interview to reporter Troy Hayden of Fox 10 Phoenix in the secure area of the courthouse where inmates are held. When asked how she felt upon hearing the verdict, Jodi said, "I think I just went blank. I just feel overwhelmed. I think I just need to take it a day at a time."

Jodi admitted she had not expected the verdict the jurors had reached. "There was no premeditation on my part. The whole time I was fairly confident I wouldn't get premeditation, because there was no premeditation."

She told Hayden the worst outcome for her would be a sentence of "natural life" in prison. "Longevity runs in my family, and I don't want to spend the rest of my natural life in one place. I am pretty healthy, I don't smoke, and I would probably live a long time, so that is not something I am looking forward to." Jodi's next statement would grab the next day's headlines and reportedly devastate members of her family.

"I said years ago that I would rather get death than life

and that still is true today," she told Hayden. "I believe death is the ultimate freedom, so I would rather just have my freedom as soon as I can get it." When asked about the moment she was driving in the desert, and came out of the fog, if she would do things differently if she had the oppportunity, Jodi answered in the affirmative. "I would turn around and drive to the Mesa police," she said. She didn't know how the outcome would differ, but said, "It would have been the right thing." Interestingly, with that question, Jodi had a chance to turn the clock back a few more hours to the master bathroom and say she would have pivoted left and out the door to safety instead of into the closet to allegedly get a gun. In other words, she could have said she wouldn't have killed Travis. But she didn't say that, perhaps because she has no regrets.

Even though the jury had found Jodi Arias guilty of first-degree murder, the trial was far from over. Ahead of the jury was the "aggravation phase" of the trial, where the very same jury who had convicted Jodi needed to decide if the murder was "especially cruel." The prosecution was delighted with the way things were going, but the next phase was just as critical if Martinez was going to succeed in getting the death penalty. He regarded the number of wounds alone as especially cruel, but he still didn't want to take any chances. He was certain that the number of wounds coupled with the defensive wounds would prove beyond a reasonable doubt that Travis had suffered a painful death almost beyond imagination. He also would argue that the gunshot was the last of the fatal wounds, and may have even been administered after Travis was already dead.

The aggravation phase was scheduled for the following day, but was postponed until May 15. Thus the next phase began at noon that day, same place, same intense Phoenix sun blazing down on the loyal crowd of trial watchers, most of whom were hoping Jodi would pay the ultimate price. Mr. Martinez only called one witness for the prosecution, Dr. Kevin Horn, the medical examiner who had performed the autopsy on Travis. He had also been the rebuttal witness a few days earlier, so the jury was quite familiar with his opinion. It was often shared with terms so graphic that the faint of heart grew queasy. His hyper-clinical language, tied to a face and a savage crime, the jumble of familiar words spoken without any emotion was actually more gut-wrenching than a dramatic recounting would have been; the descriptions of Travis's injuries morphed into something macabre, supernatural, grotesque, nauseating, and shocking. This time the focus of Dr. Horn's testimony was on how long and how much Travis suffered before he died.

Again, Dr. Horn described what he had determined to be the first fatal wound, a knife thrust to the chest that cut a major blood vessel. The stab wound probably took two minutes to kill Travis, meaning he was conscious during much of the rest of the assault on his back, head, and torso. Dr. Horn reminded the jury of Travis's defensive wounds, so important to his determination that the knife attack happened first. The cuts on Travis's hands were likely the result of trying to wrestle the knife out of Jodi's hands. The next fatal wound was the slash across the throat, which would have required considerable effort. Dr. Horn thought there was a possibility that the neck had received more than one assault before it was successful. "It could also be that there are several attempts to cut the throat in the same area," he testified. "The skin would offer some resistance to the knife, the airway itself is firm cartilage, so there would need to be some effort." In between the infliction of these fatal wounds, Travis was stabbed multiple times in his back, head, torso, and legs.

One more time, the testimony was unbearable to Travis's

family and friends. They wept openly in agony and distress as once more, the pictures of Travis, his body riddled with deep stab wounds and gouges, were slapped down on the projector and put up on the monitors around the room. After the corpse and crime scene photos were over, Martinez did something that was truly inspired. He asked everyone in court to pause with him in silence for two minutes to illustrate just how long it had taken for Travis to die. Never did any courtroom sit through a longer two minutes. The seconds seemed to go on and on and on. The already traumatized audience was shaken when the prosecutor finally began speaking again. "The last thing [Travis] saw before he lapsed into unconsciousness was that blade coming to his throat," he said. "And the last thing he felt before he left this earth was pain."

The defense didn't have much to add. Jennifer Willmott offered that the adrenaline rushing through Alexander's body may have prevented him from feeling much pain during his death. She also suggested that although the first wound was not immediately fatal, Travis's moving around would have caused him to bleed faster, thus hastening his death and shortening his period of suffering.

The jury didn't need long to come to a unanimous decision. In one hour and thirty-three minutes, they agreed with the prosecution: the murder was especially cruel. The state had proven that "the victim consciously suffered physical and mental pain, distress or anguish prior to death" and "the defendant knew or should have known that the victim would suffer."

Now that Jodi was eligible for the death penalty in the premeditated first-degree murder of Travis Alexander, next up was the penalty phase of her trial. Had the jury found the aggravating circumstance, especially cruel, was not proven, the jury's role would have been finished and Judge Stephens would have determined Jodi's sentence: natural life with no possibility of release or a life sentence with the possibility of release after twenty-five years. Now, under Arizona law, the same jury that had reigned during the guilt and aggravation phases would sit in judgment of whether Jodi would die for her crime.

The first part of the penalty phase was devoted to victim impact statements. This was the moment many in the Alexander family had been waiting for. They had watched patiently while their nemesis spewed her lies and skewered their brother. But now they would finally have their moment in front of the court and the world.

On May 16, Travis's brother Steven was the first to address the jury and the judge. He stood before the jury and kept his back completely turned to the convicted murderer. Dressed in a light gray suit, he cleared his throat before beginning to read his written remarks. With great agony, he described in painstaking detail that he learned that his big brother was dead while serving our country in the U.S. Army. Through tears, he went on to say how it had impacted him in all the years since. "The nature of my brother's murder has had a major impact on me. It's even invaded my dreams," said Steven, standing a mere six feet from the men and women who would decide the sentence of his brother's killer. "I've had nightmares about somebody coming after me with a knife, then going after my wife and my daughter. I don't want these nightmares anymore." He went on to say Travis believed he was born to do good, because that was his destiny. He would never do it now. "He was brutally ripped out of this world, my world," Steven said with anger. He softened his tone substantially as he finished his loving tribute. "Hopefully one day, I can make him proud."

Samantha Alexander, Travis's sister, was next. She too had been serving her country, as a police officer in Carlsbad,

California, when she got the news. She began by holding up a photo of Travis and his beloved grandmother. "This is a picture of my grandmother," she began through swells of tears. "She is the one who raised Travis." She went on to say how much her grandmother had suffered at the loss of her grandson, and how she had died shortly before jury selection for this very trial. There wasn't a dry eye in the house. "Losing Travis has completely destroyed the health of our family . . . Travis was our strength, our beacon of hope, our motivation. Our lives will never be the same. We would give anything to have him back." In the face of unthinkable circumstances, the Alexanders conducted themselves with dignity, grace, and courage.

And then it was time for Jodi's side to plead for her life. On May 20, court was cut short when a penalty phase defense witness, Jodi's friend Patricia, who was supposed to be providing mitigating circumstances on Jodi's behalf, suddenly withdrew. She was expected to give character witness testimony about Jodi, who was her best friend in grade school. Jodi had attended Patti's wedding and had given her a photo album as a gift. But Patti suddenly withdrew from the witness list, saying threats to her life made her reconsider. Nurmi told Judge Stephens that Martinez himself was involved with intimidating the witness, claiming he had some kind of dirt on her at a personal level. Nurmi immediately moved for a mistrial. Patti later explained that, yes, she felt threatened by anonymous online bloggers and mischaracterized by an intimidating prosecutor. But, in the end, she also felt that she didn't really want to speak on Jodi's behalf because she didn't condone Jodi's violent actions. She said the child she knew was loving and fun. The adult on trial was a stranger to her. Patti also felt bad for Travis's family.

Judge Stephens denied this latest mistrial motion, but this time the defense team seemed genuinely furious. Nurmi and Willmott angrily asked to withdraw from the case. "Ms. Willmott and I move to withdraw," petitioned Nurmi. "We cannot present a full picture [of Jodi's life] as incumbent upon us. We cannot fulfill our duties." Judge Stephens denied that request also. In a shocking move, Nurmi told the court there would be no defense witnesses for the penalty phase. The defense abandoned its plan to call witnesses in support of eight mitigating factors they had listed. Jodi's own statement to the jury, known as an allocution, was all the defense would present at this phase. The eight mitigating factors included that Jodi suffered abuse as a child and an adult. The defense had presented their evidence of this factor, ad nauseam, in the guilt phase of the trial. So it wasn't as though the jury had no evidence to consider. Other factors were that she had no criminal history, she lacked family support, she was a talented artist, and that she consistently tried to improve herself.

On May 21, 2013, slightly after noon, Jodi began her nineteen-minute allocution. She was not under oath and she could not be cross-examined. The big question was whether she would express remorse for killing Travis. She wore a black sweater-like top matched with a tailored black mid-length skirt. Her glasses were on, and she rose from the defense table to take the podium.

Jodi told the panel about charitable work she was planning from prison, including donating her hair to the Locks of Love organization. She acknowledged that the jury did not think she was battered, but she said that didn't prevent her from wanting to help raise awareness of domestic violence. With that, she held up a T-shirt of her own design, emblazoned with the word "Survivor." It was a jaw-dropping move. She was supposed to be pleading for her life. Instead, she seemed determined to get in one last dig at her dead ex-lover. Court spectators were dumbfounded by her gall

. . . and her self-destructiveness. Did Jodi really think this was going to win her points with a jury that had clearly concluded she was lying about Travis hitting her? She also said she hoped to improve literacy in prison by starting a book club and reduce solid waste by implementing a recycling program. Jodi talked about happier times. She showed pictures from her childhood, displaying ones of herself at different ages throughout the years. She had pictures of her ex-boyfriends, remembering the good times they had shared.

A weirdly comfortable and confident Jodi showed samples of the drawings she had made in jail. They were done in pencil, as that is the only medium allowed an inmate at the jail where she had been residing for almost five years. Besides no longer being able to paint in oils, she listed other life milestones that would never be enjoyed by her: being a mother, going to her sister's wedding, or spending time with her family.

Finally, Jodi came to Travis. She said she loved him. She had wanted to avoid a trial for the sake of his reputation, but she felt obligated to answer the questions posed to her truthfully. She had not wanted to expose the secrets inside the emails, texts, and phone calls, but in the name of the truth, she had honored the oath she had taken. Her presentation was perhaps the most astounding display of double-speak ever broadcast on TV. The nation's most infamous liar was speaking of honor and oaths and truth. Was she aware of her capacity to infuriate?

As for murdering Travis, "I can hardly believe I was capable of such violence; I will be sorry for the rest of my life, probably longer . . . I see with Travis's family much greater loss, one that I can never make up for. I hope with the verdict they will gain a sense of closure." While the word "sorry" was uttered, it never came in the sentence *I am sorry for what I have done. Please forgive me.* For the family of

Travis Alexander it was one more slap in the face. With that, the case came to a close.

Yet, even as jurors retired to grapple with the agonizing question of whether Jodi should live or die, she was back at the Estrella jail giving a slew of media interviews to local and national TV outlets well into the night. Amy Murphy, a reporter with Phoenix's ABC 15 TV, was one of the journalists who made Jodi's cut. Amy had actually observed the process whereby Jodi decided whom she'd talk to, describing it as "very anal, 'cause I saw the list. She had actually gone through the list herself. She took her pen and drew a line all the way across the news agency or the reporter's name. And then the ones that she wanted, she put a little check mark by." Jodi appeared wearing makeup and a civilian top and asked the reporters not to shoot her from the waist down, so as to hide her jail uniform bottoms. Amy explained, "We learned later that a local station had purchased makeup for her upon her request. She asked for waterproof mascara, foundation. And they brought that to her. And she looked like a tiny little waif of a woman . . . so incapable of doing the horrific things that she did to Travis Alexander." Amy, scoring a coup for her news station, asked Jodi the questions that were at the tip of tongues across the nation. Everybody wanted to know why Jodi's mother failed to get up and plead for her daughter's life before the jury. Jodi said that it was her defense team's decision not to have her mother talk. But, Jodi claimed, her mom had written a letter and the court had a record of it.

Amy pressed her on key issues. "Why did you say you wanted the death penalty and then change your mind?"

Jodi replied, "My cousin convinced me. The way she said it. She said regardless of what happens, there's still a lot of hope and a lot of things that can be done and don't do that to your mom."

Amy went on, "Samantha Alexander said, 'We will never get those images of our brother's neck being slit out of our minds.' How have you gotten it out of your mind?"

"It is not out of my mind, but mostly I avoid looking at it, but it is there and I've seen it." Amy Murphy said, after talking to Jodi one on one, she came away convinced that she was insane. Amy felt Jodi absolutely knew right from wrong but was, otherwise, seriously off.

After four days of deliberation, the jury failed to reach a unanimous decision as to whether Jodi should get the death penalty or a sentence of life in prison. In light of the deadlock, Judge Stephens declared a mistrial in the penalty phase of deliberations. A new trial, with a new jury, was scheduled to begin later in the summer, for sentencing purposes only. It appeared the drama would continue. We were all prepared for press conferences following the penalty phase but, because it was a deadlock, again no one talked. It was still considered a pending case.

After Jodi's penalty phase was declared a mistrial, it was revealed that the majority of jurors had voted to put Jodi to death. The vote was eight in favor, four opposed, but unanimity was required. Jurors did begin to speak out, however. Jury foreman William Zervakos, juror #18, gave several interviews, including an expansive one with HLN affiliate KTVK in Phoenix. He said he was one of the four jurors who voted against the death penalty, saying there were multiple mitigating factors, among them Jodi's age, the fact that she had no criminal record, and her "dysfunctional" family. During an appearance on *Good Morning America,* the day after Judge Stephens declared a mistrial in the death penalty phase, Zervakos voiced his opinion. "All of the testimony that I listened to, and that I actually heard as well as read,

I do believe he verbally abused her," he stated. "There was just too much evidence, that . . . you know, again not an excuse. And believe me, I'm not painting Jodi Arias a sympathetic figure."

Zervakos made it clear that Travis "didn't deserve to die." "I'm not blaming the dead guy," he said. "What she [Jodi] did was horrific, and she's got to pay for it. And she is going to . . . But Jodi is a human being. Our jurisprudence system is based on 'innocent until proven guilty.' And this girl was crucified in the court of public opinion. We didn't know that, of course, until after the fact." In return for his candor, this foreman also found himself on the receiving end of death threats as the line between free speech and harassment melted in a cyber world where anonymous bullies let loose without fear.

Jodi's fate will yet be decided by a jury of her peers, exactly according to the rules of justice we have come to cherish, saints and sinners alike.

The absolute, fiery passion outsiders had for the capital murder trial of Jodi Arias was manifesting not just at the courthouse but around the country. Networks covering the trial saw their ratings skyrocket. People in large cities and small towns were fixated on the trial's daily developments whether it was a witness blunder, Jodi's demeanor and hairstyle, or Martinez's latest rock star status. Social media exploded with opinions about *all* of the players, from the victim to the attorneys to each and every witness. Every juror, though known only by number and never shown on camera, was subjected to a character judgment. Opinions about the defendant were explosive and *overwhelmingly* negative, though she did have a following. It seemed females, especially, saw in Jodi something that was loathsome at the core, something wicked and evil. Many women who were true victims of domestic violence were *deeply* offended by her allegations.

Buzzwords from the testimony took their places in our conversations: "three-hole wonder"; "dirty little secret"; "Snow White was a battered woman," "hottie biscotti." Everyone had an opinion and purported to know what *really* happened because somehow they were better witnesses and better judges of the truth than the people testifying for either side. From the spectators' point of view, at times, *The State v. Jodi Ann Arias* was part soap opera, part circus, the other part gladiator spectacle. The trial had elements everyone could relate to and some that appealed to the voyeur in us: conflicts with religion, chastity, and secrets; kinky sex and lies; passion, obsession, jealousy, cheating, violence, and the ultimate crime of murder. Travis was murdered viciously in cold blood, killed three times over. Jodi Arias may spend the rest of her natural life in prison. However, as of this publication, she has not yet been sentenced, so she could be put to death long before she dies of natural causes. She still has the right to appeal, a process that will surely add years to any conclusion. Travis never realized his dream of "Being Better," his philosophy of constant improvement until he reached the top expressed in his blog. And Jodi? She threw away her life while robbing the world of Travis's. At least Jodi will never have the chance to murder, slaughter, or butcher again.

EPILOGUE

The trial of Jodi Arias was an absolute phenomenon. In terms of the television viewing audience, it ranked with the trials of O.J. Simpson and Casey Anthony. In those other two cases, however, the verdicts delivered were the opposite of what the public was expecting, and the calls for justice were left deeply unsatisfied. With Jodi, the verdict was both predicted and categorically hailed. Of course, a lot of things were different in this case. For one, Jodi had confessed to the killing, even though it had taken her two years to get to that point, and even then she tried to spin it.

Two years was longer than the murderess had even known Travis Alexander. She had met him on September 13, 2006, and he died a brutal death by her hand on June 4, 2008, three months shy of two years. Not including the aggravation phase and the death penalty phase, the trial lasted four months and a week, from January 2 through May 8, 2013. That was two weeks shy of the length of time the two had officially dated, which by Jodi's account began on February 2, 2007, and ended with a phone call on June 29 of that same year. Deliberations in the punishment phase of the trial lasted fifteen hours, the amount of time it would have taken for Jodi to drive from Yreka to Mesa, had she driven nonstop. Depending on when she arrived at Travis's home, she may have been there almost exactly fifteen hours. In that time Jodi managed a few hours for sleep, sex, and still more sex; a few minutes for taking nude photographs of Travis in the shower; a few long, savage minutes for the murder itself, complete with more than two dozen knife wounds, the near decapitation, plus the gratuitous gunshot to the face; and a period of time for stuffing Travis's body into the shower, cleaning up some of the enormous amounts of blood, putting clothing, towels, and the camera through the wash cycle of Travis's washing machine, and heading out of town in her rental car, into the twilight over the Arizona desert.

For the trial, tens of thousands of people tuned in to watch it, either the live stream or the evening recaps on those television networks that featured the proceedings. HLN saw record ratings for its gavel to gavel coverage, as well as its nightly analysis and debates. People could not get enough. Even at the courthouse itself, crime junkies were such regulars there that they became known by nicknames. There was "Cane Lady," and her friend Michaelann who said her father had been murdered in a knife attack and who identified with Travis's plight. One young man made a rather large painting of Jodi Arias surrounded by her lawyers, the prosecutor, and key witnesses and stood outside the courthouse showing off the canvas.

As much as people hated Jodi Arias, they were also intrigued about who she really was. During her eighteen days on the stand, everyone had their own chance to size her up. Jodi was already loathed in the court of public opinion even before she took the stand on February 4, 2013, and by almost all accounts, her "performance" during her testimony was just that. She appeared at turns smug, unrepentant, mendacious, self-serving, and even combative. She seemed willing and even eager to assassinate the character of the man she claimed to have loved without hesitation, accusing him of heinous acts like pedophilia and physical abuse. That she had murdered Travis once was horrific enough, but to attack him again in this way, under oath and in front of his whole family, was despicable.

As everyone has tried to understand Jodi, so, too, has the psychological world, and the opinions from the professionals reveal fascinating insights into the mind of Jodi Arias, perhaps shedding light on why she acted the way she did. Dr. Drew Pinsky, host of HLN's *Dr. Drew on Call,* has been an extremely valuable source of information on this topic. He is a board-certified internist, an addiction medicine specialist, and an assistant clinical professor of psychiatry at the Keck School of Medicine at the University of Southern California. Although he didn't interview Jodi directly, he did have the good fortune of interviewing multiple psychologists and psychiatrists about Jodi, and he has also reviewed the testimony of psychologist Janeen DeMarte, who took the stand as a rebuttal witness for the prosecution. Based on all of the information Dr. Drew gathered, he has a pretty good idea of what was going on with Jodi, although there is acknowledgment of the difficulty of evaluating somebody without speaking to him or her directly.

He agreed with other psychologists and psychiatrists in suggesting that Jodi has borderline personality disorder, which is what the prosecution maintained all along. About "borderlines," Dr. Drew said it best when he generalized: "They lie, they manipulate. Their point of view begs no alternative. They really can't see their role in what plays out in their life. They just can't see it. That's what personality disorders are. At its core: 'It's the world's problem, not me. I'm justified in feeling the way I do, acting the way I do because of what the world is and what the world's done to me.' That's what makes personality disorder so difficult, if not, some say, impossible to treat."

In today's pop psychology world, people love to toss

around diagnoses with abandon. But, says Dr. Drew, for borderline personality disorder, "there's very specific criteria. And you need certain numbers of these criteria: chronic feelings of emptiness, chronic feelings of preoccupation about abandonment, dysfunctional, chaotic relationships, inability to have stability in their lives, lots of suicidal ideation, extreme mood lividity. It's just a terribly unstable emotional landscape." Borderlines are prone to fierce anger and irritability. Anyone who has studied this case can look at that criteria and say: it fits Jodi to a T.

Also, by definition, borderlines seesaw between idealizing the object of their fascination and then devaluing them in the extreme. That is precisely what Jodi did with Travis. She put him on a pedestal, worshipping him socially and sexually and then—when he was unable to meet her insatiable demands—she demonized him in her mind. When she murdered Travis, she was knocking the pedestal over and smashing it into the ground.

This in no way apologizes for Jodi's behavior. As Dr. Drew and others have stressed, having a mental illness is not the same as being legally insane. Jodi understood right from wrong, as evidenced by her plotting and cover-ups. But, perhaps because she is a borderline, she felt justified to kill Travis *not* in self-defense because he was attacking her; he was not. Rather, because she felt wronged by him and felt entitled to exact revenge. She felt justified. And, some would say, she still feels justified, which is why she has shown no genuine remorse and can barely verbalize the word "sorry" in a sentence even when her own life depends on it.

Dr. Drew spoke of Jodi's "lifelong pattern of really not accepting responsibility for things, for having strange reactions, intense relationships. There was real chaos in [Jodi's] life where she would go from job to job to job. And then, very significant, was how she conducted herself in her relationship with Travis Alexander." Had she not been borderline she might have had the capacity to examine her relationship with Travis with at least a semblance of objectivity, see her part in the dysfunction and realize she was not a victim but a participant in an unhealthy situation. But Jodi never achieved that level of self-honesty or self-awareness. She was way too invested in playing the victim in the relationship and indeed engineered her own debasement by actively encouraging it, begging for ass poundings, going out of her way to be his maid, etc. She thoroughly enjoyed her pity party where she worked up her appetite for vengeance. With borderlines, relationship disillusion and bitterness are prefabricated and inevitable.

According to Dr. Drew, it is unusual for borderlines to become raging murderers. "Borderlines don't kill people, they typically kill themselves," he said, adding many of his professional colleagues suspected Jodi also had "some components of psychopathy, some problem with the ability to empathize with others, very goal directed. She's very cunning and when she really needs it, she can think about no one but herself, come what may. That, I think, is the part that the public reacts so fiercely to." That's a fancy way of saying she is likely also a psychopath. Her pathological lying also dovetails with psychopathic behavior, as the psychopath has absolutely no qualms about lying as a means to an end. Lying is child's play compared to the even more malignant behaviors in their tool kit.

Dr. Drew elaborated by saying that borderlines use a style of emotional regulation called "projective identification," paraphrased to mean, "I have a horrible feeling inside of me, so horrible I can't touch it, but I can inject that feeling into you." Thus, borderlines are terribly manipulative. "They literally can make you feel what they don't want to feel and then they manipulate you as a way of manipulating their (own) feelings."

As an example, Dr. Drew pointed to the interview Jodi gave minutes after she was found guilty of murder. She said she wanted the death penalty, saying the worst outcome for her would be spending the rest of her natural life in prison. She wasn't a smoker, and longevity ran in her family, so a lifetime behind bars would be intolerably long, if nothing else. Besides, "I believe death is the ultimate freedom, so I'd rather have my freedom as soon as I can get it," she said without hesitation to Troy Hayden of Phoenix's KSAZ. Jodi was essentially goading the jurors to execute her. In that death wish statement, Dr. Drew sees the borderline's projective identification, "She has a murderous rage, because we've all seen what her murderous rage can do. We know she has that. Her murderous rage she is now trying to put on the jury and tell the jury, 'You need to kill me. And then you'll be guilty of acting out my murderous rage.' That's how borderlines function. It's projective identification."

In a way, Jodi also engaged in projective identification sexually with Travis, encouraging him to engage in sexual conduct that she later said made her feel degraded. She was the one who felt *less than* and even worthless, but she managed to manipulate him into acting it out through sexual role playing so she could blame him.

With borderlines, dissociation becomes a common strategy as well. Jodi seemed dissociated from her *own* life, looking at her life as if it were a movie. There was a sense of unreality that allowed her to do hideous things and not really be in touch with the level of awfulness, or the hideousness of it. This is part and parcel of the emptiness and alienation that borderlines experience.

And because that dissociation makes her life feel so movie-like and unreal to her, Jodi has actually enjoyed her notoriety, as if she were starring in a movie role and not becoming a convict in real life. Journalist Amy Murphy, the television reporter for Phoenix's ABC 15 TV who conducted a one-on-one interview with Jodi Arias following the verdict, observed, "In her sick twisted little mind it is (an ego trip) absolutely . . . I asked her that question. I said, 'People think you're really enjoying all this attention.' And she goes, 'No, not this kind of attention,' but she thought about the answer long and hard. She's enjoying it. There's no doubt about it. She's enjoying it." Dissociation is what allows her to enjoy her infamy, which amounts to being famous for doing something hideous.

One thing Amy noticed about Jodi that left her with a sense of *wow, seriously mentally ill* was her eyes, what Nancy Grace called Jodi's "crazy eyes." Amy was close enough to Jodi that she could see the pupils of her brown eyes, which may have been dilated. The large pupils, coupled with the fact that she didn't blink very often, gave the sense of what people interpret as "crazy."

The reporter said she learned through her sources that Jodi was being medicated behind bars. She asked if the drugs were anti-depressants or anti-psychotic drugs, because that might explain Jodi's ability to have remained so calm, with her cold, dazed look throughout the interview process. According to the source, "I can't tell you what kind of drugs she is taking, but she is on meds for whatever it is she's dealing with." Amy wondered if Jodi had been medicated during her testimony, it being common knowledge that the defendant suffered from migraines. The source said that she got a daily vitamin, in addition to her daily migraine medication. Amy asked specifically about anti-depressants or anti-psychotics, and got a "yes" response. When she asked "which or both?" the source could not elaborate. There was speculation that Jodi's lack of affect on the stand could have been due to medications.

As for why the defense didn't do much with Jodi's mental illness, Amy was not sure. "If she's indeed a sociopath and the defense knows this, they're not going to bring that up in her defense. I think that they have downplayed the mental illness part of it for their own reasons, and who is to say if she's bipolar. If she is, then she's medicated, because nobody could sit on the stand and be that calm if they're bipolar. If she's a sociopath, that makes more sense. How can she lie through her smiles and keep her stories straight, thinking she's smarter than everyone else and not feeling any remorse?"

Given the many interviews she had done in her long career, Amy noticed she did not get an uneasy physical sensation from being in Jodi's presence. She was even looking for an evil vibe, but said she didn't get one from Jodi. "The vibe I got was a non-vibe," she said, "no emotion, a vacancy of any emotion whatsoever. It didn't matter what the questions were, she was going to stay calm and have an answer for it." Amy found it extremely odd, but not innately insidious.

Other reporters had similar opinions. Another female reporter said she hadn't been creeped out at all. In fact, she had wanted to get up and give Jodi a hug after the interview. A male reporter told Amy that he found something very captivating about Jodi and her soft-spoken manner. Amy summed it up by saying, "She's like one of those pretty fish deep down in the ocean that you are somehow drawn to, but when you get close to them, you realize 'Oh my god, they're poisonous.'" She acknowledged Jodi's looks were striking, even though she had made herself as unattractive as possible for court. She looked tiny and harmless, and it was easy to see how Travis would have been attracted to her. Jodi even seemed to flirt with her favorite reporter, the handsome Troy Hayden.

Amy came away from her own interview with Jodi convinced that the woman was out of her mind. That being said, she thought Jodi clearly could distinguish right from wrong, based on her extraordinary attempts to cover up her crime and create a phony alibi.

"I interpreted Jodi Arias as being much more seriously mentally ill than the defense ever let on," said Amy after the session.

Friends of Travis's were outraged by Jodi's postconviction media tour, and many questioned her sincerity. Chris Hughes, in particular, didn't believe her death wish for a moment. "I think Jodi's request for the death penalty is Jodi doing what she does; lying and manipulating," he stated. He said Jodi was too scared to die, and that she had been threatening suicide for years, even in high school. "If Jodi wanted to be dead, she would be," he concluded. Travis's friend Dave Hall agreed with Chris, but he thought Jodi's vanity factored in. "I think Jodi Arias loves herself too much to actually want that," he commented.

Jodi Arias herself changed her mind within a day, saying she realized her family didn't deserve the additional pain that would come if she were put to death. She said even her lawyers felt "a little betrayed" and blindsided by her interview. During her allocution, her plea to the jury, she asked the panel of twelve jurors to reject the death penalty outright for the sake of her family.

"I'm asking you to please, please don't do that to them. I've already hurt them so badly, along with so many other people," she said. "I want everyone's healing to begin, and I want everyone's pain to stop." Again, there were very few people in the court of public opinion who bought into anything she said. Even her closing seemed laced with self-pity.

"To this day, I can hardly believe I was capable of such violence. But I know that I was, and for that, I'm going to be sorry for the rest of my life." That was as far as her regret seemed to take her.

Dr. Drew weighed in on Jodi's seeming lack of remorse. "It evokes in the public a sense of rage, that we can't have this woman amongst us because we don't see her remorseful; we don't see her falling on her sword, we don't see her really empathizing with this family, we don't see her taking responsibility, which is a borderline thing. But we do see her as very cunning."

As of this writing, Travis has been gone for more than five years, but with the very high likelihood of another penalty phase in Jodi Arias's future, this case could go on interminably. Another unbiased jury has to be selected, which could take a long time, especially in light of the massive media coverage to date. The legally necessary act of bringing another set of jurors up to speed on the facts of the case is absolutely daunting.

So what will ultimately become of Jodi Arias? If the new jury in the penalty phase of the case decides on a death sentence, Judge Stephens is legally bound by that decision. But if the new jury votes for life in prison instead, Judge Stephens would have two options: one would be sentencing Jodi to life in prison with no possibility of release; the other would be sentencing her to life in prison with the possibility of release after twenty-five years. If that happens, and with time already served, she would be over fifty years of age before her first chance of release. Travis's family hopes that day never comes.

A lot of the fascination with this case has to do with the wild, forbidden sex. We are mesmerized by the infidelity, the hypocrisy, and the sexual abandon, the obsession, the games, especially in light of God's Law, the Law of Chastity. In a certain way, we are the voyeurs of a unique sexual descent into a kind of hell. Why the extreme allure of the sex lives of two strangers, beyond the fatal attraction? Maybe Nurmi hit a homerun with his observation about "dirty little secret." Secrets, sex, lies, an audiotape . . . and the obsession of a woman scorned who took a good man, by many accounts a great man, down. It may be awful, but—still—we like to watch.

The new jury that will decide the ultimate punishment is not yet seated. The court of public opinion is loud and excoriating, but fundamentally irrelevant as far as the law is concerned. Still, justice for Travis is the battle cry for most every spectator. This new death penalty phase gives room for new speculation and analysis. Only time will tell what new tactic the defense might employ to save the life of Jodi. No matter what, there will continue to be speculation about the mystery of Jodi Arias, as people pore over the evidence and try to understand what bizarre combination of chemistry and personality drove her to kill a man she professed to love.

When asked if Jodi was mentally ill, Dr. Drew concluded, "She has significant mental health issues for sure. The interesting conundrum is, it doesn't justify or mitigate what she's done, it's just a way of understanding how things like this can happen." Of critical importance, says Dr. Drew, is that Jodi be held accountable.

There are plenty of people with borderline personality disorder who do not murder, who keep themselves in check, who get help for what ails them. If there's no cure for borderlines, there are ways to contain it. Jodi had studied spiritual and philosophical movements as esoteric as transcendentalism. She must have had some awareness of basic psychology. It's hard to know why she did not seek help. People told her she had a problem, and yet she made the decision to ignore those who were undoubtedly telling her to get help. Dr. Drew's point cannot be stressed enough. "I can have compassion for an alcoholic, but when the alcoholic drives drunk and kills someone, my compassion ends."

ACKNOWLEDGMENTS

I would like to thank my dear friend of many years, HarperCollins senior vice president Lisa Sharkey, for asking me to undertake this fascinating assignment.

This book would not have come into being without the brilliant work of Lisa Pulitzer, who has a gift for seamlessly weaving facts together to form a tapestry that tells a compelling story. Matt Harper, our editor at HarperCollins, expertly steered this project through the tricky shoals of a very tight deadline and the constant storm of lies that Jodi Arias unleashed with almost every sentence. His assistant, Dani Valladares, was right there with him. Beth Karas offered invaluable assistance in keeping us factual and precise in the sea of minutia that this very long trial generated. Martha Smith was gracious and patient as she helped shape the rougher edges into a smooth narrative.

I would also like to thank those who knew Travis and Jodi and had the courage to offer their observations despite the heated passions surrounding this case. Jodi's friend Patti was one such observer. A very special thanks goes out to Sky Hughes, who really provided some of the most essential insights into Jodi's character and how she operated in Travis's world. Taylor Searle, Deanna Reid, Dave Hall, Shaun Alexander, Josh Denne, Clancy Talbot, Elisha Schabel, and Linda Ballard Boss also spoke honestly and openly, helping us paint a three-dimensional portrait of the complex yet compassionate man Travis was.

Finally, I would like to thank my amazing colleagues. I so appreciate the support I've received from HLN's top executives, Scot Safon and Katherine Green, and my fabulous executive producer Philippa Cooper Holland as well as *In Session* executive producer Scott Tufts and *Nancy Grace* executive producer Dean Sicoli. My producer in the field and the courtroom, Selin Darkalstanian, offered piercing analysis of the key players in the case. Other coworkers also helped me gather information and conduct interviews in the hot Phoenix sun and deserve my thanks, particularly Jackie Taurianen, Mary Cella, Josey Crews, Bill Hinkle, Grace Wong, and Nancy Leung. Nancy Grace, whom I consider my mentor and friend, gave freely of her time and wisdom as a former prosecutor and astute student of human nature. Dr. Drew, as well, shared the benefit of his professional experience with the deeply troubled. The accomplished photographer Joe Conrad generously shared his portraits, as did journalist Chris Hrubesh. Finally, I thank my girlfriend, Donna Dennison, for her kindness and understanding during this challenging project.